JAMES BRINDLEY
AND THE
DUKE OF BRIDGEWATER

Canal Visionaries

Victoria Owens

AMBERLEY

To Christine Richardson

Front cover: An engraving of the Barton Aqueduct made after an original drawing by Percival Skelton (*c.* 1813–1881) which appears in the 1861 and 1864 editions of Samuel Smiles's *Life of James Brindley*.

First published 2015

Amberley Publishing
The Hill, Stroud
Gloucestershire, GL5 4EP

www.amberley-books.com

British Library Cataloguing in Publication Data.
A catalogue record for this book is available from the British Library.

ISBN 978 1 4456 4966 5 (print)
ISBN 978 1 4456 4967 2 (ebook)

Typeset in 10pt on 13pt MinionPro.
Typesetting and Origination by Amberley Publishing.
Printed in the UK.

Contents

Acknowledgements

The author and publisher would like to thank the following people and organisations for permission to use copyright material in this book: National Portrait Gallery, London; Institution of Civil Engineers, London; the Brindley Mill and James Brindley Museum, Leek; Stoke-on-Trent Archives; the Wedgwood Museum, Barlaston, Stoke-on-Trent; the John Rylands Library, Manchester; University of Bristol Library; Salford Museum and Art Gallery; Richard Dean of Canalmaps Archive (www.canalmaps.net) and Bonhams, auctioneers.

Every attempt has been made to seek permission for copyright material used in this book. However, if we have inadvertently used copyright material without permission/ acknowledgement, we apologise and we will make the necessary correction at the first opportunity.

As author, I am grateful to Maney Publications for allowing me to include material from my article 'James Brindley's Notebooks, 1755–1763: An Eighteenth Century Engineer Writes About his Work', which first appeared in the *International Journal for the History of Engineering & Technology*, 83, No. 2 (2013), and its online counterpart, www.maneyonline.com/het.

My thanks go also to Paul Reynolds and the Railway and Canal Historical Society for permitting me to make use of material which first appeared in the articles 'The Private Property Debate' and 'James Brindley and the (unbuilt) Monkey Island Canal', *RCHS Journal*, Nos 222 and 223 (March and July 2015).

I would like to express my appreciation to Michael Richardson and Jamie Carstairs at the University of Bristol; Carol Morgan at the Institution of Civil Engineers, London; Lucy Lead at the Wedgwood Museum, Stoke-on-Trent, and Ian Johnston at the Duke of Bridgewater Archive, Salford University, for their practical help and immense goodwill.

On a personal note, I should also like to extend particular thanks to:
– Christopher Lewis, for his observations on the Thames chapter.
– Michael Powell, Chetham's librarian, for directing me to the December 1760–February 1762 Bridgewater Estate Accounts.
– Peter Brown, Graham Boyes and Peter Cross-Rudkin for their advice at the Railway and Canal Historical Society's 2014 canal research seminar.
– Brenda and Brian Ward of the BCN Society, for a most enjoyable trip on their narrow boat.
– My husband David, both for reading and commenting on a draft version of the text and for ensuring that family life ran smoothly while the work was in progress.

– Selina Hastings and Rick Gekoski for their encouragement.
– Christine Richardson, to whose exhaustive research and infectious enthusiasm all scholars of James Brindley's life and achievements stand indebted.

Victoria Owens,
Bristol, 2015

CHAPTER ONE

1759–60:
The Duke and the Schemer

In the spring of 1759, Francis Egerton, 3rd Duke of Bridgewater, obtained an Act of Parliament enabling him to build a navigable canal from his Lancashire home of Worsley to a site in Salford called Tenter's Croft, for the purpose of carrying coal. Coal underscored his lands in thick seams, like the stains of a vast inky thumb on a map, but there was a difficulty in getting it to market. Packhorses with panniers hardly made for efficient transport, and were the duke to ship it along the Mersey and Irwell Navigation, the high tolls would erode any gains he might make at the point of sale. Since the Worsley pits were awash with surplus water, John Gilbert, the duke's agent, cherished an ingenious idea of enlarging the existing adits to a size at which boats – narrow vessels with prominent ribs, which came to be known as starvationers – could float right up to the seams to take the coal in containers to the mine entrance. Not only did this strategy make a virtue of necessity by draining the flooded workings, but at the same stroke it raised the exciting possibility of extending a waterway out across country – in effect providing a means of transport from mine to market. Building the canal promised to be expensive, but the duke liked the idea enough to budget for the necessary outlay and petition Parliament for an Act. Perhaps because the plan had some history – his father, Scrope Egerton, the first duke, had obtained an Act to make the Worsley Brook navigable from the nearby mines to the River Irwell as early as 1737, although he never implemented it – his proposal encountered little opposition. In March 1759, his bill received the Royal Assent.[1]

Having purchased levelling staves and a spirit level, Gilbert and he recruited a labour force to make a start on the digging and then took stock. Manchester historian James Phelps conjectures that they had hit a setback; having begun to cut a trench, they 'found themselves in considerable difficulty regarding the levels, which they had not anticipated.'[2] Equally, it may not have been long before the duke and Gilbert began to think that the provisions of the Act, which enabled them to cut only as far as Salford, were rather unadventurous. While Salford would assuredly welcome the canal and the coal it carried, the real prize of a market was Manchester. Manchester was a tantalising destination – close to Worsley but out of reach on the eastern side of the River Irwell. While in theory it would be possible to convey the canal down to the river through locks, cross it on the level and then lock up on the eastern bank, it would put the canal traffic at the mercy of the Mersey & Irwell Navigation Company and their large tolls. Besides, the duke disliked locks on the basis that they were an 'obstruction.'[3] Whatever the exact reason, in the high summer of 1759 Gilbert summoned James Brindley to Worsley. It was the start of what, in both a literal and metaphorical sense, was to prove a ground-breaking collaboration. (See Illustration 1).

James Brindley

Born in 1716, for most of his adult life Brindley worked across Staffordshire, Derbyshire and Cheshire as a self-employed independent millwright. His clients included a Mr Bucknall and a Mr Warburton, for whom he made improvements to a mill at Bucknall near Stoke; the pottery manufacturing brothers John and Ralph Baddeley, for whom he converted a fulling mill in the Moddershall Valley to grind flint which, when it was added to clay, produced fashionably pale ware; a Mr George Goodwin of Monyash, for whom he put up a substantial corn mill on the River Dove near Ashbourne, and Nathanael Pattison and his business partners, who ran a silk mill in Congleton, to which Brindley made regular maintenance visits, having designed its machinery and water wheel.[4] He had also worked occasionally at Trentham Park, home of the duke's friend and brother-in-law Earl Gower, adjusting a pump and overseeing construction of a flint mill in 1758, though his connection had been more with the land agent Thomas Tibbetts than with the earl.[5] Informally, he came to be known as the Schemer, 'Not,' his descendant the novelist Arnold Bennett would explain, 'because he intrigued, but because he schemed schemes,' – in other words, he directed the practical arrangements necessary for putting large-scale ideas into effect.[6]

In addition to his mill work, he had some success in the fast-evolving field of steam engineering. By reason of its relatively economic usage of coal, the engine he built between 1756 and 1758 for the coal-owning Broade family of Fenton Vivian attracted the notice both of James Spedding, agent to Sir James Lowther of Whitehaven, and of William Brown, colliery viewer and engineer of Throckley, on Tyneside.[7] He had built further engines for Phineas Hussey's pit at Little Wyrley near Walsall, and for master potter Thomas Whieldon's mines close to Bedworth near Coventry, besides constructing a boiler at Coalbrookdale for Abraham Darby II. In December 1758, he had even taken out a patent for his,

> Invention of A Fire Engine, for Drawing Water out of Mines, or of Draining of Lands, or for Supplying of Cityes, Townes, or Gardens with Water, or which may be applicable to many other great or usefull Purposes in a better and more effectual Manner than any Engine or Machine that hath hitherto been made or used for the like Purpose ...[8]

Years later, when Brindley's devoted brother-in-law Hugh Henshall came to provide information for his entry in Andrew Kippis's *Biographica Britannica*, he maintained that Brindley would probably 'have brought the steam engine to a great degree of perfection', had not 'a number of obstacles' been 'thrown in his way' by rival engineers.[9] Brindley himself says nothing about this experience and what truth Henshall's story holds is impossible to say.

In the course of 1758 – a busy year – Brindley's steam-engine client Thomas Broade joined with Lord Anson of Shugborough and Earl Gower of Trentham in commissioning him to survey for a waterway between the potteries of Stoke and the navigable Trent at Wilden, in Derbyshire.[10] Despite some exuberant publicity, this first foray into canal work stalled for want of capital at an early stage. Although a few canals had existed in Britain for centuries – the Roman Fossdyke gave Lincoln access to the Trent and John Trew's 1563 Exeter Canal was built to enable traders to avoid paying tolls on their goods at the Countess Wear across the tidal Exe – 1750s provincial Staffordshire found the technology altogether too daring. In the absence of a charismatic promoter to talk up its usefulness, the scheme soon lost momentum, leaving Brindley to return to building steam engines in the short term.

Even before this canal adventure, he had demonstrated his flair for working with water by bringing about a triumphant transformation in the fortunes of the aptly named Wet Earth Pit at Clifton just outside Manchester. It was a site which afforded ample evidence of his skills both in surveying and working with long runs of water, and it stood less than 3 miles' distance from Worsley. In the late 1740s, the pit's owner, John Heathcote, had sunk a shaft of about 45.72 metres (150 feet) to the rich Doe seam. In an age of shallow bell-pits and open cast working, this attempt at deep mining was a bold stroke which promised much. Unfortunately, all Heathcote's hopes of seeing a profit from his enterprise foundered because water repeatedly entered the workings and overwhelmed the horse-powered chain and bucket arrangement he had installed by way of flood prevention.

According to Brindley's fulsome Victorian biographer Samuel Smiles, even at his own wedding Heathcote's thoughts turned upon his flooded mine workings. When he heard his guests mention a Staffordshire millwright named James Brindley with a reputation for showing ingenuity in the face of a challenge, Heathcote decided to consult the resourceful-sounding man without ado. On receiving an anguished summons, Brindley came at once, listened to the bridegroom's account of the pit's location, studied a plan of the coal workings and reflected for a time in silence. 'At length,' says Smiles, who assuredly was not there to see, Brindley's 'countenance brightened – his eyes sparkled, and he briefly pointed out a method by which he thought he should be enabled, at no great expense, effectually to remedy the evil.'[11]

This narrative does not stand up to scrutiny. Admittedly, no word from Brindley or his contemporaries survives to indicate how he conceived, planned and managed the work at the Wet Earth Colliery, but it is unlikely, not to say inconceivable, that he would have agreed to undertake a scheme as demanding as Wet Earth without visiting the site, making a survey, taking the levels and exploring different ways of taking the project ahead.[12] Nor for that matter would a coal owner in John Heathcote's situation employ an engineer whom he had only just met to drain his pit, and before engaging him he would at least demand a fully costed estimate of the work's likely expense, and quite possibly ask to see a few formal testimonials as well. Yet these churlish cavils miss the point of a good, if implausible, story. Whatever the actual circumstances of his recruitment, it is clear that James Brindley convinced the owner of Wet Earth pit that he could resolve the water problem, and at some point between 1752 and 1756 he designed a drainage scheme which was both imaginative and remarkably effective.[13]

For the pumping, water provided the power. Admittedly, by the 1750s steam engines were prevalent in mine drainage, their use having increased ever since the Earl of Dudley installed a Newcomen engine to pump water out of his West Midlands colliery in 1712. Nevertheless, at Wet Earth – perhaps for reasons of economy and perhaps because he wished to work with a source of energy he already understood – Brindley preferred to work with the River Irwell. The geography of the site was not entirely helpful, the mine being some 400 yards' distance from the river's nearest point (the sandstone Giant's Seat Gorge, through which it flowed some 20 feet below the level of the pithead), which precluded any question of contriving a typical short millrace. At the same time, there was one compensating advantage: the Irwell's steeply inclined course meant that there was only a short distance upstream from the colliery; even when the river was low, its water surface would still be well above the level of the pithead. Brindley settled on the hamlet of Ringley as the point at which to tap the Irwell's power. Having built a weir across the river, from the weir pool water entered a sluice to drop into a tunnel which – here the merit of meticulous surveying revealed itself – sloped, but significantly less than the natural fall of the river.

From its route it looks as though Brindley first intended that his tunnel should follow the line of the Irwell Valley Fault, anticipating that it would be possible to drive a heading through the sandstone without much difficulty. Unfortunately, at a time when there was little understanding of geology the visible rock formations proved misleading. What he appears to have taken to be the line of the sandstone fault was actually no more than an isolated sandstone outcrop. As a result, his tunnel twisted and turned through fissile shale in a vain attempt to locate the fault and to follow it. While Brindley may have experienced acute frustration at the time, the time-consuming and thankless business no doubt honed his understanding and grasp of tunnel construction. About 7 feet 6 inches square, the roof resembles a flattish arch and the invert (the lowest point of its inside) is dished to the centre, a detail which suggests someone, presumably Brindley, recognised the need to ensure that the tunnel would drain easily for maintenance. When the tunnellers – probably local miners – encountered fissures in the rock, they bricked them up to give the structure an expensive lining. Otherwise, the greater part of the labour consisted in working through the rock with hammer and chisel.

After some 800 yards (731.52 metres), the tunnel neared the northerly bank of one of the larger meanders in the Irwell's course. Here the water entered an inverted siphon, descending through one vertical shaft to cross the river beneath its bed, before re-ascending through a second vertical shaft. If the theory sounds wild, the principle was ancient; hydrologists had known for centuries that water could, in effect, flow upwards provided that its output point stood at a lower level than its entrance or input point. From the siphon exit, a leat (an artificial stream) took the water on towards the wheel chamber. The gradient – 1 in 200 – was slight, but far from descending direct to the wheel; the leat tracked the winding river, passing the colliery before turning back on itself at an acute angle to approach the site. If adoption of such a circuitous route sounds counter-intuitive, it had the merit of affording Brindley every chance to take measures to ensure that the water in the leat should remain under constant, close control. After all, were it to follow a direct line from siphon to colliery, it would take little – an obstruction, perhaps, or a jammed sluice – to cause a flood. Instead, sluice gates along its way provide access to overflow chambers leading to the river, and there is also a brick spillway. Having reached the pithead, the water entered a tunnel leading to a final sluice gate or penstock and thence to the wheel which drove the pump. It then flowed through the tailrace to return to the river.

Although no colliery ledgers are known to survive to give hard financial evidence of the flood-prone pit's transformation into a profitable concern, there is no doubt that after its uncertain beginnings, it flourished. The waterwheel remained in use until 1867, when the owners installed a turbine, and 1924 saw the introduction of steam pumping. Only in 1928 did coal production at the site cease, by which time the colliery had become uneconomic. The unique drainage scheme, to which it owed its long and productive life, had been an extraordinary demonstration of Brindley's skill, the bold introduction of the inverted siphon giving him a reputation for being able to make water run uphill.

As though to give a foil to his aptitude for solving intractable engineering problems, rumour maintained that he could neither read nor write. The allegation holds little truth, although it is fair to say that he was not on the easiest terms with the written language. During his years as an independent millwright he kept his accounts and noted progress of his works in a series of thin, paper-covered notebooks, four of which survive in the public domain. If he recorded any detail of his experience at Wet Earth pit, it does not survive, but in 1759, when he first came in on the Duke of Bridgewater's canal venture, he wrote the name 'Mr Gilbert' at the head of a page, and 'July 1 – at Worsley Hall – 6 days'.[14] The entries beneath follow an unassuming pattern, much like that of his various mill projects, with a list of dates, location and the number of days spent there. As plans for the duke's project advanced, Brindley continued to make frequent visits to Worsley, sometimes noting where he had come from and where he planned to go next. In September 1759, as though to mark his long-term commitment to the duke's venture, Brindley brought three skilled labourers – George Harrison, Samuel Adams and Samuel Bennett – to the Worsley site, and the Bridgewater Estate paid £1 9s 6d 'for the carriage of their Goods and Clothes'.[15]

The Duke of Bridgewater

The enthusiasm of Francis Egerton, 3rd Duke of Bridgewater, for canal engineering had showed itself in 1753 when he was seventeen years old and making the Grand Tour. On reaching the south of France, the Canal du Midi impressed him so much that he persuaded his tutor, Robert Wood, a distinguished antiquarian who had travelled to Palmyra, to enrol him at the Lyons Académie so he could attend lectures in hydraulics.[16] It might have remained no more than a passing interest – some polite study to complement his burgeoning interest in art – were it not that in the autumn of 1758, the duke found himself jilted.

By this time he had finished his travels and settled in London to enjoy the life of a young man about town. Having been neglected as a child, wretched at Eton and bored and restless through much of his Tour, it was the first period of solid happiness he had known. He made friends, gambled, rode in the occasional race at Newmarket and, to compound his pleasure, fell in love. She was the newly widowed Duchess of Hamilton, vivacious Elizabeth Gunning, second daughter of an impoverished Irish peer. Together with her adored older sister Maria, she had come to London in the early 1750s and before long, the two girls won the hearts of everyone who met them. Within 12 hours of meeting Elizabeth at a masquerade, the Duke of Hamilton had not only proposed but also sought out a compliant parson to marry them, thoughtfully taking with him a ring from his bed curtain with which to bless the nuptials. Having made his wedding arrangements with such zest, the impetuous husband died after only five years of married life, having caught a chill out hunting.

Widowed, Elizabeth charmed the Duke of Bridgewater, and when he asked her to marry him in early 1758, she accepted. In the months that followed, it emerged that her older sister Maria, now Lady Coventry, was having an *affaire*. Whoever her lover may have been, he was less than discreet and the pair looked set for scandal. Taking stock, the scrupulous young Duke of Bridgewater ordered Elizabeth to break off all contact. Elizabeth, not surprisingly, refused. If she had to choose between her fiancé and her sister, the sister won hands down. Here was the end of the engagement. Not long after, Elizabeth accepted a proposal from John Campbell, future Duke of Argyll and therefore the third duke in her life.

After he had generously hosted a celebratory ball for the newly engaged couple, the Duke of Bridgewater's interest in making a profit from coal surged. Although the broken engagement was not the origin of his canal enthusiasm, it may have hardened his resolve to implement the Act which enabled him to cut from Worsley to Salford. Without seeking to dispute the value of John Gilbert's practical assistance, Brindley's introduction to the venture appears to have transformed the duke's canal interest into an all-consuming passion. His great-nephew, the literary-minded Earl of Ellesmere, wrote that whereas a devout believer who had experienced a similar disappointment in love 'might have built a monastery, tenanted a cell and died a Saint', the young peer 'betook himself to his Lancashire estates, made Brindley his confessor, and died a benefactor to commerce, manufactures and mankind.'[17] The religious analogy suggests that Lord Ellesmere considered that his distinguished great-uncle's association with Brindley went beyond the decision to employ a skilled man on a demanding project; it set the seal on his life's calling. (See Illustration 2).

The meeting of minds

If the collaboration between the duke and the Schemer was at first sight surprising, both men in fact had more common ground than appearances suggested. In their early lives, both had – in different ways – defied parental expectations. For the duke, it had been a particularly stormy experience. After the death of his father Scrope, the 1st Duke of Bridgewater, in 1745, his mother married Sir Richard Lyttelton and, infatuated with her new husband, embarked on what Bridgewater biographer Hugh Malet calls 'an Indian summer of frivolity.'[18] Sir Richard took against his young stepson Francis, and in 1751 the two of them clashed so resoundingly that the fifteen-year-old duke (he had succeeded to the title of on the death of his older brother in 1748) fled home to seek refuge with his favourite cousin, Samuel Egerton of Tatton. A Bill of Complaint in Chancery followed, in which Francis had the support of his uncle, the Duke of Bedford, against his mother and made it abundantly clear that he was not prepared to make what she termed 'proper submission' to his stepfather. The proceedings had the result that when he was not away at Eton, and before he set off on his Tour, he spent most of his time at Tatton, with Samuel Egerton appointed receiver, on his behalf, of the rents and profits of the Bridgewater Estates.

Like the duke, Brindley had had a bleak childhood. His early biographers share the view that his father, a small landowner who liked the company of richer men than he, spent much of his time shooting, angling and at bull-baitings and cock-fights.[19] As for his mother, with a child born every year for seven years – and what is more, surviving – she may have been better at nurturing infants than encouraging them as they got older. Brindley grew up augmenting the family income by doing odd jobs for the local farmers. When he wasn't scaring birds or holding horses, he enjoyed visiting the mills of the district, carving small-scale wooden models of their waterwheels and gearing in his spare time. If the duke had ruffled feathers on his Tour by deciding to explore the Canal du Midi instead of visiting sites of antiquity, Brindley, aged seventeen, made an equally drastic, and no doubt unexpected, career choice. He defied his parents' expectations by spurning Lowe Hill, the family farm, which as the eldest son was his inheritance, and apprenticed himself to one Abraham Bennett, a drunken wheelwright and millwright of Macclesfield.

The seven-year term of his indentures furnished a rich seam of folklore which charts the progress of Brindley the bungler, who fitted the spokes of a cartwheel in the wrong way round, to Brindley the skilled craftsman who saved his master's professional reputation by working out how to construct the machinery for a new paper mill when Bennett was too befuddled to make sense of it. Setting aside the question of what truth the legends hold, at the end of his apprentice years he set himself up in business, renting workshop premises from the Wedgwood family in Burslem. He had emerged from the realms of engineering myth, though colourful stories would surround him throughout his life, to take his place in engineering history.

Although the construction of the Bridgewater Canal has attracted much interest from historians of engineering, there has been little exploration of the working partnership that evolved between Brindley and the duke and the reasons for its success. Once the two men, proprietor-cum-promoter on the one hand and engineer on the other, discovered how their respective interests meshed, the avidity with which (under John Gilbert's polite, mediating presence) they collaborated in the canal enterprise was remarkable. It was also subversive. In this alliance between peer and millwright, engaged as they were upon what was at once a great gamble, and a venture of immense social and commercial benefit, all social distinction dissolved. Notwithstanding the twenty-year difference in age between them, their time of collaboration would also shape the course of both men's lives: Brindley's, who was in his mid-forties when he first came to Worsley, as decisively as that of the twenty-three-year-old duke.

Brindley's notebook gives no indication of what he made of the duke's plans, or indeed what he made of the duke, who is, if possible, even less communicative, but at some point in their acquaintanceship, the duke gave Brindley a Bible. On the flyleaf an inscription states: 'The book was given to James Brindley by Francis Egerton Duke of Bridgewater', and below it a second sentence declares, 'The book was given to Anne Brindley by her affectionate mother Anne Williamson, widow of James Brindley, Longport, 1806.' Over the years it would pass, a cherished memento, through many generations of Brindley's descendants until it reached a Mr J. H. D. M. Campbell in the mid-twentieth century, a distant but genuine relative who wrote about it in 1959 for the *Derbyshire Miscellany*.[20] In 2013 it came onto the market, the photograph in the auctioneers' catalogue showing a sturdy sixteenth-century volume – the Bible, Book of Common Prayer, Day's Psalter and a concordance all bound together in faded red morocco.[21] Its present whereabouts unknown, the book's existence serves to crystallise the unlikely union between the canal visionaries – the duke who had everything to gain from showing a bold front and only his fortune to lose, and the engineer who, could he but know it, was about to scale the peak of fame.

On 23 January 1760, Brindley wrote 'Set out for London' in his notebook. Their unrecorded discussions of the autumn months had paved the way for them to embark, with John Gilbert's blessing, upon a scheme of high daring. The duke would apply for a new Act of Parliament, this time to enable him to take his canal into the very heart of Manchester. In a stroke of vast audacity, it would cross the River Irwell on a bridge – a navigable aqueduct. (See Illustration 3).

CHAPTER TWO

1761 Brindley Ascendant: The Barton Aqueduct

Brindley and the Gilberts

To the Duke of Bridgewater (1736–1803) and his agent John Gilbert (1724–95), Brindley owed the great opportunity of his life and he never forgot it. The Bridgewater Canal unleashed all his ingenuity, revealed the full height of his powers and set him on the path to fame. Yet it was not his conception, and its contribution to his reputation requires some clarification.

In both editions of his biography of the duke and the article 'Brindley and Canals', Hugh Malet sets out to correct what he regards as the erroneous inclination of historians to attribute both the Bridgewater Canal's conception and execution to James Brindley.[1] The canal's 'prime mover', Malet insists, was not Brindley at all; it owed its origins equally to the duke, who had hopes of supplying Manchester with cheap coal, and John Gilbert, who would oversee much of its day-to-day construction.[2] Gilbert was well-versed in the practical side of commercial enterprise. He had served a partial apprenticeship with Birmingham buckle-maker Matthew Boulton, father to James Watt's business partner of the same name, which gave him the opportunity both to learn a trade and to get some grounding in book-keeping and accounts.[3] Before the seven-year term was up, Gilbert's father died. He came home (Cotton Hall near Alton in Staffordshire) to run the family estates while his older brother Thomas (1720–98) completed legal training in London.

Estate management proved to be John Gilbert's metier, which was advantageous because being a younger son, he needed a career, and he took up management of the Duke of Bridgewater's Worsley Estate in the early 1750s. Meanwhile Thomas Gilbert, who never had much success as a barrister, took up the corresponding post of land agent to Granville Leveson-Gower, Earl Gower and husband of Lady Louisa Egerton, the duke's sister, at nearby Trentham. In later years Lord Gower would constitute his commercial arm, Earl Gower & Company, to exploit the coal, lime and ironstone resources of his Lilleshall estate in Shropshire, and employ the Gilbert brothers to plan the Donnington Wood Canal which gave his coal pits access to the Wolverhampton–Newport Turnpike road.[4] Working in alliance, the brothers proved to be a powerful pair; John Gilbert's engineering flair made him an ideal overseer of the duke's works-in-progress, while Thomas Gilbert, more the administrator, had great aptitude for running meetings, coordinating committees and getting decisions made. Through Earl Gower's influence and in pursuit of his wish to have an ally in the Commons, Thomas Gilbert would enter Parliament as member for the Gower pocket borough of Newcastle-under-Lyme in 1763 and for Lichfield (another Gower borough) in 1768.

To the Gilberts, as they superintended construction of the duke's canal, James Brindley was but one contributor among many upon whom the success of the enterprise depended. To Brindley himself, the canal was his entire life – at least until other canal ventures arose in its wake. It is a difference in perspective which history has tended to erode. Hugh Malet, who makes free with his opinions in his determination to redress what he see as an imbalance, says outright that 'Brindley was not an engineer of the same calibre as [John] Gilbert', yet setting aside any question about the value of this judgment, and the two men's occasional disagreements notwithstanding, in all likelihood they probably viewed one another more as colleagues than competitors or rivals.[5] In the 1750s and 1760s, the profession of civil engineering was only beginning to edge its way into public consciousness. Before the second half of the eighteenth century, the word 'engineer' belonged solidly within a military context, as Dr Johnson's definition, 'one who directs the artillery of an army', bears out. Incidentally, in his *Dictionary of the English Language* Johnson offers an equally precise meaning for the related term 'enginery', now sadly obsolete, which he defines as 'the act of managing artillery'. The change in the word's significance seems to have come about around 1760, when John Smeaton (1724–1792) of Eddystone Lighthouse fame began to describe himself as a 'civil engineer', and by implication to designate the vast range of his professional interests – millwork; design and construction of harbours, docks and bridges; planning and provision of water supply and surveying and building canals, to name but a few – as 'civil engineering'.[6] At the forefront of this fast-evolving field of activity, both Brindley and Gilbert had an interest in its success.

At the same time, in his post of land agent or steward to the duke Gilbert was a salaried employee; to Brindley, the independent contractor, the need to make a good showing of his skill was especially crucial. The Bridgewater accounts books reveal at once the esteem in which he was held, and an uncertainty about how he is to be categorised. Records of payment name him only as 'Mr Brindley' without reference to occupation, in much the same way that they name the duke's solicitor as 'Mr Tomkinson', the formality of address distancing both men from the regular estate staff such as George Armitage the blacksmith, Richard Mugg the boat builder and Charles Warburton the mole catcher. Joseph, later Sir, Banks who toured the Worsley canal works in 1767, characterised Brindley as 'a man of no education but extreemly [sic] strong natural parts', adding that John Gilbert had 'found him in Staffordshire where he was only famous for being the best millwright in the Country.'[7] Brindley himself was not unaware of the change that was overtaking his occupation. Indeed, on his 1758 patent application, he had designated himself 'millwright, of Leek'.[8] Yet when Smeaton reviewed his Staffordshire canal survey in 1761 and explicitly referred in his report (it was, for the record, extremely favourable) to the work projected by 'Mr JAMES BRINDLEY, Engineer', Brindley seems to have liked the term enough to use it four years later on his marriage bond.[9]

Even if his role within the fledgling venture was ill-defined, when the duke applied to vary the terms of his 1758 Act and to take his canal over the River Irwell it was Brindley to whom he entrusted the task of giving evidence on the matter in Parliament. On the face of it, the decision looks quite extraordinary, and it certainly throws some doubt on the validity of Malet's description of Brindley as an 'occasional consulting technician'.[10] By no reckoning does the business first of convincing the honourable members that the altered route had real merit and second that building a bridge to take the new canal across a broad, tidal navigable river by means of an aqueduct was a practicable undertaking sound like an occasional technician's task. The detail that at this point in his life Brindley could never have seen a navigable aqueduct, let alone had the experience of building one, makes his role as advocate all the more remarkable. Admittedly, he may have put up bridges in the past. Tradition maintains that he built an attractive bridge of eighteenth-century provenance over the Churnet in Leek near the corn mill he put up for Thomas Jolliffe in 1750 – now the Brindley Mill and Museum. No confirmation exists to link his name to the structure which, while it is graceful, is also modest. The bridge that the duke required would be massive in scale and dimensions. Yet Brindley's lack of experience did not deter either the duke or Gilbert from making him their aqueduct's champion, and he plainly saw no reason to turn down an adventure. Before 1756 he had never worked with steam power; two years later, he had taken out a patent on boiler design.[11] Conceivably, by propelling the 'cleverest millwright in the country' to the fore, the duke and Gilbert evinced, not for the only time, a measure of cynicism and guile. Applying for legislation enabling them to cross the Irwell and build into Manchester was in the nature of a gamble, and constructing the aqueduct a risk by any measure. For the peer and his agent to appoint an outsider to front the fraught enterprise served to safeguard Bridgewater dignity in the event of the petition's either meeting with a stormy reception or, worse, being laughed out of the House.

Petitioning Parliament

On 31 January 1760, the House of Commons heard Brindley give evidence in support of the duke's petition for a new Act. Reticent on paper, to judge from the summary of his evidence which appears in the *House of Commons Journal*, in speech he proved sufficiently frank and forthcoming to give a full and clear account of how he intended to realise the duke's proposal.[12] Some 3 miles of the canal were already built, he said, but completing the Salford route had many disadvantages. It would entail cutting for 2½ miles through solid rock and along a steep hillside where there would be much difficulty in making the channel watertight. Should it start to leak, the canal would soon empty and become unusable. Away from the rocks and hills, its route lay through 'inclosed' and 'generally good … lands', in other words, prime agricultural pasture. The new line, by contrast, would run through rough moss and morass of no value. What was more, once built the canal would help to drain the bogs and provide an easy means of transporting marl and manure to the waste of marsh so as to improve it. On the subject of the aqueduct, Brindley was shrewd enough to focus upon the practical side of construction. Building it would, he asserted, 'be no Difficulty'. The riverbed gave good foundation; he knew he had to build to a sufficient height to accommodate shipping on the Irwell; he also knew he had to provide planks (in effect, an improvised towpath) under his new arches for the men who had to haul the river vessels through the shallows.[13]

If he was sparing in his speech, he nevertheless gave the members a graphic representation of his thinking. When the MPs examining the duke's bill in committee asked, bewildered, to see a drawing of the aqueduct, Brindley apparently chose instead to produce a large Cheshire cheese and cut it in two. No eyewitness account of his performance is known to survive, although long after the Duke of Bridgewater's death James Loch MP (1780–1855), superintendent of the Bridgewater Trust and a Bridgewater insider, passed the story of the cheese on to Samuel Hughes, a Victorian engineer with enough interest in Brindley to write an article about him for *Weale's Engineering Papers*.[14] Quite what aspect of the aqueduct's construction Brindley intended his bisected cheese to represent is uncertain; perhaps he set out to illustrate the bridge's overall shape, with the halves of the cheese standing for the arches; perhaps to represent its relation to the road bridge: one half of the cheese standing for the old structure and one for the new. It may have been something to do with the path of planks. Whatever his objective, the members thrilled to the sheer élan of his performance, or, in Samuel Hughes's sober account: 'The model appears to have afforded some amusement … for Brindley was requested to leave it with the committee that they might have it before their eyes during the progress of their inquiries.' For what it is worth, Hughes relates that Brindley also gave the parliamentarians a practical demonstration of clay puddling: working up wet clay with sand, forming it into a trough, filling it with water and showing that it 'was … held in without a particle of leakage', as he approvingly notes.[15] Whether this performance also had some connection with the Barton Aqueduct is unknown.

Assuredly Brindley's showmanship did the duke's cause no harm. On Friday 7 March 1760, his bill had its third reading in the Commons without opposition and Marshe Dickinson, the committee chairman, found himself authorised to carry it 'to the Lords and desire their concurrence'. On 12 March 1760, less than a week later, the Act 'to enable the most noble Francis, Duke of Bridgewater, to make a navigable cut or canal from or near Worsley Mill, over the river Irwell, to the Town of Manchester', received the Royal Assent. Ten days later, Brindley witnessed an agreement between John Gilbert and three other gentlemen to make 'a purchase of land' and noted the sums each man contributed in the friendliest fashion, with all the parties concerned on what appear to be the most amicable terms of mutual trust.[16]

Building the aqueduct

The duke and Gilbert appear to have given Brindley pretty much sole responsibility for building the aqueduct. If he ever made formal plans for the structure at the design stage, none are known to survive. The sheer speed with which construction of both the aqueduct and the large embankment on its approaches went ahead is therefore surprising, and suggests that he took matters in hand with the utmost confidence, the labourers catching his mood. Before long, the venture kindled national curiosity. Towards the end of 1760, an excited letter in the *Gentleman's Magazine* announced that when the new navigable canal intended 'to bring coals to Manchester' was finished, it would 'be the most extraordinary thing in the kingdom, if not in Europe.' Although the writer identified himself only by his initials 'R.W.', it is likely he was none other than the duke's sometime tutor and Grand Tour companion Robert Wood. Wood, if it is he, went about his public relations role with rare gusto, asserting not only that vessels on the canal might travel underground, but also (here lies the sheer fairground wonder of the enterprise) that they would pass 'over a navigable river, without communicating with its water

[…] supported by great arches.'[17] Not surprisingly, the duke took the opportunity to exploit this aptitude for furthering the canal cause, and in March 1761 Wood was returned as Member of Parliament for the Bridgewater pocket borough of Brackley.

Despite the public interest the canal aroused, its building was never going to be as straightforward as Brindley had led Parliament to believe. The aqueduct in particular was to be a formidable structure – 200 yards long and 12 yards wide – and it would carry the canal over three great arches some 39 feet above the turbulent tidal Irwell. Across the paper cover of his 1759/60 notebook, Brindley wrote the names of two seasoned craftsmen whom he was no doubt eager to recruit: John Mainley, bricklayer of Northwich, and James Bailey, a carpenter from 'near Shatte Moss'. Since at this time the regular hard-drinking, hard-living career navvy with well-honed skills had not yet come into being, for the unskilled barrow and shovel work Gilbert appears to have assembled a direct labour organisation, drawn from itinerant farm workers on the Worsley Estate and surrounding district, together, perhaps, with any of the Romany who frequented Trafford Moss and happened to seek the security of steady employment. A surviving Bridgewater accounts book offers some indication both of the number of men engaged, and their specific skills. For 9 May 1761, for example, in the weeks when the Barton Aqueduct was almost ready to open to traffic, there was a large number of masons on the books, twenty-four in total, each paid in the region of 1s 8d per day. On the same date, a telling entry records payment of 4s to one William Boyle 'for repairing chisels'. Among other skilled trades, the accounts list miners, bricklayers and stone-getters, wood-getters, sawyers and carpenters, and blacksmiths, boat builders and millwrights. As for ordinary labourers, an entry for 16 May 1761 records thirty-nine names, together with payment, typically in the region of 1s 3d per day.[18] The recurrence over the years of many of the same surnames, for instance Seddon, Wallwork, Laughlin, Cheetham and Vallantine, suggests that having once acclimatised themselves to this new species of work, the Bridgewater labour force stuck with it.

The aqueduct progressed fast, but not without incident. One entry in the Bridgwater Estate's accounts book mentions payment of 1s 8d by one John Selley 'for ale when the banks broak'; another speaks of damage done to a barrow 'in letting the water out of the canall at Barton'.[19] To quell increasing local alarm about the potential flood risk, Brindley devised a type of gate or barrier which he intended to be placed at ¼-mile intervals along the canal bed, balanced so as to rise into a vertical position in response to a fast-flowing current and contain the escaping waters. Although it is fair to say that their efficacy was open to question, their publicity value was considerable and their installation must have helped preserve friendly relations between the canal-mad duke and his tenants and neighbours. Nevertheless, both incidents gave the Bridgewater party cause to be wary of anything that might undermine the canal embankments. It is, for instance, hardly accidental that the estate records of this time should make frequent mention of payments to Thomas Spannel and Charles Warburton 'for catching moles'.[20] On the night of 5 December 1760, an injury to the canal occurred which appeared to be the result of mindless or malicious human vandalism. An indignant announcement in the *London Gazette* stated that,

Some wicked and evil disposed persons, at present unknown, broke down the Banks of his Grace the Duke of Bridgewater's Navigation at Barton, in the county of Lancaster, which were made upon an arch over the public highway there; by which means the water was discharged from the said Navigation and considerable damage done thereto.[21]

Despite the pledge of the king's pardon to anyone providing information about the perpetrators and the duke's offer of a £100 reward, no-one ever came forward.

Whatever their cause, these incidents gave a clear warning that were the daring new aqueduct to fail, its downfall would make for greater destruction than anything resulting from a subsiding earthwork. Indeed, stories about the aqueduct's construction suggest that throughout the works' progress, people wondered how it could conceivably carry a brimming canal with boats on it above a broad river with traffic of its own. No such bridge had been built before and therefore the practicability of the scheme was suspect.

In time, circling doubts gave rise to an odd story, a story full of unnamed names and outspoken opinions that no-one cares to own. Appreciating at last that not everyone shared his confidence in his rising structure, Brindley reasoned that were a like-minded expert to weigh in on his side, the demonstration of united opinion would surely quench any rumour that the aqueduct was about to collapse. He therefore suggested to the duke that they canvass a second opinion on the work-in-progress. In response, the duke, therefore, invited an unnamed 'gentleman of eminence' to inspect the site and pronounce judgment. The outcome was not a success. Far from offering Brindley any encouragement, the visitor uttered only an incredulous snub, saying that although he had 'often heard of castles in the air, [he] was never shewn before where any of them were to be erected'.[22] This snide piece of sarcasm would resurface some six or seven years later in the form of a clunking pun around the name of the Harecastle Tunnel, but leaving aside the matter of who actually coined the castle-in-the air gibe – Smiles tentatively suggests it may have been John Smeaton – the whole episode has an unsatisfactory John-Doe-and-Richard-Roe quality. The whole question of who consulted whom about precisely what is strangely misty. Although the story purports to celebrate the utter confidence which the duke places in Brindley's judgement, notwithstanding the sneering 'gentleman of eminence', whoever he may have been, at the same time, should anything have gone wrong, it would lend itself to being turned on its head to use as proof of how Brindley, obstinate to the last, had insisted on riding his hobbyhorse into the teeth of peril, heedless of well-founded warnings of imminent disaster.

Francis Henry Egerton's record of Brindley at Worsley Old Hall

In the early days of the canal's construction, Brindley appears to have stayed with the duke, Gilbert and Gilbert's wife, Lydia, at the duke's home – Worsley Old Hall. There was nothing unusual about skilled craftsmen of the eighteenth century lodging in the homes of their clients. Capability Brown, for instance, resided as a guest at Stowe, Croome Park, Sherborne Castle et al, houses whose grounds he landscaped. At Chatsworth, the painter Antonio Verrio immortalised his quarrel with the housekeeper Mrs Hackett by depicting her as Atropos, eternally grey-faced and scowling as she wields her shears from the ceiling of the Great

Chamber. At Worsley, the unsought intimacy between the Duke of Bridgewater, John and Lydia Gilbert and James Brindley around the time of the aqueduct's building seems to have given rise to a fairly febrile and acrimonious atmosphere. The sole record of how Brindley acclimatised himself to this ménage comes from Francis Henry Egerton (1756–1829), third child and second son of the duke's first cousin John Egerton (1721–1787), bishop successively of Bangor, Lichfield and Durham.

Following his father's clerical calling, albeit without much enthusiasm, the Hon. Rev. Francis Henry Egerton, 8th Earl of Bridgewater, became absentee rector of Whitchurch in Shropshire, a Prebendary of Durham Cathedral, Fellow of All Souls, Fellow also of the Royal Society, and spent most of his life in Paris.[23] A reputation for genuine scholarship notwithstanding and an excellent memory to boot, his eccentricities were prodigious. He filled his house on the Rue St-Honoré with poodles who wore shoes and dined with him at his table, and by way of relaxation, would shoot the birds in his garden, having first ordered his servants to clip their wings so as to give him every chance of hitting his prey. It is not easy to know how much value to place on his 1819 memoir, *A Letter to the Parisians and the French Nation upon Inland Navigation containing a Defence of the Public Character of his Grace Francis Egerton, late Duke of Bridgewater, and including some notices and anecdotes concerning Mr James Brindley.*

Since the very title signals Egerton's wish to bolster and protect the reputation of his relative and namesake, it goes without saying that he is hardly a disinterested commentator. According to Strachan Holme, librarian at the London Bridgewater House in the 1920s and author of an unfinished biography of the duke, he wrote the work in order both to encourage the Parisians to build more canals and to respond to 'a French review which had minimised the duke's work and given too much credit to Brindley.'[24] Biased from the outset, Egerton was not a witness to the events he describes. Insistence that his remarks about Brindley derive from 'what passed in conversation' between himself and the duke does not alter the fact that what he repeats is hearsay and open to all the charges of imprecision, prejudice and downright error that the term implies. Smiles's description of his work as 'singularly incoherent' is not entirely unfair, but it misses the point. True, Egerton rambles around his subject, digresses often, and fills his voluminous footnotes with wild theological speculations. At the same time, despite its manifest capriciousness and prejudice, the *Letter to the Parisians* emanates from the very heart of Bridgewater Canal history and is not by any means lacking in entertainment value. For these reasons alone it merits attention, while inviting a certain amount of circumspection in the reading.

It portrays Brindley in the domestic sphere as a law unto himself. For all their gossipy tone, Egerton's Brindley anecdotes show the engineer making his mark with the duke in a way that goes far beyond the purely business aspects of their working relationship.[25] Egerton tells a story of his attempting to cure toothache by washing his mouth 'with very Cold water, and then again, with Very Warm, and then again, with Cold, Till he roared with pain.' At meals Brindley eats until the pressure of his stomach upon his waistcoat palpably tightens the buttons. He causes mild dismay under cross-examination by a parliamentary committee by demanding to know what the Earl of Sandwich, at that time First Lord of the Admiralty, means by the term 'ships'. When Gilbert's rig of a horse – that is, an imperfectly gelded colt - gets Brindley's mare in foal, Brindley refuses to believe,

That Mr John Gilbert did not contrive This, on purpose to prevent his (Mr Brindley's) using his mare in going in pursuit of his business.

In the earlier version of his Bridgewater biography, Malet gives rather a sentimental picture of the three men sitting up 'late over their port, studying rather primitive maps', with Mrs Gilbert putting 'her head around the door from time to time, [to] scold them for the late and irregular hours they kept.'[26] In all likelihood, living at close quarters the chances are that the three men found one another's foibles irritating beyond belief; if, as a result, the atmosphere between them sometimes soured, it was only to be expected.

Egerton's charges hit hardest when they touch directly upon Brindley's competence. For instance, he slips in the sly suggestion of a drink problem. 'At first,' he claims,

[Brindley] Lived in the House at Worsley; and was sober: He used to drink, only, a Bason of Milk in the morning, before He went our among them Work-Men: He, afterwards, left the house at Worsley and removed to Stretford, where he became drunken. He carried in his pocket a little Brandy-Bottle wattled, called a Pocket-Pistol.

It is a mischievous allegation, framed as though to convey the impression of Brindley's regularly giving way to massive benders in the solitude of his lodging, but it may be that Egerton views the pocket pistol with excessively prim eyes. While no account of his own drinking habits is known to survive, alcohol played a large part in all walks of eighteenth-century life, as the frequent references to 'ale for the labourers' in the Bridgewater Estate accounts bear out. Indeed, when the Northumbrian engineer William Brown of Throckley visited Fenton Vivian in September 1759 to view the steam engine Brindley had built for Thomas Broade, his first action was to give the resident labour force 'drinking money' by way of persuading them to show him Brindley's patent design of boiler.[27] As for the duke, during his Grand Tour, he descended often enough into total stupor to alarm Robert Wood into writing some anxious letters to his charge's guardians. Indeed, when he discovered that the duke had secretly 'hired a country house', laid in copious amounts of champagne and proceeded to neglect his guests, insult Wood's brother and give way 'to the lowest pleasures below redemption', Wood, who was neither an innocent nor a fusspot, tendered his resignation and agreed to relent and remain in his post only on condition of receiving £300 a year thereafter for life as a matter, he said, 'of Justice, not of generosity'.[28] With time, the champagne trouble blew over, but the whole episode makes Brindley's impromptu hipflask look rather tame.

It is the aqueduct, rather than any eccentric or intemperate behaviour, which gives rise to Egerton's gravest charge. In his memoir he claims that, together with the locks at Runcorn and the stretch of the canal that crossed the River Bollin and ran through meadows by the Mersey, it is one of three works of Brindley's which, in the duke's opinion, were 'liable to animadversion'.[29] Conscious that some defect in the design manifested itself in the course of the bridge's construction, Egerton claims that Brindley,

Ran away from it, to Stretford: and He, Never, appeared again, until the Bridge was become secure:

Heavy Rains came; and, Mr Brindley feared it would fall:
He did very ill: for, he weighted the Sides:

Something, it appears, had gone wrong with calculating the stresses upon the structure, and during the bad weather, the fault came to light.

In attributing the error to Brindley, future generations have accepted without question the views of Egerton and Malet, whose assertion that John Gilbert 'doubtless drew the engineering plans' invites some expectation that he might also shoulder some responsibility for the mishap. Yet the events are not as clear-cut as readers of the *Letter to the Parisians* have sometimes made out. For all the ominous plodding of his sentences, Egerton does not actually say that the bridge showed signs of imminent collapse, or even that it 'appeared to begin to buckle'.[30] He states only that Brindley was anxious about its stability. Whether or not his concern was justified, it was certainly understandable. The generation of self-taught engineers who flourished in the mid-eighteenth century forged their understanding of the theory of their work through hands-on endeavour. Not surprisingly, mistakes dogged their efforts. William Edwards's 1756 bridge in Pontypridd, its 140-foot single-span arch sweeping gracefully over the river, came into being only at the fourth attempt. As his fellow clergyman Edward Vaughan Pughe was to reflect, being 'No master of the rules of Architecture' Edwards 'had to buy his knowledge by experience and pay dear for it'.[31]

Whatever trouble threatened or befell the arches of the Barton Aqueduct, Gilbert was well-placed to see what preventive measures were necessary in anticipation of trouble and was quick to act. Brindley did not have a record of consistent first-time success with aqueducts, as his future experience at the Bollin crossing would show; neither, for that matter, did William Jessop, canal engineer of the following generation, so he was hardly alone. In a sense, the episode demonstrates Gilbert and himself in the act of collaborating rather effectively, Brindley making the first attempt at a crossing which, when it turns out to be flawed, Gilbert is quick to remedy. Egerton, nevertheless, hot to uphold family reputation, depicts the potential disaster as a triumph, if not precisely for the duke (his first cousin once removed, to whom he was clearly much attached) then assuredly for the Bridgewater interest as represented by John Gilbert. Where Brindley, Egerton explains, had weighted the sides of the arch, Gilbert,

Took just the contrary Method: he weighted the Arch in danger: and, Lightened the Sides:
He removed the Weight from the Sides: and Laid it, Regularly on the Arch: then He clayed it
again: And afterwards, He let the Whole remain till late the following Spring, to 'Settle'.

Not content with analysing Gilbert's action in engineering terms, Egerton also passes moral judgement upon Brindley, making the damning charge that as soon as disaster threatened, he fled from the scene. He is, in other words, an abject craven who cannot face the consequences of his miscalculation, whereas John Gilbert is a good and faithful servant whose prompt action saves the day.

Not everyone has found this transparent determination to turn the circumstances into an affirmation of Bridgewater honour persuasive. Samuel Smiles comes briskly to Brindley's defence, insisting that any allegation of faintheartedness on his part 'is at variance with the whole character and history of the man.'[32] He might have added (it being a well-attested piece of the Brindley folklore) that when he needed undisturbed peace in which to grapple with work problems, it was always Brindley's habit to take to his bed. There is perhaps rather more at stake here than acquitting James Brindley of the charge of fleeing the scene of a potential disaster of his own making. After all, had that been his intention he would surely have gone further than Stretford. Besides, the remark about leaving the repair until 'late the following Spring, to "Settle"' does not fit with the chronology of the bridge's construction. The Act of Parliament authorising the Barton Aqueduct had received the Royal Assent on 12 March 1760. Admittedly, at that date work on building it may have already begun, but even if it proceeded fast the chance of its being so nearly complete by the autumn or winter of 1760 that Brindley could form a view of its stability by that time, which is what Egerton's talk of leaving it 'till late the following Spring' suggests, seems remote. Whether Gilbert, with a relatively inexperienced workforce, could have substantially rebuilt the aqueduct between the spring and early summer of 1761 so as to have it ready to open to traffic by 17 July is equally questionable.

When the Bridgewater Canal's Bollin Aqueduct collapsed in the heavy autumn rains of 1767, newspapers in the Midlands were swift to report the calamity.[33] By contrast, whatever trouble befell the aqueduct over the Irwell at Barton in 1760 passed off quietly, almost without notice. For what it is worth, the 1760–62 Bridgewater Estate's account book dating from then contains three entries which conceivably might touch upon the aqueduct's modifications. On 25 March 1761, a quarter day, John Gilbert records payment to Brindley of £19 5s 'for 55 days at [...] as per bill', an entry which not only confirms Brindley's salary as 7s per day, but also suggests that he was in good standing with the duke and his agent at the given date. On 13 June 1761, there is a note of an extraordinary payment of 2s 5d to the workmen Wallwork and Laughlin 'for Ale when the Lab[rs] was in the water at Barton Bridge'. Reference to some sort of flood trouble near Barton, together with the record of a gratuity, does not necessarily touch upon the aqueduct, but someone has seen fit to flag up the place on the page with pencil lines in the margin as though to emphasise its import. Then on 26 September 1761, in his distinctively sloping handwriting, without any accompanying comment, John Gilbert notes the sum of 10 guineas 'Pd workmen to drink by his Grace's order when the water went over the Bridge.' Although by this date the canal crossing the aqueduct had been open for some two months, the bonus was no doubt welcome. Brindley, meanwhile, let his tally of days spent in the duke's service run from 26 March 1761 until 24 July 1762, more than a year, before he 'satled the old a count', receiving £116 12s 8d in respect of 309 days' work at 7s a day.[34]

It is probable that the misadventure which befell the aqueduct at this time was relatively minor, its detail known only to Brindley himself and Gilbert; how much truth there ever was in Egerton's tale of an incipient calamity, for which he holds Brindley entirely responsible, it is difficult to determine. Were Brindley's form really as volatile as Egerton and Malet make out, it is hard to see why the duke should have placed such confidence in him. It was Brindley, after all, who provided evidence concerning the canal's route to Parliament, and Brindley to whom (as Joseph Banks observed in his 1767/8 journal) he entrusted 'most of the engineering work of the canal'.[35] The bond between them was strong. On Brindley's side, if the aqueduct had caused him anything resembling embarrassment it is hard to see why he should have arranged for the painter Francis Parsons to depict it in the background of his portrait, the foremost achievement of his life, bathed in the light of a glorious enlightenment dawn over his left shoulder. (See Illustration 4). Whatever his thinking, whatever cracks may or may not have appeared in the masonry and whatever steps Gilbert may have taken towards guaranteeing the aqueduct's stability and safety, the Barton Aqueduct had its ceremonial opening on 17 July 1761 in front of an eager crowd which included the duke himself, the Earl of Stamford and 'a great number of spectators'.[36]

CHAPTER THREE

Summer 1761–Autumn 1763:
The Bridgewater Canal

Growing ambitions

The terms of the 1758 Act which enabled the duke 'to make a navigable cut or canal from … Salford, to or near Worsley Mill' precluded him from selling coal from his mines in Manchester or Salford for any higher price than 4*d* per hundred weight. Although the 1760 Act enabled him to alter the canal's course, it did not change the 4*d* per hundred weight coal clause. To coal-hungry Manchester, the promise of cheap fuel was immensely welcome and one of the reasons why the aqueduct inspired such excitement. Nevertheless, the duke did not conceive the canal for reasons of altruism alone, and he knew that its long-term commercial success required more than a spirit of philanthropy and a daring bridge.

Exactly when the ambition of building on towards Liverpool crystallised in his thinking is uncertain. Brindley biographer Christine Richardson suspects that he may have had the 'lucrative and burgeoning Liverpool-Manchester trade' conducted over the Irwell and Mersey Navigation in his sight, even when he obtained his 1758 Act, and aspired to make the Mersey Estuary his eventual destination.[1] Not only might it be a profitable step in itself, but it could also pave the way for even larger things. Although the expansive navigation in Staffordshire for which Brindley made surveys in the late 1750s had stalled at the planning stage, it nevertheless touched closely enough upon the Duke of Bridgewater's canal enthusiasm to heighten his interest in commerce, and he must have seen that maritime, mercantile Liverpool on the Mersey was a likely place in which to make money.

He did not commit his thoughts to paper and there was good reason for his reticence. The fate of the pamphlet *A New Scheme for Making Inland Navigations*, in which Thomas Broade had divulged the 'many and great Advantages' of the proposed Staffordshire Navigation, showed just how easily publicity could misfire. In his eagerness to publicise the proposals, Mr Broade had employed some sleight of hand. Although he referred in his opening sentences to a 'Scheme … now on foot, for making a communication between Liverpool and Hull', it soon became apparent that what was actually proposed was a very much less ambitious 'cut … from Stoke upon Trent … to Wilden'. He made a bold announcement that it would be 'possible' to make this waterway 'communicate with the Cheshire Rivers', but was conspicuously vague about how exactly the communication was to be achieved. As for his claim that building 'a new Road for Carriages and Horses … thro' Harecastle Vale' would give rise to 'no great Difficulty or Expence', if the financially astute tradesmen of Staffordshire should be rather cautious about taking such a glib assurance at face value, it was hardly surprising.[2] In practical terms, the skills behind the venture were untried, and inflated accounts of its merits only drew attention to the potential hazard of investing in it. For the short term at least, the Staffordshire promoters allowed their scheme to fade out of the public view.

Wary and well placed to learn from the experience of his brother-in-law, Earl Gower of Trentham, on the Staffordshire venture, the duke disclosed the full scope of his canal visions to no-one except the people who would be directly instrumental in bringing them into being. These trusted confidants included Lord Gower himself, whom the duke regarded as a good friend as well as a family connection; the Gilbert brothers with their shrewd understanding of how to manage large ventures; solicitor William Tomkinson and James Brindley the engineer.

By an irony of history, it is the supposedly illiterate Brindley who provides the fullest record of the early phases of the Bridgewater Canal's progress. If his journal-keeping of the 1750s had been a wayward mix of accounts, memoranda about his workmen's wages and occasional comments on a project's progress with the occasional remedy for back trouble or other ailments thrown in, by autumn 1761 his records had become relatively methodical. He had by now abandoned his old practice of assigning a new page to each undertaking and noting the costs incurred at more-or-less regular intervals, and instead he ruled a margin down the left hand side of each double page, wrote the day's date inside it, and proceeded to make brief chronological daily entries. Often, they consist of nothing more than place names, Longford and Worsley occurring most often, but on 30 September 1761 he mentions setting out for Dunham 'to level for Liverpool'. This initial survey which Brindley terms 'Levveling' and 'Reconnitoring' occupied some ten days, from 1 September until 10 October when he writes 'Finished the uper level to Hempstone' – Hempstone, also known as 'The Hempstones', being a point on the tidal Mersey a short distance upstream of Runcorn.[3] Over the following weeks it appears that John Gilbert also visited the place, since a note of the 2s paid 'a man for 2 days with us at Hempstones' and a further shilling paid to 'the old fisherman at the Hempstones' appears in his handwriting in the estate accounts.[4] It marked the start of the duke's preparations for making good his grand aspiration.

At the end of November 1761, Brindley came to London to give evidence in support of the duke's application for a new Canal Act. He informed the House of Commons that it would not only be possible to extend the duke's canal, which had now reached Longford Bridge, as far as the Mersey, but also that it would 'facilitate' the transport of coal, stone, timber and other goods between Manchester and Liverpool and greatly reduce the expense of their carriage.[5] In a subtly qualified statement, he also stated that the landowners and tenants of the district 'with whom he had conversed' gave every sign of welcoming the canal, pronouncing it 'very serviceable ... and a great service to the country in general'.[6] His assurance on this matter apparently satisfied the honourable members, since the House gave the duke leave to bring in a bill to extend his canal from Longford Bridge to the Mersey at Hempstones.

In January 1762, when the bill came up before the Commons for debate, it soon became clear that his confidence in Cheshire's eager anticipation of the canal's promised benefits proved less than well-founded. The proprietors and shareholders of the Mersey & Irwell Navigation petitioned against the duke's bill passing into law on the grounds that, having spent large sums on making the river navigable, if the canal should be built they stood to lose by their investment; Sir Peter Warburton of Arley alleged that it would render his mills on the River Bollin useless; the townsmen of Warrington opposed it because they feared that it would deprive the rivers Mersey and Irwell (their links with Manchester) of water; some of the Manchester merchants and traders objected to it on account of its potential damage to the Mersey & Irwell Navigation, and a group of Cheshire landowners headed by the Hon. Richard Barry and Peter Legh, joint Lords of the Manor of Grappenhall, and including the canal's doughtiest opponent Sir Richard Brooke of Norton Priory opposed it because they maintained that it was not necessary.[7] That this party included several trustees of the River Weaver Navigation – Cheshire's existing route to the Mersey, which it joined below Frodsham – was hardly coincidental. One James Gildart, the gentleman entitled to take 'tolls and benefit' from the ferry that gave Hollins Ferry on the Mersey its name, realised belatedly that the canal promised to put him out of business and reduce the value of his farm. He offered to sell his land to the duke and at the same time petitioned the House to grant him 'such relief as the nature of his case merits'.[8]

These objections to the canal, many of which came from parties with a clear interest in preserving the river navigations' hold over Cheshire's water transport, were perhaps predictable. What neither the duke nor, perhaps, Tomkinson foresaw was the arrival of a petition from another set of Cheshire landowners, opposing the canal on the ground that they had been misled about it. The duke's agents, this faction maintained, had 'prevailed' upon them to give their consent to the scheme, before they were 'fully apprised of the Consequence thereof', and having 'maturely considered' the canal's likely impact, they found it 'very prejudicial' to their interest.[9] The *Journal of the House of Commons* does not name the petitioners, saying only that their names 'are thereunto subscribed, but it seems likely that they included another steadfast opponent of the canal, namely Mary, the Countess of Stamford.

Wife of Harry Grey, 4th Earl of Stamford, Mary had inherited Dunham Massey from her father, the Earl of Warrington. Although by law both the house and estate passed to her husband on their marriage, she continued to live at Dunham and to oversee its management while Lord Stamford spent most of his time at his other residence, Enville in Worcestershire, where he devoted himself to landscaping the grounds. Among the countess's papers is a transcription of Brindley's evidence on the duke's petition, complete with some revealing annotation. To his claim that local landowners considered that the canal would be serviceable, someone – possibly the countess herself – has added the terse comment 'very few'. His remark about the tenants being pleased with the proposal meets the written response 'Quite ye contrary'. Even his assertion that no coals reach Manchester 'but what comes on horseback' receives a contradiction from the margin: 'None are so carried but by Gardeners' horses of Altrincham, who take Garden stuff to Manchester … [and] bring back Coals'.[10]

The argumentative thrust of these allegations was plain. Brindley, the duke's witness, they imply, had deceived the landowners of Cheshire and the Members of Parliament alike. Although it was a serious allegation, the countess seems to have preferred not to pursue it, relying instead on her near neighbours, the Weaver men (she had great confidence both in Sir Peter Warburton and Lord Strange), to press home her claim for full compensation from the duke. It is an episode that reveals the precarious nature of Brindley's role in the duke's concerns. By virtue of his standing, he was well-placed to view the situation with professional detachment and to disregard the landowning gentry of Cheshire's attitude to the duke's proposed canal as wholly irrelevant to the question of whether its construction was practicable in engineering terms. At the same time, he could hardly avoid knowing that he might in future find himself either working for some of these same Cheshire gentlemen, or having to call on them in connection with future land purchases. Although the establishment of turnpike trusts and their commissioners had gone some way towards setting a pattern for negotiation about compulsory purchase of land and appropriate compensation for its loss, neither the country aristocracy nor the millwrights-turned-engineers of the 1760s were entirely *au fait* with these matters. Being at the forefront of the new technology required a measure of discretion and knowingness, as Brindley was beginning to discover.

One aspect of the thing was having the right clothes. His notes of the time include a couple of London shopping lists, the first detailing the 'Shirts, shues, stockins, nackcloths, buckles and gloves' [sic]; the second mentioning new britches, new shoes, cloth coat and waistcoat, and 2 guineas of broadcloth from which he presumably arranged to have a coat made up.[11] He also paid a shilling to be shaved four times over, had his shoes blacked and acquired a knife. Why he should have wanted his last item is a mystery; otherwise, it is a revealing account of what early 1760s propriety deemed appropriate garb for a member of a new profession to don before testifying to the legislators of the nation.

Despite the brevity of his entries, his record of the Bridgewater Canal Bill's passage through Parliament shows his keen eye for the telling detail. For instance, he highlights the 4½ hours' solid questioning endured by William Tomkinson, the duke's long-suffering solicitor; notes the 250 letters the duke sends to canvass the honourable members' support; remarks on the 'grate vigor' of the House's deliberations and, mischievously, records how excess of strong feeling leads one MP inadvertently to vote on the wrong side. Terse as they are, his comments reflect both a shrewd appraisal of the parliamentarians' deliberations and a thorough appreciation of the passions riding upon their outcome. On the right-hand side of the page, he provides a skeletal commentary: '3 divisions – The Duk carr[i]ed by numbers every time – a 4 division moved, but Noes yielded.' On 8 March he states, 'This Bill past the House & was carried to the Lords', where it would pass without opposition. Lord Strange, he observed, was 'sick with grief'.[12] (See Illustration 5).

He was not always such a contented spectator. Besides canal business, among the records of his weeks in London during the early part of 1762, towards the end of January Brindley writes 'at the play'.[13] The story that maintains he was persuaded to see a performance of Shakespeare's *Richard III* with David Garrick in the leading role, which might well have made for a blood-curdling entertainment, is open to question; Brindley's biographer Christine Richardson researched Garrick's engagements of the time, only to discover that they did not include playing Richard III.[14] With Brindley himself, the specific production perhaps counted for less than the stirrings of a queasy conscience inherited from his Quaker ancestors, to whom theatrical glamour had been rank abomination. His evening out proved disastrous, the whole experience shocking him to the core. Afterwards, he 'complained for several days … that his ideas were disturbed', and all his notebook entries for the first fortnight of February read either 'not well', or, more succinctly, 'ill', which suggests that even before he set foot in the theatre, the onset of disease may have clouded his capacity for enjoyment. What is certain is that once he had recovered his health and spirits, having gone to church by way of devout thanksgiving, he put the whole disagreeable business behind him and announced that under no circumstances whatever would he watch a play again. It was an extreme reaction and one which Brindley's friends, particularly Josiah Wedgwood, who had a boundless capacity for enjoyment, were inclined to deplore. Years later indeed, Wedgwood and Bentley would attribute Brindley's early death to his inability to derive any pleasure either from 'miscellaneous reading' or 'the polite and elegant arts'.[15]

The day's work

The Bridgewater Canal Act of 1762 brought the duke, his agent and his engineer a new surge of encouragement. By late 1763, the canal had reached Corn Brook, about 1 mile from Castlefield where it was to terminate, and its course lay dead across that of the Corne Brook, the tributary of the Irwell that gave the place its name. Brindley's notebook entries by this time do not just to record place names with an occasional word of comment, but relate events as they unfold in the manner of a personal journal. He no longer ruled out a grid across the page to make it accommodate up to a month's worth of entries, but instead allowed himself to allocate a page to a day, with discrete notes – admittedly always very concise – for morning and afternoon. Only one volume, if that term does not over-aggrandise the slight, flimsy notebook that holds the records he wrote between 31 October and 27 November 1763, survives from Brindley's diarist phase, but its pages reflect the raw stuff of his life during the canal's construction.[16] (See Illustration 6).

Since the duke's enabling legislation precluded any diversion of the tributary of a navigable river, Brindley planned to take the Corne Brook under the canal. His plan, as Christine Richardson describes it, was to feed the stream,

> Into a large circular basin, from where it would fall gradually into a smaller basin within it. From there it would flow into a tunnel under the canal, the exit of which was at a lower level than the entrance, thereby forcing the water to find a level and rise into its natural channel for further passage down to the river.[17]

Like the siphon at Wet Earth, the structure fitted a need which the precise local conditions dictated, and Brindley appears to have arranged to supervise its building in person. Unfortunately, just as the work was about to begin, a bridge collapsed on land nearby which belonged to one of the canal's keenest opponents – Mr George Lloyd of Hulme Hall. 'Monday October 31, 1763', Brindley wrote, 'at Cornhill',

> At Breckfast a man cam to let me no Mr Loydes Bridge was fall at Corn Brook. Orderd Loyd's Bridge to be suported again foor Noon.

Recognising the gravity of the situation, he despatched carpenters to set about the repair work at the first opportunity. Once they had matters in hand, he once more gave his attention to the stream, and on 4 November 1763 recorded his order that the brook be dammed as a preliminary to diverting it through the new siphon. The morning did not progress without incident. 'Rock' wrote Brindley, before adding that an injured collier was 'sent to the infermery [sic]'. He then recorded the 8*d* spent on dining in the Bull inn. Finding himself short of labourers, in the afternoon he went to Cornhill to despatch four men to the site of the new weir at Cornbrook. Work advanced steadily. Brindley devoted the afternoon of Thursday 10 November to planning 'the size of the Arch over the River Marse [Mersey]' and noted its dimensions: '66 foot span And rise 16.4 feet'.[18] A couple of days later, Thomas Gilbert visited the site to announce that he 'had coming the Dutchis of Malbrou to Manchester'. This early celebrity visitor was in fact Caroline Spencer, Duchess of Marlborough, born Lady Caroline Russell and the cousin of Earl Gower. What she made of the canal Brindley, it is sad to say, does not relate.

Although a degree of tension between himself and John Gilbert colours some of Brindley's journal entries, it is less prevalent than the Bridgewater Canal folklore makes out. On Sunday 13 November, for example, Brindley despatches a messenger from Gilbert in short order and with the rather disobliging message, 'No more society', for no obvious reason except that it is 'a fine sunshine daye' in which he is enjoying the company of one P. Nickes. Less than a week later, on 18 November 1763, Gilbert and he disagree over the employment of the estate carpenters and Gilbert is 'displesd' with Brindley's arrangement and layout of the canal's drains. Smiles suggests that his coolness sprang from the time when his mare was found to be in foal, allegedly by Gilbert's rig, yet if there was much reserve and rivalry between them, it is more likely to come about as the result of each man's viewing his work from a different perspective than from any inept horse-husbandry.[19] According to his friend Joseph Banks, Gilbert brought such 'indefatigable industry' to his duties as agent as to be constantly 'overlooking every part' of the work in progress, 'and trusting scare the smallest thing to be done except under his own eye'.[20] While the duke no doubt valued this vigilance, since long years of self-employment had accustomed Brindley to trusting in his own judgement, if he found Gilbert's micro-management of his work more irritating than helpful it would hardly be surprising. Yet on occasion the colleagues could set aside their differences and turn companionable. '17 Thursday Novm 1763', writes Brindley in unusually chatty vein,

> Past 7 o clock at Night Mr Gilbert and son Tom called on mee at Gorsehill & I went with them to the Cock then stayed all Night.[21]

It is an entry from which Hugh Malet makes much narrative capital, asserting in both of his biographies of the duke that the Gilberts took Brindley 'on a drinking spree' specifically in order to placate him after the business with the in-foal mare.[22] In fact, Brindley's spare account of the evening furnishes no evidence whatever to support this version of events which, to all appearance, was no more than the colleagues' decision to spend an evening at the nearest inn. (See Illustration 7).

One of the disappointments of reading Brindley's notebooks is that he rarely gives any detail about his inventions. By chance, on Wednesday 23 November he makes a brief reference to the stop gates, or 'stops' as he succinctly calls them, which he had contrived in order to prevent the loss of water after a breach. 'Noon. At Cornhill,' he writes. 'Ordered the stop to be finished as soun as posable.' Two days later, on Friday 25 November 1763, again at Cornhill, he adds that he,

Made the carpenters to alter the props of the stop to rasst in the fasha [fascia] of the stonework and to lay a plank above the beam level with the surface of the water to walk upon.

On neither occasion does he say anything to illuminate their function or operation. The gates were designed to lie on the canal bed, usually in pairs in a horizontal position. The idea was that if the canal were breached, the flow of water would cause one of the gates to pivot into a vertical position where it would be supported by a post so as to retain as much as water as possible.[23] They probably worked better in theory than in practice, but when the agriculturalist Arthur Young visited the Bridgewater Canal towards the end of the 1760s, he found them immensely impressive both in terms of conserving canal water and as a flood prevention measure.[24]

Mr Lloyd, by this time, had started defiantly helping himself to the available building materials, and on 25 November 1763 Brindley found him in the act of 'piking [stealing] the paving stones.' Challenged, Lloyd brazenly claimed that he had a 'right' to take them. On the following day, with what seems remarkable restraint in the circumstances, Brindley 'left word' with the labourers Palton and Samuel to let Lloyd know that he forbade him to remove any more large stones or gravel, at least until Gilbert had been consulted on the matter.

The weather, previously mild, altered and Brindley watched the crosswinds stir waves on the water's surface. Before long, snow and frost made canal digging impossible, although 'Cheetham's men' – presumably the labourers employed by an independent contractor – continued at work mending roads. On the morning of 22 November, Brindley despatched the 'old 20 tun boat' to Worsley to break the ice before ordering Thomas Morris, the carpenter, to dismantle a crane at Cornbrook.[25] Before long there came the fresh hazard of a rapid thaw. 'Grate rains', noted Brindley on 26 November, and observed that the canal had risen by 2 inches. The following day, a Sunday, he 'Lay in bed till Noon' but on venturing out to check the water levels, found the Longford Brook had risen to 6 inches of the centre of the weir. On that note of concern, with an updated tally of his days on the site, Brindley's November diary closes, its circumstantial detail reflecting the very pith and texture of his days spent overseeing the progress of the Bridgewater Canal.

Cash flow

Stories of the duke at this time tend to concern the financial straits to which the canal brought him. The wish to keep the whole enterprise under his direct control prompted his decision not to form a joint stock company, but treat the canal, like the mine which it served, as part of his estate. This hands-on approach to managing his affairs came at a cost and although large, his resources were far from limitless. At one point in the construction phase he had the embarrassment of discovering that no banker either in Manchester or Liverpool would cash his bill for £500, so convinced were they of his imminent ruin.[26]

His working capital he raised largely through the issue of bonds – agreements naming the lender, the amount of money he or she had loaned to the venture and specifying the rate of interest it incurred, while he pledged his name and estates as security for each loan. Someone in the Bridgewater Estate – perhaps the self-effacing John Gilbert, but more likely the ruthless lawyer William Tomkinson – was evidently rather effective at brokering these agreements, since bonds were issued to some far-flung and unlikely lenders. They include, for instance, the spinster Frances Piggott of New Bond Street, who lent the duke an initial £5,000 which increased by a further £1,000; the widow Ann Cowley of Surrey who combined with London apothecary Robert Cowley, perhaps her relative, in a loan of £1,200, and a clergyman named Levett who loaned a further £1,000. While issuing bonds increased the available funds, it was not without problems. Not only did the task of keeping records for a large number of small loans increase the estate managers' administrative workload, but also there was the risk that if the canal should fail, the duke's only means of paying off his creditors would be through the sale of his estates – a course of action which, as Hugh Malet drily observes, would have 'reduced' him 'to … poverty scarcely consonant with his impressive titles'.[27] As an interim measure, he raised additional small sums from his tenantry, round whose homes John Gilbert often rode to solicit loans when the labourers' pay-day was imminent. If he found requesting money on behalf of his aristocratic employer distasteful, anecdote makes out that he had the consolation of being able, on one occasion, to swap his work nag for a fine horse belonging to a highwayman on the run who thought that a change of mount might conceal his identity.[28]

In truth, the duke's circumstances may not have been quite as parlous as the stories make out. At the same time as work advanced on the canal, he built not only the elegant Brick Hall – an airier and more graceful dwelling than the dark and sprawling Old Hall – in which to stay on his visits to Worsley, but also the commanding Bridgewater House near the locks in Runcorn. His palpable eagerness to see the canal advance led him to take a reckless approach to land purchase, of which vendors were swift to take advantage. Not only would he buy out George Lloyd of Hulme Hall, thief of the paving stones, for £9,000 and then mortgage his estates back to him for £4,500, but he also paid the large sum of 30 guineas to the owner of a minute plot of land complete with a pear-tree which happened to stand in the canal's path near Lymm.[29] Seeking to raise funds through the orthodox channels, the duke approached London banker, Sir Francis Child who – proving rather more amenable to these overtures than his opposite numbers in the north – advanced him loans totalling a value of £25,000.[30]

A strange, inconclusive story about this uncertain time came to light when plans to build a Liverpool and Manchester Railway were afoot and the brothers George and John – later Sir John – Rennie came to Manchester to make a survey. Robert Haldane Bradshaw (1759–1835), trustee for the Bridgewater Estate and superintendent of the Bridgewater Canal, took them to his house near Chat Moss and, in a rare turnabout for a man who usually viewed railways and railwaymen with implacable opposition, entertained them most hospitably. Bradshaw had regularly fired shots above the heads of George Stephenson's surveying party but apparently respect and affection for the older John Rennie, the engineer responsible for building both the Lancaster Canal and the Kennet and Avon Canal, brought out his more genial side, and the two young men found him at his friendliest.

Pointing, in the course of conversation, to a distant white-washed house, Bradshaw related how it had once been an inn where the duke and Brindley met to discuss how to raise enough money to pay their labourers' wages. While it is not unlikely that John Gilbert joined them, Bradshaw's portrayal of himself as one of the party is unconvincing, since he was born in 1759 and at the time of the duke's cash-flow crisis would have been no more than an infant. According to Bradshaw, the duke confronted Brindley with a demand to know where they were to find the money for completing the canal. Brindley, by way of answer, gave short shrift to the duke's pessimism in the face of mounting debts. He could not tell where the money was to be found, but he was certain once the funds were located, he could finish the canal and pledged that 'it would pay well'. Wanting something more constructive than empty optimism, the duke repeated his enquiry about where the money was to come from.

'Don't mind, Duke; don't be cast down', was Brindley's less than helpful answer, 'We are sure to succeed after all.' Remarkably, according both to Bradshaw and Sir John Rennie, who repeats the anecdote in his *Autobiography* without casting any doubt whatever upon its veracity, with this airy assurance the duke was content.[31]

According to Rennie and Bradshaw, 'It happened shortly afterwards that the duke managed to get money enough to complete the canal', which was a happy outcome, but feels rather too convenient to make for a satisfying narrative. Viewed in the light of a fable, the tale is decidedly slippery; does Bradshaw set out to illustrate the merits of perseverance by indicating that the duke does not give up in hard times? Or to praise his courage in having confidence in new and untried technologies and taking Brindley's word that the canal will pay well without objection or quibble? The story's moral never becomes wholly clear.

How much, if anything, the anecdote owes to fact rather than myth is a diverting but unanswerable question. Yet even if the tale is pure folklore, it has the distinction of providing a rare if not unique account of a conversation between the duke and his engineer. In its shadowy way, what is more, it bears revealing witness to the social changes afoot in the 1760s. There is something rather refreshing about seeing the duke, straitened circumstances notwithstanding, frequent a remote pothouse and finding Brindley so much at ease in his company. His wild claims would prove prophetic after all, for the canal would prosper indeed. It would also, although this detail is hardly likely to have been in Bradshaw's mind when he soliloquised to the Rennie brothers, presage the arrival of an age in which graft, skill and commercial know-how would count for as much as inherited wealth and status.

CHAPTER FOUR

1762–64: Rivers

Brindley's accounts books-cum-diaries reveal the extent to which, from about 1760 onwards, the duke's canal absorbed him. It would not be long before Josiah Wedgwood succeeded in reviving interest in the dormant Staffordshire Navigation scheme, but in the meantime, Brindley's skills caught the attention of proprietors of a number of existing river navigations. The work took him away from Worsley, which may have caused the duke and, more particularly, John Gilbert some irritation, but he was self-employed after all, and the duke's canal venture had boosted his reputation and honed his skills, for which river navigation work provided an obvious outlet.

Besides, it strengthened his conviction that canals were more advantageous. He expressed his view of rivers in a remarkable image in which he compared their 'water … flowing down a declivity' to 'a furious giant, running along and overturning everything before him'.[1] The conception of a river as a vast, sprinting form, whose uncontrolled force disturbs or destroys anything and everything in its path, makes its point in strong terms. Assuredly, no trader in his senses would wish to entrust a cargo to this untamed and destructive element. As the allegory develops its detail alters, the river-giant changing from runner to wrestler and, showing a certain understanding of prize fighting, Brindley asserts that if 'you lay the giant flat upon his back, he loses all his force, and becomes completely passive, whatever his size may be.'

Dissection of his simile is, admittedly, slightly ridiculous since it hardly needs exposition to reveal its thrust. At the same time, Brindley's insistence that through the application of art and skill the undisciplined force of water can be rendered serviceable begs large questions. After all, since people had always used rivers for transport, the hesitation of eighteenth-century manufacturers and traders to invest in untried canal developments begins to look understandable. Brindley's river work may have had no direct bearing on his association with the duke, but it gives some indication of the path his career might have taken if the canal idea had not proved so successful.

The Don Navigation, 1762

In the third week of June 1762, some sixteen months before he came to record his day-by-day supervision of work around Cornhill and Cornbrook, Brindley recorded travelling from Lancashire across the Pennines and into South Yorkshire.[2] Having reached Rotherham, he spent three days apparently surveying the western stretches of the Don Navigation before heading into Doncaster for a meeting of the General Assembly of Proprietors of the Don Navigation Company on Midsummer's Day, 24 June 1762. What he may not have appreciated at the time was that he had walked into what, commercially speaking, was a hornets' nest.

Having had its lower reaches re-routed through Cornelius Vermuyden's Dutch River in the 1630s, and the length from Doncaster upstream to Tinsley near Sheffield made navigable by progressive straightening and deepening in the 1720s, by the 1760s the River Don navigation was a patchwork of different improvement projects.[3] At its upstream end, waters drained down into it from the Pennines; downstream, it was tidal. Taken as a whole, the Don exemplified all the disadvantages to which river navigations were prone. It was the source of power for a number of enterprises situated along its course, and when the Don Navigation Company summoned Brindley, they were apparently struggling somewhat to keep up with consumer demand.

Over the summer of 1762 the Don Navigation Company were in the thick of an acrimonious feud with the ambitious brothers Jonathan, Samuel and Aaron Walker. Before establishing a small ironworks at Grenoside near Sheffield, Jonathan (b.1710) had managed the family farms; Samuel (b.1715) had been a schoolmaster, while Aaron (b.1718) experimented with casting and smelting. Within five years their foundry had outgrown its site, and in 1746 the Walkers moved their operation to Masbrough where they built casting houses, furnaces and a smithy, relying upon the nearby Don for both water power and water transport.[4]

To the Don Navigation Company, the Walker Brothers proved demanding neighbours. Not only did they seek preferential rates for their vessels, but in the course of establishing their Masbrough operations they built a weir across the river so as to provide a steady flow of water to their mill dam along a stream called Holmes Goit.[5] While the weir helped to ensure that the Walker wheels turned efficiently, it can hardly have assisted navigation. In 1757/8, the go-getting brothers made a navigable cut from their works to the Don so as to avoid the need for their vessels to use Holmes Goit. At much the same time, local landowner Lord Effingham leased a building – 'not being an iron forge, blast furnace or slitting mill' – on the Goit to the Don Navigation Company and magnanimously offered to build a weir across the stream by way of providing it with water. Interpreting this proposal as a direct threat to their own water supply, in order to forestall the Navigation Company from building anything resembling a dam across Holmes Goit the Walkers began to use it for their boats again and blocked their own cut. Conciliatory, the Navigation Company suggested making a new channel which would both accommodate the Walkers' transport vessels and serve their premises on the Goit.[6] The proposal came to nothing, and the attempt to lodge a bill in Parliament 'for the Restoring, perfecting, continuing and preserving the navigation from Rotherham Dam into Jordan Dam' failed, having encountered such powerful opposition from Messrs Walkers, 'that the Company's sollicitors [sic] and agents were advised that it would be impossible to obtain such a Bill, and therefore it was desisted from.'[7]

Some two years previously, the Navigation Company's Assistant Manager, William Martin of Tinsley, had taken a party of boatmen to 'Manchester and other places in that neighbourhood in order to keep up correspondence with the traders in those parts'.[8] In all likelihood, while Martin was in the Manchester area he had met Brindley, remembered him and, in the face of the strife with the Walkers, summoned him to a meeting of the Don Navigation committee where the minutes refer to him as a 'judicious engineer'.[9] Exactly what Martin and his colleagues thought he might do to resolve the impasse with the Walkers, it is impossible to say, but they evidently hoped that where the law offered no remedy for their troubles, the schemer might find some engineering solution.

Whether engineering judgement could ever have settled this particular dispute is doubtful. The iron-founding brothers continued to divert water for their own usages throughout the 1760s and in August 1770 their extraction of navigation water to supply a new rolling mill at Thrybergh had the effect of halting all shipping. Taken to task by the Don proprietors, former schoolmaster Samuel Walker announced that since he considered himself to be 'aggrieved by the Company', until 'those Grievances were removed' he and his brothers 'shou'd take every Opportunity to impede the Navigation' and that 'he hoped his Children wou'd do so after him' – an attitude which suggests that he was never likely to be amenable to reason.[10]

If the Don proprietors hoped Brindley would intervene with the Walkers on their behalf, their hopes were vain. Far from defusing the 1762 imbroglio, he distanced himself from the aggrieved parties. To attempt to mediate between the Navigation Company on the one hand and a set of pugnacious brothers with a thirsty iron business on the other was not part of his job. At the same time, to have some idea of what he made of the energetic Walkers would be instructive, not least because their experience of building a flourishing business from nothing but their skills was not entirely alien to his own.

He spent only a week in South Yorkshire before he returned to Worsley, but he evidently regarded his business with the Don Navigation as unfinished because in September 1762 he spent a fortnight in the market town of Thorne, roughly midway between Doncaster and Goole. While he was there, he arranged to 'reconter' – reconnoitre – and survey a possible canal route between the Don and the Trent, and to design and make a sample model for bridges that would open 'either with leaves or by a swivel' to be built at Goole, Rawcliffe and a site designated only as 'The New Bridge' on the Dutch River.[11]

Neither project was strikingly successful. Like the waterway from Stoke to Wilden which Thomas Broade and his aristocratic friends planned in 1758, Brindley's Thorne canal venture was too far ahead of its time to garner much immediate public support, although it may not have been entirely coincidental that a canal was later built from Stainforth on the Don to Keadby on the Trent, which opened in 1802.[12] The bridges did not come up to expectation either. Local carpenter Martin Wolstenholme built a bridge at Rawcliffe to Brindley's design in August 1763, but initially refused to put up the other two because the construction costs of the first had vastly exceeded Brindley's estimate.[13] Since at this time the old Goole Bridge was 'much in want of Repairs', the proprietors of the Don Navigation authorised Mr Wolstenholme to proceed with the other two swivel bridges 'and [...] to employ as many workmen and labourers ... to expedite this business as the work will admit'.[14] On the subject of Brindley's over-optimistic forecast of the expense, in the company minutes book at least they maintained a tactful silence.

The Lower Avon Navigation, 1763

If the surviving facts concerning Brindley's involvement with the Don Navigation Company are sparse, information about his contribution to the Lower Avon Navigation is skeletal. The sole documentation comes in a pair of entries in the notebook in which Brindley details his employment on the Bridgewater Canal from 31 October to 27 November 1763. One, which is undated, occurs on a page of accounts and reads 'Mon[ey] La[i]d down before I went with guge parat into Worcestershire – Spent at sundre times 2s 8d'; the other mentions '10 days spent with the Judge Parratt.'[15]

'Guge Parat' or Judge George Perrott, Baron of the Exchequer and resident of Pershore in Worcestershire, was the sole owner and proprietor of the Navigation of the River Avon between Tewkesbury and Evesham.[16] The Avon owed its early improvement to one William Sandys of Fladbury, who in the 1630s made it navigable from Tewkesbury to Stratford-upon-Avon. Having acquired the navigation rights in the 1660s, Lord Windsor was to employ the energetic engineer Andrew Yarranton 'to set the river in order and to repair the Pershore Sluice'.[17] The early eighteenth century witnessed a split in the river's ownership, the upper portion from Evesham upstream to the river's source in Northamptonshire being separate from the lower Avon between Tewkesbury and Evesham. In 1758, Perrott, whose greatest distinction at that time lay in having been elected a bencher of the Inner Temple, acquired the Lower Avon Navigation which flowed past Pershore.

It had, by this time, fallen into disrepair and the rising lawyer was to devote some ten years to making it useful – not to say, profitable – once more. On precisely what aspect of his renovation of the old Avon navigation the Judge sought James Brindley's advice, and what talk passed between the two men, is now a total mystery. Brindley's notes about the venture are too brief to be informative, and George Perrott's personal records – assuming that he kept any – do not appear to have survived. The silence is frustrating. It would be illuminating both to know what recommendations Brindley offered the judge and what impressions he formed about the work of his engineering predecessor Yarranton. (See Illustration 9).

The River Weaver Navigation: 1764 and earlier

For much of 1764, Brindley vanishes. If he kept up any regular notebook at this time, it is not known to survive. Work on the Bridgewater Canal advanced, with the duke purchasing land which the canal would cross, and it is possible that when his river navigations work permitted, Brindley took some anonymous part in its valuation. In June 1764 the Liverpool town clerk summoned him to survey the city docks with a view to finding 'some method of cleansing [them] one by another'.[19] The mission went well enough for Bentley, Wedgwood and Henshall to remember it when they compiled Brindley's entry for Andrew Kippis's *Biographica Britannica*, although how much of his time this work occupied is uncertain.[20] Then, after a summer of invisibility, he appeared in Cheshire on 4 October 1764 on the River Weaver Navigation.

The 1721 Act of Parliament that first authorised improvements to the Weaver, an important route for waterborne traffic between the Cheshire salt fields and Liverpool, included provision to make its modest tributary the Witton Brook navigable from its junction with the river to Witton Bridge.[21] In fact, the brook received little attention before 1756, when the commissioners of the navigation put the task of deepening it out to contract. The team of contractors chosen – John Barrow, Richard Heyes, John Mort and William Antrobus – agreed to do the work for the rather modest fee of £700, which they were to receive in instalments.[22] Having made a start, they received £400 for their efforts in March 1757 with a further £200 reaching them in July 1758. Then, for some unknown reason, things appear to have stalled. On their mettle, the commissioners asked Henry Berry, engineer of the nearby Sankey Navigation, for a survey and report. Something in Berry's findings prompted the commissioners to withhold the final £100; whatever the difficulty was, the work remained unfinished.

By now, a party of Liverpool merchants had grown sufficiently concerned about the Weaver's condition to persuade the Liverpool Corporation to finance a full survey of the river. A reorganisation of the navigation's management (an Act of 1760 passed its administration to a newly elected committee of trustees) and presence of the Liverpool men breathing down their collective necks encouraged the Weaver party to take action.[23] It took little time for the newly elected trustees to turn their attention to their over-stretched contractors. The 1760 Act obliged them to provide water to a depth of 4½ feet in the river navigation, and while in strict terms this condition applied only to the river, there was clear wisdom in completing the cleansing and deepening of the brook at the same time.[24] In the spring of 1763, the Weaver trustees' patience with the contractors who were supposed to be doing this work ran out, and on 7 April 1763 they gave the task to the inspector and superintendent of the navigation, Robert Pownall.

Pownall produced his plans for the necessary works in September 1764.[25] At this point, Brindley became involved; the trustees, who clearly had great respect for his judgement, wanted him to appraise Pownall's scheme and make an estimate of its likely cost. Therefore he attended their committee meeting on 4 October 1764 and not only approved Pownall's overall plan and choice of location 'for fixing the new lock', but went as far as to say that he 'could not think of a properer method of compleating the navigation on the [...] Brook but what would be attended with a much greater expence.' It is a generous tribute from one engineer to another and what seems particularly to have appealed to Brindley was the sheer ambition of Pownall's thinking; his idea was to construct a whole 'new trench or cut' alongside the existing brook, intended to 'take off the waste water and keep the ... Brook free from sand.'[26] Here, after all, was something like a small-scale canal. Pownall's trench might not be intended to be navigable, but next to the shallow brook it served to demonstrate what, in terms of tidy efficiency, a man-made channel might achieve. (See Illustration 8).

Incidentally, Brindley's estimate of £3,000 as the sum required cost for completing Pownall's proposed scheme proved almost £1,000 short. In the event, the Witton Brook improvements cost a total of £3967.[27] As Martin Wolstenholme had discovered with the River Don Navigation swivel bridges, Brindley's estimates tended to err on the small side.

The Calder Navigation, 1764–66

By the end of 1764, Brindley had seen a number of river navigations at first hand. Although a lack of records makes it impossible to form much impression of conditions on George Perrott's Lower Avon, maintaining the Weaver and its tributaries in a navigable condition and accommodating the needs of local manufacturers by the River Don graphically illustrated the troubles to which they were prone. He assuredly did not put himself forward for the post of engineer to the Calder Navigation (incidentally, the name 'Calder and Hebble Navigation' dates from an Act of 1769, which had the effect of incorporating holders of loan stock in the enterprise into a Company of Proprietors), but took the job when it was offered to him after a management coup.[28]

In etymological terms, the name 'Calder' signifies a stream of stones. By the beginning of the eighteenth century, the shallow river had been made navigable from its confluence with the River Aire near Castleford to Wakefield and provided power for a number of mills along its upper reaches. Nevertheless, when promoters approached John Smeaton to discuss potential improvements in 1751, he concluded that more of it could be made navigable 'with very little disadvantage to mill owners'.[29] In 1758, he took up the appointment of engineer to the navigation; works began the following year and by late 1764 it was open to traffic from Wakefield to Brighouse, a modest 4 miles or so from Halifax.

Although many of the Navigation's Yorkshire-based proprietors found its approximately 16 miles' length sufficient for their purposes, since the 1758 legislation already enabled the Navigation Company to build west as far as Sowerby Bridge, their Lancashire colleagues appear to have harboured the prospect of extending the navigation right into their own commercial heartland. After some disagreement, on 6 December 1764 the question of whether to terminate at Brighouse, which was the plan that Yorkshire favoured, or adopt Lancashire's preferred strategy of building on to Sowerby Bridge – only 24 miles, or a day's carriage journey from Manchester – went to a vote.

The fact that the meeting to decide the navigation's future and western terminus took place in Rochdale may have contributed to Lancashire's carrying the day.[30] Halifax curate John Watson – not, perhaps, a local man – gives a revealing exegesis of Lancastrian thinking, in which he foresees that even if commodities such as 'flax and lin-yarn' had to be transported some distance by road, extending the navigable length of the Calder had the potential to improve east–west communications out of all recognition. Perhaps his, and Lancashire's, optimism overran. He states, for instance, that 'On this extended plan', goods travelling,

> From Hull to Liverpool and from Liverpool to Hull would have only seventeen computed miles to travel by land; and those two sea-ports would have a very cheap and easy communication ... which would not only be of great benefit to all the interjacent country ... but of public utility in general, as an inland communication by water (save for the small space aforesaid) would therefore be formed between the eastern and western sea.[31]

Victorious, the Lancashire faction's next move was to dispense with the services of the Yorkshireman Smeaton, and the Navigation Company minutes book records the resolution:

That the Clerk of the Navigation do by letter acquaint James Brindley that he is fixed upon as a proper person to undertake the works for perfecting the Calder Navigation and that he be desired as soon as possible to survey the Works, and propose the plans and estimates thereof […] and that Bill of Expenses and his Charges be paid by the Treasurer of the said Navigation for the time being.[32]

Whatever near disaster may or may not have attended its building, the Barton Aqueduct had brought him into the public eye, and the Lancashire men among the Calder Navigation's proprietors saw it as confirmation that Brindley had the daring and vision to meet the ambitions. Over the winter of 1764/5 the Bridgewater Canal works proceeded under their care of on-site overseer and Brindley took the chance to make surveys and prepare estimates. Finding the outcome entirely to their satisfaction, on 31 January 1765 (less than two months after they commissioned his survey) the Calder commissioners minuted their decision to appoint him 'Surveyor, Manager and Undertaker' of the Navigation.[33] He was to be paid 1½ guineas 'for every Dayes attendance', which probably worked out as rather less, all told, than the £250 per annum salary that Smeaton had received, but which was still rather more than the 7s a day he had from the Duke of Bridgewater. Smeaton, incidentally, took his discharge in courteous spirit. Not only did he decline to claim any salary after 15 November 1764, but also made the frank admission:

[I] shall never envy any Man the praise of doing better than myself while I am conscious of having done as well as those that have trod the same (or perhaps less difficult) steps before me.[34]

Hindsight may colour interpretation, yet this remark carries the strong sense that Smeaton foresaw the professional rivalry that was to exist between Brindley and himself throughout the second half of the 1760s. By this time, the two engineers had already come across one another in the professional context. Not only had Smeaton appraised Brindley's survey for the putative 'Navegation in Stafford Shire' in 1760, but two years later they measured 'the Duk's pools', probably sough water, together, and both of them gave evidence to Parliament in support of the Duke of Bridgewater's 1762 Canal Act.[35] Despite the frequency of these encounters, evidence of what they made of one another is sparse. Although in his 1760 report on the proposed Staffordshire canal Smeaton describes the 'tracts of ground' over which Brindley plans his route as being 'well-chosen' and its course 'judiciously designed', by 1768 his magnanimity is exhausted. In his 'Review of several matters relative to the Forth and Clyde Navigation', Brindley's proposals for its route and dimensions brought him to such high frustration that at one point he enquires rhetorically, 'Pray, Mr Brindley, is there no way to do a thing right, but the way you do?'[36]

Although his relations with Smeaton were apt to be volatile, during his association with the Calder Navigation Brindley formed one of the most productive professional connections of his life. Robert Whitworth (1734–99), eighth of the nine children of a Sowerby comb smith, born in the same year as Hugh Henshall, proved a formidably able engineer and draughtsman.

While his reasoning on the subject is lost – a discreet man, he never discussed the subject – it is significant that having worked both with Smeaton and Brindley, Whitworth saw fit to throw his lot in with Brindley. Perhaps it was on account of a preference for Brindley's style of engineering; perhaps Whitworth shared Brindley's conviction about the superiority of canals to river navigations, or it may have been down to immediate friendship. Before long, they would join in setting out what, in time, would become the Huddersfield Broad Canal, also known as Sir John Ramsden's Canal, thereby forming an association which would serve both of them well. It was perhaps the greatest benefit that Brindley derived from his entire Calder experience.

In March 1765, some two months after his appointment, an advertisement for 'a proper person or persons to undertake the cutting of the Canal (about two Miles and a half) from Brooksmouth near Halifax to Sowerby Bridge' appeared in north of England newspapers.[37] Brindley, it appears, had first planned to cross the Calder on an aqueduct before taking the new length of navigation on to Sowerby Bridge on the river's south side. On 20 June 1765, for reasons not immediately apparent, the commissioners instructed him to continue as far as Brooksmouth, then resurvey the remaining couple of miles to Sowerby Bridge on the Calder's north side. Brindley's response was to cut on to Brooksmouth on the river's north side with a branch running up to Halifax, and then across the Calder 'and continue to a basin opposite the Ryburn at Sowerby'. How much the arrangement and construction of the staircase locks at Salterhebble owed to Brindley before Smeaton reconfigured them in 1782 is open to question, but if the original locks at Salterhebble followed Brindley's design, they may well have been the first with which he had any involvement.[38]

One consequence of Brindley's tenure of the post of surveyor to the Calder Navigation was that it had the effect of generating a surge of canal ambition in Manchester, where he was already well known, and the nearby towns. Led by Harbord Harbord, Richard Towneley and Roger Sedgwick, towards the end of 1765 a group of enthusiasts met in Rochdale and opened a subscription with a view to promoting a canal intended to link the navigation at Sowerby Bridge with the Duke of Bridgewater's Canal.[39] At their behest, it appears that in January 1766, between planning Josiah Wedgwood's nascent Trent and Mersey Canal and testifying against the Macclesfield Canal Bill at the duke's instigation, Brindley found time to make some initial surveys. One was for a relatively direct route, the cost of which he estimated at £78,180; for an alternative route via Bury which added an extra 8 miles, he gave the figure of £102,625.[40] In the short term nothing came of either plan, and it would not be until 1794 that the Rochdale Canal got its first Act, with John Rennie as its engineer-in-chief, and William Jessop as his resident. Nevertheless, the episode demonstrates the strength of mid-1760s zeal to see an east–west waterway take shape, and it is perhaps surprising to find that the total funds subscribed for the venture amounted only to £237.[41]

Equally unexpected is the discovery that by the middle of 1766, clerk Thomas Simpson was appointed superintendent to the Calder Navigation, indicating that Brindley by this time had moved on.[42] Whatever the circumstances – did he resign? Was he dismissed after some unrecorded clash with the committee? – by December 1767, the navigation commissioners were advertising for 'a SURVEYOR … properly qualified and well-recommended'.[43] In the spring of 1768, by which time major winter floods necessitated a new survey of the river, Smeaton resumed his former post. On his return, he observed that had the commissioners installed the floodgates as he advocated in his previous term of employment, the resulting damage might have been significantly smaller, 'though probably not entirely prevented'. Brindley may have left in some disappointment, having hoped his work on the Upper Calder Navigation would coordinate with overseeing the Rochdale scheme to which the funds subscribed had been so sparse. He may well also have experienced a degree of frustration with the navigation's commissioners vacillating about which side of the Calder they preferred their route to take.

For what it is worth, in 1776 (four years after Brindley's death), a strongly worded letter from Richard Towneley appeared in the *Leeds Intelligencer* which may cast some oblique light upon the circumstances in which he quit his Calder Navigation post. 'You will remember', Towneley begins,

> That a few years ago, a Proposal was made for extending the Navigation from SOWERBY BRIDGE to MANCHESTER, and thereby rendering a short and easy Junction between the East and West seas, and a Navigable Communication betwixt the two great Commercial Ports of HULL and LIVERPOOL. That Levels were taken, Plans drawn and Estimates made of the Undertaking, by that very able and honest Engineer, Mr Brindley – who is now alas no more! - You will also remember how exceedingly desirous the Country in general was, to have this plan carried into immediate and effectual Execution, and will reflect with Indignation, how a Scheme, so very beneficial to all your Interests […] was obstructed, and at last render'd abortive thro' the unreasonable Prejudices, sordid Self-interest, or imaginary Grievances, of a few individuals who, from some unfortunate Warp in judgment, had taken a disgust to Navigations in general and to this intended one in Particular.[44]

Precisely how these individuals' 'Prejudices … Self-interest … Grievances' and 'Warp in judgement' manifested themselves Towneley does not relate, but it is not impossible that their concerted opposition contributed to Brindley's departure. After all, the need to deal with factions, particularly when they arose among persons who viewed 'Navigations in general' with open 'disgust', was never going to make for straightforward construction and as his image of the uncontrolled giant illustrates, he conceived his work as a process of regulating water systems, not wrangling with adversaries. Towneley not only applauds Brindley's ingenuity and integrity, but as his letter proceeds it emerges that he even preserved the very 'Plans, Levels and Estimates' which Brindley had prepared some ten years previously, in the hope of that these documents will spur the revival of a 'very practicable as well as useful Design.'

Neither the Don nor the Calder and Hebble Navigations gave Brindley an entirely satisfactory experience, with the ironworking Walkers contriving to hold the proprietors to ransom at Rotherham and the Calder and Hebble men splitting into Yorkshire and Lancashire factions over every twist in the line, without a thought for its engineering implications. By the middle of the 1760s, Brindley had developed an unassailable confidence in canals' capacity to provide better, more advantageous water transport than rivers. Advising the commissioners for the River Soar in 1766 on the best means of carrying into execution an Act for making the

Soar navigable from the Trent to Loughborough, he bluntly urged them to think of building a canal instead, on the grounds that it would have the virtue of avoiding the 'shallows, etc., in the river', besides being, as his letter states, 'not only more commodious' but also saving 'a considerable expense'.[45]

Such conviction, though steadfast, was not readily communicable. Wary, profit-hungry manufacturers were, not surprisingly, sceptical about the merits of an untried technology. The notion that a manmade waterway might pass through hills and cross valleys on the level was outside their experience and therefore beyond their belief. The Duke of Bridgewater, championing his canal, had in a manner of speaking proved a point, but cautious businessmen wanted more certainty before committing their finance to canal building. It took the triumphant rebirth of the Staffordshire Navigation, a canal which wooed and at last won the commercial hearts of the Midlanders, to demonstrate the worth of manmade waterways to the nation.

CHAPTER FIVE

1765 Setting the Trent on Fire:
Promoting the Canal from the Trent to the Mersey [1]

The Duke of Bridgewater would play a part in shaping Brindley's next major canal venture, but only from the side-lines. On this occasion, Josiah Wedgwood the potter took the lead in reviving interest in the Staffordshire Navigation for which Brindley had made surveys in the late 1750s. Although the scheme appeared to have fallen out of favour by the early 1760s, frustrated by lack of investment, the pottery towns' wish to see themselves linked with the ports of Hull and Liverpool had never entirely burnt out. (See Illustration 10)

Josiah Wedgwood

Professionally speaking, since the safe carriage of goods made a vital contribution to his commercial success, it was inevitable that Wedgwood should take some interest in transport. At the start of February 1765, in tones which reveal his acute awareness of the shortcomings of existing provision, writing to his rich older brother John he mentions bringing all his energies to bear on improving the available roads. Specifically, he hoped to promote a plan 'to have the Utoxeter [sic] and Burslem Turnpikes join'd & to have the road made Turnpike from Buxton & Bakewell to Leek & from Leek to N:castle'.[2] At the same time, roads – even turnpike roads, with funds from tolls to maintain them in good condition – were less than ideal. Wedgwood could not help but see that water offered a better means of conveyance for his pottery than roads ever would. By the spring of 1765 he had taken up the cause of building a canal from the Trent to the Mersey. Where documentation is sparse, it is difficult to establish a clear chronology of events, but Wedgwood's letters give at least some outline of the thinking which led to the decision to petition Parliament for a bill to bring in an Act enabling the canal's construction.

Wedgwood clearly had the idea under consideration by the early spring of 1765, and on 8 March he asked Brindley to dine with him before they went on to a public meeting at the Leopard Inn in Burslem 'on the subject of a Navigation from Hull, or Wilden Ferry'.[3] Describing the evening afterwards in a letter to his brother John, his tone is matter-of-fact, even laconic; he says nothing about the conversation which presumably passed between Brindley and himself, introducing his companion, 'Mr Brindley, the Duke of Bridgewater's engineer', as though he is not sure whether John Wedgwood will recognise the name. Nevertheless, he cannot conceal his satisfaction at the sheer strength of local support for the canal that he encounters at the public meeting, observing that 'Our Gent seems very warm in setting this matter on foot again', and allowing himself to boast a little about the numerous and 'pressing solicitations' he receives from those present to ride around the district in order to garner support throughout Staffordshire. 'We are', he continues, once more self-contained and to-the-point, 'to have another meeting at Hanley tomorrow & per Wednesday's post you shall know the result.'

Brindley had had some dealings with the Wedgwood family in the past. Around 1750, he built a wind-powered flint-crushing mill at the Jenkins in Burslem for Josiah's uncles John and Thomas, which caused much consternation when its sails blew off on its first day of operation.[4] In the following years both Brindley and Wedgwood lived for a time at Fenton, where Brindley built steam engines for coal owner Thomas Broade and Wedgwood went into partnership with master potter Thomas Whieldon, for whom Brindley would build an engine in 1759 to drain his Bedworth coal pits.[5] He also had a close family link with Wedgwood's line of business, his younger brother John being a potter to whom Wedgwood sometimes applied to fill large orders for ware.[6] On occasion – for instance, when he claimed that the Trent and Mersey Canal's conspicuously convenient course through Wedgwood's Etruria 'estate' smacked of favouritism in the planning – John Brindley could be a thorn in his older brother's side.[7] Nevertheless, they appear to have been on excellent terms most of the time and having a family ally within the Staffordshire pottery trade could hardly have done James Brindley any commercial harm.

In the mid-1760s it was the engineering brother, not the potter, with whom Wedgwood was chiefly concerned. Looking to James Brindley's early survey for a Staffordshire Navigation, and the success he was making of the Bridgewater Canal, Wedgwood determined to secure his services. At this time, their association was entirely a professional matter, conducted with civility but not as yet friendship. After all, although both men followed their respective callings with skill and flair, they hardly resembled kindred spirits. Wedgwood, a compulsive letter-writer, enjoyed family life, conversation and exchange of opinions; Brindley – uncommunicative, solitary and as yet unmarried – gave a strong impression of living for his work alone.

Promoting the idea

In the weeks following the Burslem gathering of March 1765, Wedgwood called on the landowners of the district to outline his plans and held a number of public meetings to discuss them. These meetings were hugely successful. Having toyed with the canal for so long, now the prospect promised to become an earth-and-water certainty and the Midlands manufacturers gave it their backing. Visiting Birmingham in early April 1765, he 'made it appear pretty evident' to the city's manufacturers that once it was built, the canal promised yearly savings of £10,000 'in the article of Land Carriage to and from the River Trent'.[8] It may have been a rash pledge, but Birmingham's fast-expanding industries needed the transport, and the town's manufacturers liked what they heard. One of them, Samuel Garbett, whom Wedgwood describes as 'a very intelligent gentleman' pointed out the advantages the proposed canal held for trade with Russia in iron and flax. 'We have not yet been with the Gent. of Liverpool',

Wedgwood observed to his brother, before remarking that his great friend Thomas Bentley, a Liverpool resident, had already advised him on what line to take in addressing meetings in that city.[9] Warming to his role as promoter, he concluded his reflections with the statement that 'This scheme of a Navigation' was 'undoubtedly the best thing that could possibly be planned for this country.'

Whatever its merits, to gain parliamentary approval the canal had to have powerful friends. Besides his interest in future commerce with Russia, Garbett had been delighted to learn that Wedgwood had made an overture to Lord Gower, 'whose countenance', that is to say, potential influence, he regarded as being 'of extreme consequence'.[10] Garbett's argument was that provided that the canal enjoyed the support of men like Lord Gower and the Duke of Bridgewater, who had what he terms 'ministerial weight', any argument that the 'common landowners' might levy against it would only 'be laugh'd at' and dismissed. In the sycophantic climate of the time it was sound reasoning no doubt, Gower being by any measure a potent choice for the role of the new canal's guardian-protector, and although his wife Louisa, the duke's favourite sister, had died in 1761, the two men were firm friends, united by their shared interest in canals and horse-racing. In fact, Garbett seems to have been under some misapprehension about Wedgwood's movements. Although Wedgwood may indeed have made some approach to Lord Gower in the spring of 1765, nothing would come of it for many months. Given how valuable an ally to the cause Gower promised to be, it is somewhat surprising that Wedgwood was not more insistent about canvassing his immediate support. Perhaps he judged that it would appear over brash and run the risk of having have the opposite result to that which he intended.

A figure with whom Wedgwood was in correspondence by this time was Erasmus Darwin of Lichfield. Poet, physician, champion of Enlightenment ideas about natural history and philosophy, Darwin's many enthusiasms included engineering and improved transport. Writing to him on 4 May 1765, Wedgwood relates that he happened to meet John Gilbert on his way to Trentham. As they fell into a discussion about canals, Wedgwood produced a map of the proposed Staffordshire Navigation, to find Gilbert at once asking 'if it could not join the Duke [of Bridgewater]'s Canal, now authorised to join the Mersey at the Hempstones'. It would, Gilbert observed, 'Be almost as near a way to Liverpool, & much nearer to Manchester and save our locking down into the River.' In return, the Trent and Mersey men 'might afford to give his Grace a small tonnage'.[11] Coupled with Garbett's convictions about the usefulness of having friends in high places, these points were persuasive indeed. Wedgwood promised to pursue enquiries.

The chief obstacle he foresaw in implementing Gilbert's idea lay in opposition from the River Weaver Navigation trustees. The Weaver Navigation was expensive to maintain. It joined the Mersey downstream of Frodsham and, at a time when the new canal's western terminus had not yet been decided, the trustees understandably hoped that canal traffic bound for Liverpool would pay tolls to travel over their navigation on its way to the Mersey. Having recently attended a meeting at Northwich where the Weaver trustees deliberately set out to 'convince' the Wedgwood party that it was in their interest to join the Weaver Navigation, Wedgwood was well placed to warn Darwin about the slippery relations between the Weaver men and the

Staffordshire canal lobby.[12] Not only had the Weaver contingent made much of their readiness to alter their locks and make other adaptations as necessary but also, thrusting matters ahead, they sent Robert Pownall, who the previous year had drawn up such impressive plans for improving the Witton Brook, on a survey 'from Winsford Bridge to Lawton'.[13] This apparently well-intentioned step was not as innocent as it looked. Brindley's assistant Hugh Henshall was already engaged in surveying a line for the duke from Harecastle, where Brindley's route of the 1750s had ended, to the Hempstones, and the Weaver trustees' despatch of Pownall to 'attend and assist him', by pointing out routes for joining 'the most convenient part of the Weaver', was a blatant attempt at persuasion. If Wedgwood had misgivings over these tactics, on paper at least he gave them short shrift and insisted that he was confident of remaining on friendly terms with both the Duke of Bridgewater and the Weaver party.

By mid-May there was a new development. Wedgwood and Brindley – 'Brindley *the great*', as Wedgwood dubs him – had held a meeting at Newcastle-under-Lyme where they learned that the Macclesfield brass magnate and silk manufacturer Charles Roe proposed to build a canal from his town to link with the Bridgewater Canal. The duke, what was more, took enough interest in it to ask to see Roe's plans, although admittedly that had been before John Gilbert mooted the possibility of the Bridgewater Canal's being 'made to coincide' with Wedgwood's.[14] Henshall's survey-in-progress which the Weaver men sent Robert Pownall to gate-crash was intended to assess the Bridgewater/Staffordshire connection's practicability. Competition for the Liverpool-bound trade, in other words, was growing fast. Wedgwood decided to pay the city a visit and talk up the Staffordshire canal plan. Once there (he had an unpleasantly hot and dusty journey) he found his scheme greeted with immense good will. The mayor not only invited him to meet the local merchants over dinner where they drank 'with glee' to the canal's success, but also offered to open a subscription to raise funds for 'carrying the Bill through the House of Commons'.[15]

Finding influential friends

Encouraged by this favourable reception and mindful of Samuel Garbett's counsel, Wedgwood spent the summer of 1765 wooing the Duke of Bridgewater and Lord Gower. Scenting a potential advantage, and notwithstanding the interest he had already expressed in Charles Roe's idea, the duke set out to charm him. When Wedgwood and Newcastle-under-Lyme solicitor John Sparrow called at Worsley, he showed them some Roman pottery that the labourers had unearthed at Castlefield, ordered a fine cream-ware table service, and arranged a pleasure cruise 'thro' a most delightfull vale to Manchester' on the ducal gondola.[16] As a social occasion it was pleasurable without question, but it is striking that Wedgwood's account of the day's events says nothing to suggest that the duke, the solicitor and he actually talked business, let alone reached any formal agreement concerning one another's canal plans. Instead, he reflected in rather bleak tones that the commissioners of the River Weaver were happy to 'use their interest in favour of our design, provided we fall into their Navigation' – in other words, join it, although he preferred to put little concerning this delicate matter into writing.

In the course of the summer he met Lord Gower and the duke more than once at Trentham, each occasion following the same amiable, inconclusive pattern with the exchange of many expressions of goodwill, but no clear commitment.[17] Deference, tact and the wish not to appear to nag a nobleman prompted Wedgwood to hold his peace, although frustration may have laced his silence.

In September 1765 a minor dispute occurred among the canal's supporters. Wedgwood had asked the literary-minded Bentley – he was the uncle of the novelist Ann Radcliffe and a frequent contributor to the *Monthly Review* – to write a promotional pamphlet about the canal to encourage to potential investors.[18] Invited to read the first draft, Darwin criticised it in such barbed and high-handed terms that it took all Wedgwood's emollient humour and diplomacy to persuade Bentley not to give up: '*nobody*', Darwin claimed, 'writes *Grace* & Rt honourable but Taylors and such like folks.'[19] 'Be it remembered that he [Darwin] himself is a Poetical Genius,' Wedgwood teased, dismissing some of Darwin's more waspish remarks in his anxiety to restore Bentley's good will. Squabbles among allies wasted time and this disagreement occupied much of Wedgwood's attention while it lasted. Autumn advanced, and in October Garbett wrote to the Secretary of the Society of Arts, suggesting that they take up the cause of promoting inland navigation.[20] Despite these many and various distractions, Wedgwood could not help but be aware that the duke remained silent.

Then, on 2 November 1765, with Bentley's much revised 'Pamphlet on Inland Navigation' newly published in the *St James's Chronicle*, Wedgwood wrote to say that Thomas Gilbert had asked on the duke's behalf how the canal scheme progressed.[21] It was only an enquiry, not a promise of support, and the Weaver trustees still had hopes of capturing all the Midland's traffic on their navigation, but nevertheless it was an encouraging sign. Careful not to make too much of little, Wedgwood remarked only that he was glad to find the duke had not forgotten the Staffordshire canal scheme and hoped he would remain its 'steady and potent friend.' Precisely what form the duke's thinking took at this time is uncertain; his 1762 Act enabled him to join the Mersey at the Hempstones near Runcorn, although he probably had the Liverpool trade in his sights. As a result of his efforts, Wedgwood had seen enthusiasm for the new canal grow. Yet the question of where its western terminus was to be (specifically, whether it would go to Liverpool as Bentley and John Tarlton, the mayor, confidently expected) remained unanswered. With the duke so reticent, Wedgwood, anxious to keep him as an ally, hoped and waited.

By 12 December 1765, Wedgwood decided that he had learned all that he could from the duke, the Gilberts and Brindley who, incidentally, had married Hugh Henshall's sister Ann only four days previously. It did not amount to much. The only point on which he could be certain was,

> That his Grace intended to bring ... a Canal to Liverpool some way & some time, neither of which Circumstances were determin'd.

Whether the Duke was inclined to have any other canal join his, let alone explain how such a junction might be made was 'much doubted by Messrs G[ilbert] & B[rindley].' By now, he could contain his frustration no longer. 'I most sincerely wish,' he bursts out mid-letter,

Our great Patron may prove in every respect the Patriot we both would be glad to find in him. He has done great things for our country & for us ... it grieves one to suspect such a Character shod mean to serve himself only at the expence of what is most dear to a people by whom he is so much beloved. I hope his views are more liberal, more extended & more worthy of a Character so greatly respected.[23]

Even before he had finished writing, word arrived from Bentley full of justifiable concern that they were all 'intended to be humbug'.[24] Stung, Wedgwood abandoned his earlier deference and decided 'to insist' upon Lord Gower's 'PUBLICLY' – the capitalization is his – putting himself 'at the head' of the canal venture to take it 'under his protection'.[25] By this strategy, not only did he safeguard himself and his allies from the duke's double-crossing them, but also, having secured the patronage of a local aristocrat, reckoned that he could be confident that his scheme would assume enough 'importance with the Landowners and Country Gentlemen' to warrant his applying to take the 'grand design into Parliament this Session'.

Having settled on tactics by which to address the duke's evasions and equivocations, Wedgwood wanted to talk to Brindley. The conversation, he recognised, demanded careful handling. Being party both to the duke's and to Wedgwood's thinking, Brindley was required to show the utmost discretion. 'Was there,' Wedgwood enquired, 'a way, without incurring undue expense – for the new Staffordshire canal to join the Duke's canal?'[26] Brindley assured him that there was. Wedgwood's next question, 'whether, when other People's business is done, it is meant that we should be permitted to do our own?', sought, in its oblique way, to establish whether the Staffordshire men would have freedom to manage their canal as their own concern when it was complete and open, without finding themselves in hock to the duke. Taking Wedgwood's enigmatic wording in his stride, Brindley replied 'It is so meant', in other words, yes. To all appearances, Wedgwood's closing questions turn on practical matters. Would the duke, he asked, 'cause an estimate to be made of crossing the Dane?' Would he also enable 'any engineer' to undertake to build the aqueduct 'in a given time and for a certain sum', or did he prefer to do it himself? Insofar as these enquiries held a hidden agenda, it amounted to asking whether the crossing of the River Dane would be on the duke's canal, or the Trent and Mersey Canal? Again, Brindley recognised what was afoot. He 'could not answer for the Duke', he said, meaning that he could not, or would not, say whether the duke proposed to provide an aqueduct over the Dane, but he 'would consider of the subject himself.'

After Brindley's death, Wedgwood would describe him as a 'sensible friend', the adjective in its eighteenth-century usage denoting not only what was 'reasonable, judicious and wise', but also signifying 'quick intellectual feeling' and swift and sure understanding.[27] In the shadows and silences surrounding the somewhat delicate questions about who was to build the canal, how it was to negotiate the Weaver Navigation and its disputatious trustees, and how, where and if it was to cross the Mersey, intuitive apprehension counted for much. From the outset, Brindley appears to have guessed that Wedgwood was angling for information about how far the duke was willing to help the Staffordshire canal men and taken care not to supply it too freely. At the same time, he had no reason to discourage Wedgwood and the other Trent and Mersey Canal promoters from pursuing their scheme – it was, after all, a venture which had many merits, not least that it held out the promise of future employment. Wedgwood and Brindley, Brindley and the duke could grasp the tenor of one another's thinking without having to distil it into words. This mutual understanding would contribute greatly to securing the Wolseley Bridge meeting's unanimous resolution of 31 December 1765 to petition Parliament for leave to bring in a bill for the Trent and Mersey Canal. (See Illustration 11).

Management and administration

The unspoken plans almost fell through at the last moment with an event which revealed the potential fracture-lines in the unanimity of the canal's supporters. Reaching home on the eve of a crucial public meeting after an exhausting day's travel, Wedgwood found a pamphlet outlining proposals which, to his mind, were 'dark, mysterious and ungenerous'.[28] The work of Thomas Gilbert, it advocated that the new canal be administered by commissioners – that is to say, by officials drawn, roughly speaking, from the same moneyed stratum of society as jurors and magistrates, and for that matter, the Weaver Navigation trustees.[29] To Wedgwood, the idea was anathema. While adopting the commissioner scheme might enable Gilbert himself and his well-to-do gentleman-commissioner friends to draw a profit from the canal tolls while satisfying their consciences with occasional repairs to its fabric, it would bring no benefit whatever to the small tradesman-investor. Not only, in Wedgwood's view, were Gilbert's notions about the proposed canal's managerial framework completely wrong-headed, but he also had the effrontery to prescribe terms for its future administration without consulting anyone else involved in its promotion. Intensely irritated, Wedgwood bundled a group of his allies (by chance, they included the newly wed James Brindley) into a post chaise and headed at once for Thomas Gilbert's Lichfield base.

The Burslem party arrived to discover Thomas Gilbert in the act of threshing out the commissioner scheme in all its fine paternalistic detail with Earl Gower and the Birmingham industrialist Samuel Garbett. Having jettisoned any polite reservations which, in other circumstances, he might have harboured around 'consenting to intrude … unasked upon a Junto' in which he might not be wanted, Wedgwood allowed his companions to thrust him 'in the forefront of the battle'.[30] It proved good policy. In the account of the evening's events that Wedgwood gave Bentley afterwards, what follows is his record of a triumph. 'I am not reasoning now,' he confesses; 'only huzzaing and singing Io' after a conquest.' Since he had given more consideration than anyone else to the question of how the canal company was to be run, he was ideally placed to quash all idea of management-by-commissioners before it gained ground. Launching a direct appeal to Earl Gower's 'candour and humanity', he asked if it would not be 'very cruel, when a set of men had employed their time, their talents and their purses for ten years together' to find 'a new sett of Masters … raised up to controul both them & their works?' The words hit home. 'It would be hard', Earl Gower agreed, pleading with his protégé, 'Gilbert, it would be very hard …', and the conquest was complete.

What Brindley, scooped up at short notice from his wife's company, made of Thomas Gilbert's trouncing is a matter of conjecture. He was more accustomed to taking orders from the Gilbert brothers than wrangling with them, and he could hardly have avoided seeing Wedgwood get his way by sheer force of conviction. It was, by any standards, a striking instance of what a committed individual might achieve against all odds by determination and shock tactics.

Wolseley Bridge

The gathering which took place at Wolseley Bridge on Monday 30 December 1765 was the culmination of the series of public meetings that had taken place over the year to garner interest among potential investors in what would become the Trent and Mersey Canal. It held enough national significance for several newspapers to carry reports of its proceedings and outcome. In tenor and outline, all these accounts resemble one another so closely that it looks as though someone with an aptitude for news management on the Gower/Bridgewater staff (probably one of the Gilbert brothers) undertook to circulate an agreed version of events. The *Leeds Intelligencer* provides a fair example of the type of report that they wished to make public. 'At a meeting held in Wolseley Bridge in Staffordshire on Monday sevennight', it opens:

> It was unanimously resolved to apply to Parliament for leave to bring in a Bill for making a navigable canal from Wilden, in the County of Derby, through Staffordshire, to the river Mersey. Earl Gower, Lord-Lieutenant for the County of Stafford: Lord Grey and Mr Bagott, Members for that County; Mr Ashton Curzon, Member for Clitheroe; Mr Anson, Member for the city of Litchfield; Mr [Thomas] Gilbert, Member for Newcastle-under-line, and many others of the principal Gentlemen and Landowners of that and the neighbouring counties, as well as several merchants and tradesmen from Liverpool, Birmingham, and other great trading towns, were present: Lord Gower opened the meeting, with a very sensible and elegant speech, in which he expressed his satisfaction in seeing so many Gentlemen met together upon so great a design; that he looked upon it as of the utmost consequence to the manufactures of that and the adjacent counties, and to the kingdom in general, and that ever since he had heard of the scheme, it had been his determination to support it with all his interest, both provincial and political; for he was satisfied that the landed and trading interests were so far from being incompatible, that they were the mutual support of each other; and therefore, his Lordship hoped, that every Gentleman present would concur with him in endeavouring to carry so noble and useful a design into execution. Mr Brindley, engineer to the Duke of Bridgewater, was then examined, and the heads of the plan were also produced, and agreed to, with very little alteration. The necessary steps are now taking for the intended application to Parliament.[31]

Except for the meeting's resolution, this bland account reveals little beyond its writer's interest in the Members of Parliament who were present. Far from charting any debate, let alone dispute among participants, it insinuates that the meeting reached its consensus as a matter of foregone conclusion, without quibble or hitch. Whoever composed the piece had a powerful flair for public relations; the arts of canal building were still in their infancy and presenting the idea that this ambitious venture commanded universal support was crucial to its success.

At the same time, any idea that it gives an accurate impression of what took place at Wolseley Bridge that Monday is open to question. One significant detail which the report avoids mentioning is the fact that although the company present resolved to petition Parliament for a bill for making a canal 'from Wilden to the Mersey', the exact site of the western terminus is specified in only the loosest terms. The Mersey, after all, is a sizeable river with a long estuarine reach, and the point at which the canal was to join it, supposing that it joined the Mersey at all, occasioned some heated exchanges. By chance, a letter in which one John Stafford, a Macclesfield solicitor who was present at Wolseley Bridge describes the meeting to his friend and fellow lawyer Samuel Wright of Knutsford gives a rather different version of events. Mr Stafford's unvarnished account of the day not only calls into question the accuracy of the anodyne press reports, but also reveals much about the eighteenth-century arts of politicking.[32]

Stafford spent the evening before the meeting at an inn in Stone. With him were a Mr Tarleton (probably John Tarleton, a merchant and ship-owning slaver who became Mayor of Liverpool in 1764) and Mr Scrope Colquit, Liverpool city councillor and attorney at law.[33] Probably at the same time that Josiah Wedgwood thrust himself into the Garbett, Gilbert and Gower 'junto' in Lichfield, Tarleton and Colquitt told Stafford that they had 'subscribed £200 out of the publick purse' towards obtaining the new canal's Act, because they were 'of the opinion that canal navigations are much preferable to river navigations.'[34] They also mentioned that a petition had been circulated by the duke's lawyer, William Tomkinson, which had initially led them to think that the canal would not actually go to Liverpool – at least, not in the short term – but join the duke's canal at Agden 'and so go into the Mersey at the Hemp Stones'. Guided by Colquitt, Tomkinson had recognised that a canal which terminated before it reached their city was not at all what the city's corporation wanted and had altered the wording with the result that the document was 'signed by several'. Perfectly sanguine about the outcome of the meeting on the morrow, Colquitt remarked to Stafford that a canal which terminated at Hempstones had limited usefulness, being 'liable to the same objections with respect to stoppages by the neap tides as the Weaver Navigation.'

It was therefore with visible consternation that on the following day, when Thomas Gilbert produced his petition 'ready ingrossed for leave to bring a Bill into Parliament', Tarleton and Colquitt realised that it said nothing about the canal's going to Liverpool, but only 'to the river Mersey in the County of Chester'. Tarleton at once objected that the Mersey was in Lancashire, not Cheshire, and demanded to know how a scheme conceived 'to carry on the canal over the Mersey to the town of Liverpool' was to be executed if the canal stopped short at the Mersey. According to Stafford, who shows a shrewd appreciation of the arts of legalistic wrangling, 'Mr Gilbert' (he probably means Thomas) answered with a suave and unsatisfactory pledge to the effect that while the Liverpool connection 'might be done afterwards', taking the canal 'to the Mersey' was all that was planned for the present. Colquitt immediately pressed him on the precise significance of the phrase '*to the Mersey*' [Stafford's italics] and demanded to know which 'particular part' of the river he had in mind, but Gilbert 'very artfully parried them off', changed the subject to finance and requested Brindley to estimate the canal's likely construction costs.

Fluent and compelling upon all subjects relating to practical engineering works, Brindley promptly explained that the most expensive section of the canal would be the stretch which negotiated Harecastle Hill, the most conspicuous natural obstacle in its course, through which he proposed to build a tunnel. Immediately questioned about the 'practicability of the subterraneous passage at Harecastle Hill' – it was an extraordinarily bold undertaking, if not downright foolhardy – he gave the impression that the tunnelling option had won the approval of Smeaton. In fact, when Smeaton had reviewed Brindley's 1758 line, he suggested making 'a deep cut through the summit' of Harecastle Hill in order to create a reservoir from which, he conjectured, it would be relatively easy to build, both to east and west.[35] Telling the company 'that Mr Smeeton as well as himself had … viewed the ground and that they both thought it practicable to drive the canal through it in such a manner as to answer the purposes of the navigation effectually' was not only truthful in part, Smeaton had certainly viewed the ground, but also enabled him to allay the meeting's qualms by invoking the name of an engineer who was at least as well-known as himself, if not rather more distinguished. It was sleight of hand, but it served his purposes. After all, Brindley no doubt guessed that were he to describe the actual business of sinking shafts across the hill, gauging their depth with a plumb line and driving headings from the base of each shaft to the next with powder and pick, it would only invite hostile questions and objections on the grounds of impossibility. Since John Stafford was unlikely ever to have read Smeaton's report, in common with the other Cheshire gentleman he no doubt took Brindley's assurances at face value.

Although the meeting concluded triumphantly with the decision to apply to Parliament for leave to bring in a bill, Stafford was certain that its resolution owed more than a little to *suggestio falsi* and *suppressio veri*. 'I cannot forbear thinking', he observed wryly to Samuel Wright, 'the Liverpool gentlemen have been rather hum'd in this business.' Admittedly he was no impartial witness, having in the past done a certain amount of legal work for the Weaver trustees. Nevertheless, his portrayal of the Gower and Bridgewater faction's skilful, not to say ruthless, manipulation of the discussion is not readily argued away. The mystery around the location of the canal's western terminus ended only when the Trent and Mersey Canal Bill was making its way through Parliament. On 12 March 1766, the Duke of Bridgewater suddenly and publicly applied for permission to vary his course.[36] It meant that the canal from the Trent to the Mersey would never reach the Mersey; instead, the Bridgewater Canal would in effect intercept and pick up the new canal at Preston Brook, from where the duke would build the waterway west towards Runcorn without touching the Weaver. (See Illustration 12).

At this point, seeing an end to their hopes, the Weaver Navigation trustees erupted. The gist of their splenetic pamphlet *Seasonable Considerations on a Navigable Canal Intended to be cut from the River Trent to the River Mersey* (1766) and its accompanying *Supplement* is that the canal promoters have treated them most unjustly. Besides being unnecessary, the pamphlets argue, the proposed canal represents an invidious attack upon the river navigators' incomes. After all, they had improved and maintained their navigations on the understanding that they would enjoy some benefits from their investment. Now they stood to gain nothing.

In their indignation, the pamphleteers make Brindley a prime target for their mud-slinging, portraying him as an unprincipled opportunist who has led the young Duke of Bridgewater astray. 'If Engineers', they assert,

Have encouraged a Profusion of Expence in former Schemes, which have not answered, surely they ought not to retrieve the Miscarriage, (however essential to a Continuance of Favour and Confidence), with the Vitals of innocent Individuals.[37]

Not content with almost bankrupting his client, they claim that the unprincipled Schemer's appetite for self-enrichment knows no bounds. Had he not joined Gilbert in purchasing 'Mines and Estates' near Harecastle specifically 'In expectation of this new Canal being cut from the Trent to the Mersey'?[38] Worse, the Trent and Mersey proprietors allow him to defraud every property owner along the new canal's intended line by systematically valuing land 'at ten pounds per acre, which is beyond all Dispute worth FORTY GUINEAS'.[39] So bumptious is he that no-one can tell him anything; indeed,

> This wonderful Projector has arrived to such a Pitch of *Self-Infallibility* that he has presumed, that no one would venture to cast up a Sum after him; and that the grossest Impositions would be implicitly swallowed.[40]

For all the pamphleteers' understandable sense of grievance, their invective tells only half the story. That Brindley should make light of the errors in his mathematics is totally believable; how would he get any work done, if he lingered over the fine arithmetical detail of the costs of a venture still under discussion? His sums might slip, his insistence on building to an exacting standard prove expensive, and he might on occasion take the chance of buying up good land in a prime location. Nevertheless, what emerges from the insinuations and allegations is a powerful picture of a man who overcomes difficulties by relying on his own judgement.

If the pamphleteers had reservations about Brindley's abilities and cast aspersions on his integrity, Wedgwood – soon to be appointed treasurer to the committee of the proprietors of the navigation from the Trent to the Mersey – trusted him implicitly. On 14 May 1766, the 'Act for making a navigable Cut or Canal from the River Trent, at or near Wilden Ferry, in the county of Derby, to the River Mersey, at or near Runcorn Gap' received the Royal Assent. Some two months later, in front of a crowd of potters on a heath outside Burslem, Josiah Wedgwood solemnly cut the first sod of the new waterway and James Brindley wheeled away the earth in a barrow. The public action set a seal upon their friendship. Unlike the duke, with his fey goodwill and frequent demands, Wedgwood regarded Brindley with steadfast affection. The Grand Trunk gave rise to a warm friendship, nurtured not only by commerce, but humour, hospitality and mutual respect. This comradeship would leaven the frustrations, illness and disappointments that attended Brindley's years of fame; it would end only upon his death.

CHAPTER SIX

Interlude: Leisure and Love

For all the aspersions the Weaver pamphleteers cast upon his character, Brindley was not without integrity and his conscience was keen. His appointment to the post of surveyor general to the newly formed Company of Proprietors of the Navigation from the Trent to the Mersey on a salary of £200 per annum did not erode his loyalty to the duke, his great patron, to whom he was quick to give his assistance on canal business when it was required. Nevertheless, the sod-cutting ceremony on Burslem Heath marked the subtle changes that were beginning to overtake Brindley's and the duke's professional relationship and it is a convenient point to examine how the two men spent their time when they were not engaged upon canal business.

The duke at leisure

Bloodstock, building and collecting paintings were, canals apart, the duke's lifelong interests. The interest in art manifested itself during his grand tour, when he developed an interest in the works of Richard Wilson (1714–82), a Welsh landscapist with a taste for classical subjects who resided in Italy throughout the 1750s. Around the same time, he arranged for Anton Raphael Mengs, court painter to Charles III of Spain, to paint a portrait of Robert Wood as a memento of their travels.[1] Buying paintings was an expensive pastime and during the years of building the canal, he abandoned it. His enthusiasm resurfaced in 1797 when, now in his wealthy middle age, he purchased the Orleans collection jointly together with his nephew George Granville Leveson-Gower and the Earl of Carlisle. This stupendous assemblage of Renaissance art came on the market in 1797 and included works by Durer, Raphael and Titian. At first, the duke appears to have viewed the purchase as a useful investment and arranged with the other members of his art syndicate to exhibit the paintings at a couple of London galleries with the intention of selling them off. Yet there may have been more than commerce at stake. Certain favourite paintings, notably Titian's *Diana and Actaeon* and *Diana and Callisto* he chose to keep, displaying them in his London residence, Cleveland House.[2]

If his interest in art fluctuated according to his means, racing absorbed him throughout his life. A founder member of the Jockey Club, he chose garter blue for his racing colour – an attractive, if muted, shade. The story goes that riding a race on a windy day as a slight young man, spectators laid bets on whether he would be blown out of the saddle before he had completed the course.³ Even in the late 1750s and early 1760s, when the cost of canal building was beginning to make economy look prudent, he did his utmost to maintain his racing stable, although he sold off a few horses in 1764.⁴ (See Illustration 13).

Such was the dominance of Dennis O'Kelly's Eclipse in racing circles of the second half of the eighteenth century that the phrase 'also-ran' describes other horses and owners all too precisely. Nevertheless, the duke achieved some successes. At Newmarket in April 1765, his horse Boreas beat Lord Orford's Ghost for 300 guineas, and at the same meeting, his Tartar beat Lord Rockingham's Rowzer for 500 guineas.⁵ The following October was less propitious, his filly being beaten by a Mr Shafto's filly in a sweepstake, while the Duke of Ancaster's Sultan beat Boreas for 300 guineas.⁶ Boreas and Tartar were his most consistent horses, although their stablemates Gingerbread, Thumper, Calculator and Needle all won races from time to time.

Besides building Brick Hall in Worsley, (he intended it to serve as his Lancashire *pied-a-terre*, but allowed John Gilbert and his family to treat it as their home) and the imposing Bridgewater House in Runcorn, he also spent the not inconsiderable sum of £2,946 11s 7d on improving the Egerton estates at Ashridge in Hertfordshire. Between 1762 and 1768, just when the ducal cash-flow may have been at its tightest, Lancelot Capability Brown landscaped the grounds of Ashridge House and Henry Holland, Brown's son-in-law, replaced the sprawling medieval buildings with a decorous stone manor.⁷ The nineteenth-century Egertons would alter it again, commissioning James Wyatt to redesign the house in Gothic style and Humphrey Repton to lay out the gardens.

Art, turf and building projects aside, insofar as pocket boroughs lent themselves to sound management, the duke managed his borough of Brackley with great energy, if variable success. On the advice of his uncle the Duke of Bedford, he put forward London lawyer Marshe Dickinson who was duly elected in 1753. In 1761, as Brackley's other MP, he introduced his former tutor Robert Wood who had witnessed his canal enthusiasm at first hand in France. Both Dickinson and Wood proved stalwart allies in the years when the duke's first three Canal Acts made their way through Parliament. Dickinson died in 1765, and in his place the duke nominated the twenty-two-year-old John Montagu, Viscount Hinchingbrooke; as an MP, Hinchingbrooke did not impress, although in time he made his mark as master of his majesty's buckhounds and ranger of St James's and Hyde Parks.⁸ On Wood's death in 1771, the duke arranged for his relative William Egerton to replace him, but once again he appears to have mistook his man. Where Wood had been an energetic parliamentarian, Egerton is 'not known to have spoken in the House'.⁹

By about 1765, the young duke had acquired many of the tastes and habits that would sustain him for the remainder of his days. His sister Louisa and her husband Lord Gower, who shared his interest in racing, were his closest confidantes and most companionable relatives. Among his family he was known as 'Dux', and in a letter to James Loch, MP, clergyman John Fenton gives a vignette of him attending some family party throughout which he engaged John Sparrow, solicitor to the Trent & Mersey Canal Company, in a most 'earnest conversation about canals', the two gentlemen ensconced together on a sofa, while the festivities went on around them.¹⁰

Brindley's marriage

If the pattern of the duke's life began to settle into a pattern by the time he reached his mid-thirties, James Brindley, around the age of fifty, would encounter all the turnabout of marriage and acquiring a settled home. Always uncommunicative on paper, while his notebook entries give some indication of his engineering and managerial responsibilities, not to mention his somewhat uneasy social and professional relations with John Gilbert, they say nothing whatever of more intimate friendships, let alone courtship. In the face of his own total and impenetrable silence, it is possible from the surviving circumstantial evidence to form some picture of the events as they unfolded.

In the first week of September 1762, having inspected Nathanael Pattison's mill at Congleton and spent a couple of days with his parents in Leek, Brindley mentions pausing at 'New Chapill', where he 'Satled with Mr Hansal'.[11] Bent Farm in Newchapel was home to the Henshall family: John, his wife, Ann, their son Hugh and a daughter named Ann after her mother. Jane, an older Henshall daughter, had married wealthy landowner William Clowes in 1750: brother, by chance, of the Josiah Clowes who would later design the Thames and Severn Canal's Sapperton Tunnel.[12]

Paterfamilias John Henshall seems to have combined work as a surveyor with a modest legal practice. He witnessed a number of indentures, deeds and other legal documents for Josiah Wedgwood's rich relative, the widow Catherine Egerton, besides being one of the executors of her will.[13] He also bought books and had an interest in art. A surviving copy of Alexander Browne's 1669 work *Ars Pictoria: or, An Academy Treating of Drawing, Painting, Limning and Etching* bears John Henshall's name together with various corrigenda made in his neat hand, and also, marking it as a paternal gift, the inscription of his son who writes 'Hugh Henshall's Book, 1752' on the front page.[14] John may have brought Hugh (1734–1816) to Brindley's attention when his earliest surveys for a 'Navigation in Staffordshire' were in hand. By 1765 Brindley judged him sufficiently competent to survey a route from the Weaver Navigation at Winsford to Lawton, via either Middlewich or Nantwich, never guessing that the Weaver Navigation's man Robert Pownall would shadow his steps.[15] Two years later would find Hugh on the Bridgewater Canal, causing himself some consternation by failing to distinguish between Cheshire measure and stature measure.[16] It was a rare error; Hugh Henshall was, like Whitworth, both Brindley's colleague and friend. Wedgwood in one of his letters shows the two of them arriving at his home on business: 'I have now about some five hundred things to do,' Wedgwood expostulates, 'Messrs Brindley and Henshall are in the house, & I must go to them.'[17] It was clearly a thoroughly inconvenient time, but they evidently made a powerful combination, too formidable to be easily dismissed.

Born in 1746, Hugh's sister Ann was around sixteen years old when Brindley called at her parent's home in September 1762; he, at this time, was about forty-six. When they married on 8 December 1765, they were respectively nineteen and forty-nine. In some embarrassment over the thirty-year difference in the respective ages of bride and groom, Brindley's twenty-first century biographers have rushed to comment on the available evidence about the different ages at which men and women respectively embarked on wedded life in the 1760s.[18] While illuminating in sociological terms, this information adds nothing to our understanding of what James Brindley and Ann Henshall made of one another before the nuptials, or indeed, what brought them together. It is by contrast both touching and ironic to discover that Samuel Smiles, stern proponent of self-help, portrays the marriage entirely in the light of romance. Brindley, he says, took 'a special liking to Anne', which in time 'ripened into an attachment' and when he proposed, she promptly accepted him.[19] Smiles is fond of Ann. On the evidence of a 'portrait of her as a woman', which he had the good fortune to see (it is now apparently lost), he judges that she 'must have been a comely girl' and relates how Brindley, on his visits to the Henshall household, was accustomed to bring with him 'gingerbread for Ann in his pocket'.[20]

Of course, what Smiles sentimentally presents as a courtship may in truth have been the prolonged preparation for a union which the hard-headed Henshall parents saw every reason to promote. Not only was it a chance for Ann to marry wealth, but it also offered every prospect of securing professional advancement for Hugh, and Ann, seeing exactly what her father wanted, may have thought it wise to allow him to broker the nuptials without objection. Whatever the circumstances, bride and groom exchanged vows at St Margaret's, Wolstanton, the Henshalls' parish church, on 8 December 1765.

Josiah Wedgwood, who placed immense value upon a happy marriage, once said that it ought to be the custom 'for new Married Men to hear, see, feel or understand nothing but their Wives for a handfull of the first months after Matrimony'.[21] Any wish to spend the early months of married life in Ann's company that James Brindley may have harboured was vain. After his and Ann's wedding, the business of promoting the cause of the canal from the Trent to the Mersey – in particular, the delicate task of conciliating the proprietors of the Weaver Navigation – loomed large enough to override all other considerations. Malet quotes a letter dated Saturday 21 December 1765 from Brindley to John Gilbert which is full of canal business. 'On Tuesday', he writes,

Sir George [Warren] sent Nuton [sic] into Manchester to make what interest he could for Sir George, and to gather ye old Navigators [Weaver Navigators, that is] to meet Sir George […] to make a Head against His Grace.

I saw Dr Seswige [Dr Roger Sedgwick, a future supporter of the Rochdale Canal] who says he wants to see you about payment of his land in Cheshire.

On Wednesday there was not much transpired, but was so dark I could scarce do anything.

On Thursday Wedgwood of Burslem came to Dunham and sent for me and dined with Lord Grey & Sir Harry Mainwaring and others. Sir Harry could not keep his temper. Mr Wedgwood came to solicit Lord Grey in favour of the Staffordshire canal, and stayed at Mrs Latoune [?Leighton] all night and I went with him, and on Friday set out to wait on Mr Egerton and wait on him. He says Sparrow and others are endeavouring to get the landowners' consents from Harecastle to Agden.

I have ordered Simcock to ye length falls of Sankey Navigation.

Royle wants to have coals sent faster to Altrincham, that he may have an opportunity to drain off ye Sale Moor canal in about a week's time.[22]

Making plans for the imminent meeting at Wolseley Bridge, conversing with Lord Grey and the irascible Sir Harry Mainwaring and issuing directions to his brother-in-law-cum-assistant Simcock was never going to leave Brindley much scope for contemplating the delights of marital bliss, yet despite this inauspicious start to their married life, the couple appear to have been very happy. Ann was clever, strong-minded and energetic. True to his bookish instincts, her father had ensured that she received a thorough and wide-ranging education, which provided her with the skills her husband lacked, most notably a fluent command of the written language. Smiles claims that she took charge of her husband's correspondence as though her assumption of the role of clerk were somehow remarkable. In fact, eighteenth-century history suggests that it was not at all unusual for the wives of artisans to undertake clerical and administrative work for their husbands. Throughout the working life of silversmith John Bateman, for example, his wife Hester kept his accounts. Indeed, when John died in 1760 of tuberculosis and left Hester his tools, she taught herself his craft and enjoyed great success in it.[23] Ann Brindley showed a similar taste and aptitude for business. Not only was she active in managing the earthenware manufactory which her second husband, Robert Williamson, established, but widowed twice over and in her seventy-eighth year, she would take out a fourteen-year lease on the Astbury Lime Works near Mow Cop.[24]

She often travelled with her husband, and on 19 February 1769 when the weather was foul enough for the *Oxford Journal* to draw attention to the persisting 'rain and snow', they attended the first general meeting of the proprietors of the Coventry Canal together.[25] After the meeting, during which James Brindley informed the company that 'the whole communication with the Staffordshire Canal would be accomplished in four or five years at most', they stayed on their way home with the Wedgwoods at Etruria Hall. 'Mr Brindley & his Lady call'd here in their way … lay with us and are just left us this morning', Wedgwood chattily informed Bentley afterwards, adding that he and his wife Sally were going 'to spend tomorrow with them at Newchapel'.[26] A letter dated to 1769 from Brindley to Richard Richardson, sometime mayor of Chester, brims with business detail and ends tenderly with Ann's warm-hearted compliments to Richardson's wife, with whom she is clearly on friendly terms.[27] Clearly, their union was one in which affection and commerce went hand in hand.

Not only a useful clerk and amanuensis, Ann also knew how to stand up for herself, and in the matter of her husband's portrait she would do so with grace and insistence. Towards the end of February 1770, shortly after the baptism of his first child – a daughter, named Anne after her mother – Brindley went to London on various canal concerns and arranged while he was there to sit for the fashionable portraitist Francis Parsons. It went disastrously wrong. When the painting, in itself impressive, was on the point of completion, Brindley appears to have fallen prey to Quakerish qualms about the morality of what he was doing, just as he had when he went to see the play in January 1762. No Quaker himself, he had nevertheless inherited his ethics from Quaker ancestors to whom portraiture was every bit as abhorrent as the theatre.[28] It was an expensive way of indulging personal vanity which, to a God-fearing individual, could look suspiciously like idolatry. Whatever course Brindley's tortured reasoning took, the sittings left him stricken, and when Parsons got round to requesting his rather large fee (it was 60 guineas) he refused to pay.

There followed a fractious exchange which Josiah Wedgwood diplomatically described as 'a little fracas about the terms'. Brindley, he is certain, always intended to pay for his picture, but did not care for Parsons' 'mode of demanding so much from him.'[29] Portraitist and sitter parted, without money changing hands. The painting remained in the artist's Great Ormond Street studio.

Ann was understandably upset. It was not at all the outcome for which she had hoped. Wedgwood, a prime source of information about the Brindleys' married life, maintains that she 'always wish'd to have the picture.' Unlike her husband, she had no inherited Quaker ideas about the immorality of portraiture, and wanted for every reason to own a painting of him at the height of his skills. There was no question of her purchasing it herself, which would anyway have been singularly tactless, since she had no money of her own except what he allowed her.

Things reached an impasse which lasted for about two years. Perhaps in this time Brindley experienced a certain amount of inner conflict between reluctance to back down and the recollection that he had not behaved at all well, and Parsons had every reason to feel aggrieved with him. Whatever his reasoning, on his deathbed, he had a change of heart, and gave Ann both his permission, and presumably funds, to buy the painting. Wedgwood, in whom she must have confided, instructed Bentley, who was by now his London agent, to purchase it from Parsons without ado. 'Mrs Brindley ... begs you would be so good to see Mr Parsons', he writes, at his most paternal and solicitous. 'She readily complies with his terms, & hopes he will not refuse her the picture ... She has set her heart much upon having it, so if Mr Parsons has any new terms to propose, you'l please send them...'[30] Parsons, once he had arranged to have an engraving taken of the portrait, was happy to despatch the original to Staffordshire. It arrived in December 1772, by which time James Brindley had been dead for three months.

Turnhurst Hall

Since he died without making a will and for years the probate records of his estate were lost, the domestic detail of Brindley's home life has received little attention. In fact, the meticulous inventory of his estate which Hugh Henshall drew up after his death is in the National Archives, and gives an impression that Turnhurst Hall, the Brindleys' marital home, was an unpretentious, comfortable home, intended to be reasonably self-sufficient.[31] (See Illustrations 14 and 15).

After years of living in lodgings near his works-in-progress, while making occasional visits to his parents in the farmhouse near Leek, Brindley seems to have taken to settled domesticity with zest. The house, or rather, the portion of it in which they lived, contains a great deal of solid, stylish furniture. There were, for example, ten mahogany chairs and a mahogany leaved dining table in the 'Best Parlour'; a 'clock and mahogany case' in the 'Little Parlour'; a counterpane, rather more fashionable than an ordinary bed rug, and white dimity hangings in the white room on the first floor.[32] It may not be entirely coincidental that construction of the Staffordshire and Worcestershire Canal, which passes though that prime centre of carpet manufacture, Kidderminster, should have encouraged the couple to support the town's trade. They have both a 'Scotch carpet' (a reversible carpet woven without a pile), valued at a guinea in the first floor blue room, and a Wilton carpet valued at 4 guineas in the best parlour.[33]

As for household linen, there are thirty-four pairs of sheets; fourteen pillow coats; twelve table cloths; eleven breakfast cloths; twelve kitchen towels; ten old towels and forty-three napkins. It seems a most generous supply, although perhaps these quantities are no more than what was adequate. As well as the family bedrooms – the blue, white and green rooms – Henshall also mentions a little garret (habitable attic); a 'Garrett over the white room' and a men's garrett, which presumably were where the servants slept. Each garret contains a fair amount of miscellaneous bedding. The range and quantity of crockery is not given with such precision, but Henshall's valuation of the 'China' values at £4, as distinct from the inferior 'Earthenware' which commands only 10s, suggests again the quantities are lavish. In the china room, which is separate from the kitchen, there are also glasses, a tea chest valued at 7s 6d, which might have been a large wooden container sub-divided into compartments for different types of tea, or a small, ornamental caddy. With a storage vessel for tea, it is no surprise to find trays, in this instance 'one old japanned tea board'; four small tea waiters – that is, salvers; a mahogany tea board and an oak table tray. Henshall's inventory gives the sense that the Turnhurst china room was probably something of a glory hole; among its other contents there are 'three cloathes – hard' (5s), a tin candle box (8d), a 'cloathes brush' (1s 6d) and 'One dozen knives and forks', to which Henshall adds the comment 'odd ones' although their 15s valuation suggests that they may well have been silver.

The range, with its grate and fender, heads the list of contents of the kitchen proper. There are also fire irons, a 'smoak jack' for turning the two spits, a broiling gridiron, 'two frying pans and two tin dripping pans' and an 'old dutch oven' – a term which could refer either to a cast-iron pot or a brick oven beside a fireplace. One of the more mysterious contents, 'A cocier for the horse store', may, at a guess, have been a tool for repairing broken saddlery.[34] The smaller utensils include two toasting forks, a pestle and mortar, a 'cleaver and chaving [sic] dish' and an 'Iron ladle and slice'. There is also a white table and '4 old chairs and one stool'. Supposing that this room was where the servants ate, it suggests that in total they numbered five, which seems a great many people to look after one married couple and their two infant daughters.

The livestock in the inventory included three horses – a 'bay horse' valued at the substantial 15 gns, the 'old mare' (5gns) and the 'little black mare' (£3 16s) and 'A cow called Grisel', whose estimated value of 6 guineas suggests she was a good milker. Garden implements such as rakes, hoes, a spade and forks are in good supply. Within the grounds, there was also (a mark of practical foresight) a hotbed; which was a bed of earth surrounded by a robust wooden frame with a glazed top, and heated by fermenting manure with a view to forcing and raising early vegetables and perhaps exotic fruit like pineapples. In an outbuilding which Henshall calls the 'Brewhouse' there were two churns, a milking can and a cheese press and board, which suggest that it served as much as a dairy as it did for brewing the household beer. The cellar, incidentally, held some 10 guineas' worth of liquor and an assortment of barrels and casks of different sizes.

The Turnhurst establishment was clearly comfortable and well-stocked but not perhaps overly luxurious. For instance, decoration is minimal, consisting of little more than the

'India print over the chimney piece' in the best parlour, which was probably a decorative block-printed square of calico, and the 'three small pictures' in the white room, their subjects unknown. As for the 'two worked stools' and two bedside carpets which commanded a modest valuation of 4 shillings, they may have been intended for the younger Anne and her small sister Susannah. It is frustrating to discover that Henshall does not list the 2 guineas' worth of books that he mentions in the same section of the inventory as Brindley's case of mathematical instruments, beam compasses and ivory rule. To have some indication of their titles would shed rewarding light upon the scope and range of technical literature available to an engineer of the 1760s.

Henshall's inventory closes with a list of investments and other property: 'a property in the Birmingham Canal' valued at £540; the sum of £1,750 'advanced upon the Oxford Canal'; a debt of £379 owing 'from the Chesterfield Canal' and other miscellaneous sums owing, which together with the contents of house and grounds, not to mention 'four common spirit levels, one black one, and a small one, two pair wanting legs', which Henshall values at 16 gns, brings the total value of Brindley's estate to £8,609 4s 2d. While it may not be on a par with the vast fortune of Sir Richard Arkwright who once boasted that he could pay off the national debt, it is assuredly a tidy sum, and no doubt one with which James Brindley was more than content.

CHAPTER SEVEN

1766: Beginning to Build the Staffordshire and Worcestershire Canal

As the country's interest in canal building grew, Brindley found himself in much demand. By this time, work on the Bridgewater Canal had built up its own momentum. Supervision of day-to-day progress rested with a number of foremen appointed to oversee construction at different sites along the route – Richard Owens at Worsley; Thomas Wallwork at Bollen; Thomas Laughlin at Castlefield; Adams at Broadheath and Cheetham at Stretford.[1] Of Brindley's constant presence on site, there was no pressing need. That is not to say that he and the duke parted company, but more that he began to undertake new ventures, nevertheless pledging to come whenever the duke needed his assistance. This book's remaining chapters will focus largely upon the schemes he pursued at the height of his career when he was independent of the duke's patronage, although quick to give his help when the need arose, as it often did. Examination of his attempts, which were not always wholly successful, to adjust to working with the canal committees rather than for one clear-sighted individual goes a long way towards explaining why, despite its occasional storms, his collaboration with the duke was so successful.

Promoting the Staffordshire and Worcestershire Canal[2]

Somehow, despite the ferment of half-truths and deceit which surrounded the deliberations of the December 1765 Wolseley Bridge meeting, by the New Year a surge of confidence in canal technology had begun to emerge. While Wedgwood and his friends applied to Parliament for a Trent and Mersey Canal Bill, a set of manufacturers, merchants and minor gentry of Wolverhampton decided to investigate the possibility of linking their town with both the new canal proposed for Staffordshire and the River Severn. Potentially, it would connect them with Bristol, Hull and Liverpool – three of the country's major ports – and within a month of the Wolseley Bridge decision, James Perry, merchant, and John Baker, gentleman, both of Wolverhampton, convened a public meeting to explore the possibilities.

'A scheme is on foot', announced the *Derby Mercury* in January 1766,

> For making a navigable canal from Redstone's Ferry on the river Severn, through Kidderminster to Autherley near Wolverhampton, Staffordshire, and from thence down the river Penk, in order to join to the canal intended to be made from Wilden-Ferry near

Shudborough to Liverpool [sic], which will … be attended with great advantage to those parts, as well as to the trade and commerce of the kingdom in general.[3]

Exactly when Brindley's involvement with the scheme began is unknown. Hugh Malet claims, somewhat improbably, that John Gilbert made an initial survey for the Wolverhampton gentlemen with some assistance from his son, and then piloted the Staffordshire & Worcestershire Bill through Parliament.[4] While, admittedly, an entry in the 1766 Bridgewater accounts book notes payment of £118 to Gilbert 'For levelling etc in Cheshire' with his son, and 'attending the Staffordshire Navigation Bill as a witness through both Houses of Parliament', both tasks would seem to have more connection with the Trent and Mersey Canal, which at this time was often, if confusingly, known as the Staffordshire Navigation rather than the putative canal intended to link the Severn with the Trent.[5] It is not impossible that the Wolverhampton party saw no need for making a formal survey in the early stages of the canal's planning, since a provisional line of sorts for their route already existed. Fifty years previously, one Thomas Congreve, a medical man of Wolverhampton, had outlined the route by which a waterway, making use of existing brooks and rivers and joining them by short lengths of manmade canal, might run from the Trent to the Severn by way of Wolverhampton and Kidderminster.[6] By February 1766 Brindley was in Worcestershire, spending 'a day at the request of a group of Stourbridge people surveying a line from that town to Stourton' and it is likely that at this time, he at least looked over the country through which the new canal would pass.[7]

On 15 February, when the Staffordshire & Worcestershire Bill came up before the Commons, petitions in its support arrived from the townsmen of Walsall, Stourbridge, Kidderminster, Dudley and Bewdley.[8] Giving evidence to the Commons on 20 March, Brindley informed the House both that the plan was practicable, and that it would 'be of great benefit to the country in general', by 'reducing the price of Carriage Three Parts in four at least'.[9] Perry, who also appeared as a witness, strengthened the arguments in its favour with a deft calculation that while producers of coal and lime currently paid 'Eight shillings per ton for Ten Miles' in carriage costs, once they could move their goods by water, the price of carriage would drop to 'about One Shilling and Nine pence' per ton, while Baker confirmed that it would be of 'advantage to the iron works on the Stowr.'[10] Their representations carried the day and on 14 May 1766, having passed swiftly through both Houses of Parliament, the Staffordshire and Worcestershire Canal Bill received the royal assent. (See Illustration 16).

The last of the Weaver Navigators: Charles Roe's canal for Macclesfield

For Brindley, talking up the new canal's merits in the Commons coincided with a demand for help from the duke. It was not a matter of onsite engineering, but a question of giving evidence to suppress the ambitions of a rival. Aggrieved at finding all hope of Wedgwood's Staffordshire canal's joining the Weaver Navigation quashed at Wolseley Bridge, Cheshire (in the person of Charles Roe of Macclesfield) had not been slow to fight back.

Only a fortnight after the fateful meeting, disappointed that the duke had lost interest in his plan for a link between Macclesfield and the Bridgewater Canal, Roe changed strategy. Backed by much Cheshire support, he petitioned Parliament to bring in a bill to build a canal which would go from the 'great trading town of Manchester', in other words, the duke's commercial stronghold, to Witton Bridge on the Witton Brook and thence by the Weaver to the Mersey. On its way, it would pass through Knutsford, Mottram Andrew, Macclesfield and Stockport, much to the satisfaction of their residents.[11] (See Illustration 17).

On 10 February 1766, at the Commons' committee stage, Manchester surveyor Hugh Oldham and John Golborne, an engineer from Chester, gave evidence to the effect that Roe's Knutsford Canal scheme was 'very practicable'.[12] Oldham gave the dimensions as 5 yards at the top, 4 yards at the bottom and 'from 3 to 3½ feet deep', and reassured the committee that the quantities of water available were 'sufficient for the navigation of vessels from 15 to 20 tons burthen at all times', while Golborne estimated that the expense 'including everything' would amount to 'about £44,000', or £1,200 a mile. Describing its potential benefits to the locality, Roe himself pledged that it would reduce the price of slate, flags, cheese and salt, and supply the Macclesfield silk works and copper mines with cheap coal. Everything augured well for its success. The only opposition came in the form of a petition from the 'Gentlemen, Merchants, Manufacturers, Tradesmen and others, from Manchester and the nearby towns of Lancaster, Middlewich, Congleton and Stockport' who wished to draw attention to the duke's proven experience and success in canal building.[13] The Bridgewater Canal, they argued, had proven 'public utility' and was demonstrably 'the best mode of navigation in this Kingdom'. Surely, in the light of the duke's success, it would be best for the nation if Parliament enabled him to extend his existing canal from Sale Moor to Stockport and join with the canal between Wilden Ferry and the Mersey, rather than authorise Roe's scheme. It may not have been coincidental that at this point in the deliberations a petition arrived from the owners and occupiers of mills along the route of Roe's Knutsford Canal, who could not see that it had any public utility and opposed it because they were 'apprehensive' lest it should prove 'prejudicial' to their interests.[14] The House ordered that counsel be heard for the respective petitioners, but nothing occurred at the hearing, which took place on 25 March 1766, to impede the progress of Roe's bill. With a few small-scale amendments, it passed the Commons and was ordered to be engrossed for despatch to the Lords. To the Bridgewater and Wedgwood camp, it was a setback. To make good their bold pledges at the Wolseley Bridge meeting, it was necessary to quash Roe's scheme – popular in Macclesfield and Stockport – before it gained any more support. What followed suggests that in the first fortnight of April 1766 some intense discussion took place between the duke, his solicitor William Tomkinson, his fixers the Gilbert brothers and his engineer James Brindley of which unfortunately no record survives.

At a time when canal legislation was in its infancy, to employ a lawyer with the ability to draw out the logic from a tangle of competing objectives counted for much. By way of counsel for the duke, Tomkinson briefed John Dunning of the Middle Temple who, according to his political patron Lord Shelburne, possessed 'such a faculty of arrangement that he would take an absolute chaos of matter and return it to you in an instant, so clear and distinct as of itself to present a proper judgment without need of discussion.'[15] On 14 April 1766, the duke petitioned the House of Lords for leave to oppose Roe's bill.

At the core of his petition was the allegation that if the House of Lords were to allow Roe's bill to pass into law, they will fatally jeopardise works in progress on the Bridgewater Canal. The general grounds of the duke's objection were firstly that whatever Roe might claim, his proposed canal offered no great benefit to commerce, nor was it of public utility; second, trade between Manchester, Stockport and the port of Liverpool would be better served by his canal, for which Parliament had already passed 'several Acts', than it would by Roe's and third, there was insufficient traffic to justify 'the injury ... to individual and to the public', to which the construction of Roe's waterway would give rise. What was more, having 'at great risque and at an immense expense completed a great part of the Navigation', to the duke's dismay, the bill recently passed by the Commons allowed Roe 'to cut off and divert' three streams which feed his canal – the Medlock, the Hough End Brook and the Corn Brook.[16] Since 'experience' had shown the Bridgewater Canal 'to be of very great benefit to the Country', he concludes, he trusted that the Lords would not undermine the 'powers' they had already granted him for its extension and completion.

The Lords heard the arguments for and against Roe's bill on 18 April 1766. Although by this time Brindley had considerable experience of testifying in Parliament, be it on behalf of the duke or Wedgwood or the Staffordshire & Worcestershire men, it had always been in their ventures' support. To give evidence against a rival scheme was rather a different proposition. As he discoursed under Dunning's questioning upon Roe's canal's utility and practicability, the number of locks it would need and its carriage costs compared with those on the duke's canal, he emerged as a highly proficient and reliable witness. Dunning gave especial prominence to Brindley's evidence concerning the three streams. Insofar as it is possible to judge from the extremely brief summary of his evidence which the *House of Lords Journal* provides, his exposition of the engineering issues surrounding the three streams was lucid. If the new navigation were to divert their courses, the duke's canal would be likely to receive great injury as a result. To build the new navigation without diverting them was wholly impracticable. Not only would their diversion have a detrimental impact on the local corn mills; it would also make it impossible for the duke to extend his canal.

Under cross-examination by Roe's counsel, a Mr Graham, Brindley answered questions about the possibility of building the new navigation without 'taking in' the three crucial streams and the extent of damage to the duke's canal if the streams were not taken into it. Frustratingly, no record of his answers to these significant questions survives, but the fact that Roe's witnesses Golborne and Oldham meanwhile received cross-examination from Dunning about their 'knowledge of Mr Brindley as an engineer' is a revealing detail. Were he less than confident of Brindley's bona fides authority, he presumably would not take the risk of posing the questions. Other witnesses gave evidence concerning the shortage of coal in Macclesfield, the cost of stone and lime, and the use of the canal to transport them. Once their cross-examination had concluded, the hearing was adjourned.

At this point, it appears that some clandestine negotiation occurred, for the Knutsford and Macclesfield Navigation Bill vanished from the parliamentary agenda. Whether something, perhaps not unrelated to the duke's decision to despatch Brindley on a survey (for which he was paid £105) for a branch canal intended to run from Sale Moor to Stockport persuaded Charles Roe to abandon his canal project, or whether – to offer a more cynical conjecture – money changed hands, it is impossible to say. Whatever agreement the parties reached, on 2 May 1766 an inconspicuous paragraph in the *Derby Mercury* announced that 'The plan … for some time in agitation for making a navigable canal from Witton Bridge to Stockport and Macclesfield … is dropt.' Although the duke obtained an Act to authorise his Stockport extension he never built it, and the Macclesfield Canal running from Marple through Macclesfield and Congleton to join the Trent and Mersey near Kidsgrove did not get its enabling Act until 1826.

Overtures from Hesse-Kassel

As though to burnish his growing fame, around this time Brindley apparently received a rather flattering overture. Samuel Smiles, who admittedly is not the most reliable chronicler, claims that the 'Prince of Hesse' who was 'meditating a canal through his dominions in Germany' apparently offered Brindley the work on any terms he cared to name – a chance which his family 'strongly urged' him to take up.[17] Smiles' 'Prince of Hesse' was actually Frederik II, Landgrave of Hesse-Kassel from 1720–1785, who made himself rich by hiring out troops known as Hessians. He was married, not entirely happily, to Princess Mary, daughter of George II and Caroline of Ansbach. Marital discord notwithstanding, in 1745, he had supported his father-in-law by landing some 6,000 Hessians in Scotland to suppress the Jacobite uprising.

In the early 1760s, he had turned his attention to matters nearer home by seeking to improve navigation on the Fulda River and at this point, history offers some corroboration for Smiles' tale. The River Fulda rises near Wasserkuppe in the south of Hesse, to flow in a northerly direction through the towns of Bad Hersfeld, Bebra and Kassel before joining the Werra river at Hannoversch Munden to form the Weser. Having opened the Fulda from Munden upstream through Kassel to Bad Hersfeld, in May 1765, his plan to continue the works hit opposition from the Bad Hersfeld shippers, who relished the advantages of operating from 'the last navigable port on the river'.[18] Downstream, meanwhile, shipping multiplied and, scenting an opportunity, the townsmen of Hannoversch Munden increased the tariffs. This outbreak of local protectionism was not at all what Frederik had intended and, incensed, he responded by investigating the possibility of circumventing Hannoversch Munden by building a canal.

It may not be entirely a matter of chance that early in 1766, Mary hoped to visit her royal nephew George III in London.[19] Although by now she and Frederik were estranged, her plans may have drawn his attention to England's rising industry and new canal schemes. If the combination of circumstances led him to consider approaching Brindley with the intention of enticing him out of Bridgewater clutches, it is not entirely beyond belief. At any rate, the timing would fit. For Brindley to turn down an offer of work was unusual, if not unknown. What apparently deterred him from accepting Frederik's lucrative job opportunity was an appeal from the duke which, claims Smiles in one his purpler passages, 'counted for more with him than all pecuniary considerations'.[20] His decision was fortunate since in reality the Hesse-Kassel canal venture held out less golden promise than his relatives may have supposed. In the face of local hostility, Frederik abandoned his canal aspirations and soon lost interest in the Fulda.[21]

The Staffordshire and Worcestershire Canal: construction

Whatever the truth of his potential employment in Germany, by the early summer of 1766 Brindley's new venture in the West Midlands had become a certainty. On 24 June, the newly constituted company of proprietors held their first general meeting at the Swan Inn in Wolverhampton, and elected their officers – a clerk, treasurer, surveyor, clerk of works and an underclerk of works. The elected clerk, John Jesson of Graisley, described only as 'gentleman' took charge of the necessary land purchase. The role of the treasurer, James Perry, merchant of Wolverhampton, was obvious: the management of the company finances. Lest he should in any way misuse the shareholders' funds, the Company required him to give a bond to the immense value of £10,000.

Brindley's appointment as the company's surveyor marked a decisive change of employment climate. Having worked for most of the previous seven years within the Bridgewater shadow and often under the probing eyes of John Gilbert, together with his Trent & Mersey appointment, this post brought a new measure of independence to his canal practice. On both the Trent and Mersey and the Staffordshire and Worcestershire Canals, he would now oversee construction on his own terms. In Wedgwood he had a loyal, not to say devoted, ally at committee level; with the Staffordshire and Worcestershire work, ostensibly responsibility for seeing that the works were carried out according to the surveyor's specification rested with the clerk of works – one John Baker, gentleman of Wolverhampton. In practice, Baker delegated this task to his deputy, under clerk John Fennyhouse Green.

Green is a mysterious, even obscure figure, but he was a conscientious record keeper and his notebooks provide a remarkable chronicle of the Staffordshire and Worcestershire Canal's construction. In the course of a commission from the Canal & River Trust, formerly British Waterways, to interpret the canal's Stourport basins, the artist David Patten discovered that Green was born in Lapley in Staffordshire in 1727 and would be buried there in 1774. Before his appointment as under clerk, he assisted Samuel Simcock – the husband, as it happened, of Brindley's sister Esther – with levelling near Tettenhall Bridge.[22] Peter Cross-Rudkin, in his authoritative paper on the canal's construction describes him as a 'competent, neat and methodical surveyor'.[23] From an early stage, the committee insisted that Green should write down all Brindley's orders and that Brindley should sign Green's record to confirm its accuracy. It was a fussy managerial requirement which, in respect of Brindley's counter-signing, was not always met, but it served to minimise the risks both of misunderstanding, and of committee members taking the wrong sort of initiative.

Green's record of Brindley's instructions, together with his day-book entries, chart the cut's advance and the various setbacks encountered over the six years of its building. One typical small-scale calamity was the repeated flooding of a partially built lock-chamber near Stourton. Green writes:

By Mr Brindley's orders set out length of about 6 yds into the temporary road at Stewponey to be cut down to bottom of canal for a Drain […] The great Springs of water in cutting for the lock pit have spoiled the pump, tho' twice repaired. We made an attempt to Thurl, [cut through] but the rock being very wet, Mr Brindley gave it his opinion it would be cheapest to cut a drain.[24]

In his 'Orders' Brindley often makes free with his opinions and makes no attempt to hide his annoyance at some of the treasurer's ill-judged economies. He does not, for instance, conceal his concern over aspects of the treasurer's ill-judged frugality; Green faithfully records his frustration on finding:

That the banking between the Aquaduct and the Lock above receives a great injury from the Moles and which is owing to a refusal with my Orders before given for having a Mole catcher employed.[25]

The impatience with which the on-site workmen regard Brindley's stringent standards of building could have repercussions. An episode which occurs in the course of building a culvert near Acton Trussell speaks for itself. 'Order given by Mr Brindley 20th September 1770', writes Green,

That Gabriel Featherston, a bricklayer, be discharged from the Company's service for his unfaire keyeing up the Arch in the culver[t] at the water course at Shutt Hill which he, Mr Brindley, this day saw himself.

A statement follows indicating that Brindley has a change of heart, and,

Featherston promises that for the future he will neither begin, carry on nor finish any kind of work at any place in a sleighly manner in any respect, neither by himself nor his servants, for which reason Mr Brindley agrees Featherston shall be continued on during his good behaviour.
Signed Gab. Featherston

James Brindley [not his hand][26]

The word 'sleighly' by which Brindley characterises Featherston's workmanship is probably a form of the archaic adjective 'sleighty', denoting something that is crafty or akin to sleight of hand. Perhaps Featherston guilefully contrived to conceal the deficiencies of the brickwork in the culvert. How much Brindley's decision to reinstate him after his dismissal owes to goodwill and how much to a shortage of skilled bricklayers in the Acton Trussell district is open to question.

Tradition has it that the lock at Compton to the west of Wolverhampton and at the southern end of the Staffordshire and Worcestershire Canal's summit is the first lock that Brindley built. The statement is slippery, both on account of the similar claims made for locks on the

Calder Navigation and because it is hard to know what weight to give to the verb 'built' in circumstances where Brindley's role, as engineer or surveyor-in-chief, turned more upon overseeing construction as the contractors took it ahead than any stone-and-mortar activity.[27] For what it is worth, among the craftsmen whom the Staffordshire & Worcestershire employed was one Thomas Dadford – originally a carpenter and joiner, later an engineer and father of engineers. Brindley would instruct Dadford, who had possibly been 'trying to undertake work not allocated to him' that his 'sole employ' was 'to attend to the building of lockes'.[28] Whatever the circumstances, it was a sound piece of delegation. Locks, as Klemperer and Sillitoe note in the account of their quest for Brindley's own experimental lock supposedly in the grounds of Turnhurst Hall, confronted their builders with sophisticated challenges. First there was the need 'to balance sound construction against high unit cost', and second, the structure had to withstand the threefold forces exerted by 'water pressure, variable ground conditions and the stresses of daily use'.[29] Dadford, evidently versatile and ambitious enough to undertake work which lay outside his immediate experience, would contract in 1771 to put up the solid stone aqueduct on which the canal crosses the River Sow at Milford.

A distinctive feature of the Staffordshire and Worcestershire Canal is the circular spill-weirs, which stood to one side of the upper entrance to each lock. Conceived to convey excess water to the lower pound either by an underground culvert or an open leat, as L. T. C. Rolt explained, the 'outer rim' of the round structure 'forms the cill of the weir, its centre being the mouth of the culvert'.[30] Not only was the design elegant, it also, Rolt observed, had the advantage of taking up less space than a straight weir and being less susceptible to becoming 'fouled by floating debris'.[31] At the same time, the round weirs proved expensive to build in terms both of cash and time. While Rolt's statement that the Staffordshire & Worcestershire design 'was never repeated' is not strictly correct (there is a round 'tumbling' weir on the Droitwich Canal alongside lock No. 6 at Ladywood and Linacre Bridge), financial considerations precluded any widespread adoption of the design.[32]

The Staffordshire & Worcestershire was not a wealthy canal company and, circular weirs apart, its financial condition was not such as to give Brindley scope for the type of experiment and invention that he pursued under the duke's auspices around Manchester. Nevertheless, Green's record indicates that the route's challenges required ingenuity in the solving. A number of *ex gratia* payments authorised by Brindley gives an idea of some of the hazards that the contractors encountered. 'One guinea extraordinary on account of the side slipping into the canal' notes Green, keeping a record of disbursments; 6 guineas 'for quicksands cutting drains and keeping 'em open' and 12 guineas extra 'for quicksands below Tettenhall Bridge' and 'Getting of 2 great rocks out in Mr Gough's land'.[33] As usual, in planning the canal it was necessary to take the needs of local land and business owners into account. A long-lived tradition has it that the canal broadens dramatically as it nears Tixall Hall because the hall's owner, Thomas Clifford, thought that the more it resembled a lake, the better it would chime with Capabilty Brown's improvements to his grounds. Precise details about the construction of Tixall Wide have been impossible to locate; Green does not appear to mention the feature and Brown's biographer Jane Brown rather confusingly claims that Thomas Clifford paid 25 guineas 'for widening the River Sow'.[34]

A greater challenge than meeting the needs of a finicky landowner lay in the question of how the canal was to accommodate the Smestow Brook. This modest tributary of the Stour powered a surprisingly large number of mills, ironworks and furnaces in the vicinity of Wolverhampton. Since their owners showed understandable concern about the possible effect of diverting the stream, Brindley and Green conceived the Dunstall Water Bridge – a combined aqueduct and footbridge – as a means of keeping it on a level course. Its occasional spelling 'Tunstall' may owe something to Brindley's and his North Staffordshire associates' recollection of Tunstall near Stoke, most northerly and by chance closest of the six towns to Turnhurst. What is striking about the directions from Brindley concerning the water bridge that Green recorded is their precision. The 'Top water breadth in Canal', writes Green, is 'to be nine feet'; the breadth of the towing path, 4 feet.[35] The batter of the abutment (the extent to which it slopes away from the perpendicular) is to be '8 or 9 inches on a side'; the arch is be 'a sixth part of a circle', its inside 'to be nine feet above top water', and Green enjoined to take care that 'there be a sufficient height for a man to ride under the Bridge.' In terms of its dimensions, the breadth of the bridge 'from cut to cut' – presumably side to side – is to be 20 feet; the thickness of the parapet walls 'to be 2¼ feet and to be 3 Bricks up to a foot above top of the Arch'; the parapet walls are to be 3 feet in height and there is 'A good water way to be made off the Bridge into the old water course.' The significance of this last instruction is somewhat elusive but becomes apparent from the bridge's appearance; to minimise the risk of the brook's flooding the bridge deck in times of spate, there is ample means of escape for excess water. (See Illustration 18).

The junction with the Severn

The early phases of the canal's construction went ahead before the site of its junction with the Severn had been agreed. When Perry and Baker first met to canvass support, they stated in their publicity that the canal would join the Severn at Redstone's Ferry, a vast sandstone rock face overlooking a remote stretch of the Severn in Worcestershire. Caves pitted its surface, home in the Middle Ages to successive hermits who ferried travellers over the river as an act of charity; by the eighteenth century, they had become infamous for harbouring thieves.[36] Local notoriety apart, the place was not well known and when they petitioned Parliament, the promoters glossed over the junction's exact location, indicating only that it would be 'at or near Bewdley'. After all, mention of a prosperous inland port promised to inspire confidence among prospective investors.

Although a neat fable of commercial retribution alleges that the fastidious townsfolk of Bewdley refused to have Brindley's 'stinking ditch' only to see their fortunes decline thereafter, this version of events does not entirely stand up. As the site of a canal junction with the Severn, Bewdley had irremediable disadvantages. The fact that orchards occupied much of the land around it would make it dear to purchase, with the expense of acquiring the populated district of Wribbenhall on the Severn's northern bank and clearing it to make way for wharves and basins swelling the costs.[37] What was more, the town's geography stood against it. Bewdley stands at the heart of a range of hills; the River Stour, a tributary of the Severn, is close by, but the town has no direct access to the Stour Valley.[38] For the cost of tunnelling through Harecastle

Hill, Brindley had given an estimated figure of £10,000; the cost of tunnelling through Summer House Hill to Bewdley promised to be of much the same order. Quite how sanguine he would have been about taking on two formidable tunnelling projects simultaneously, with all the associated difficulty of finding competent contractors and seasoned labour, is open to question; a tunnel would also commit the new and rather hastily formed Staffordshire & Worcestershire Canal Company to massive expenditure at an early stage. What was more, since the stretch of Severn downstream of Bewdley towards Lower Mitton was notoriously shallow and difficult to navigate, it made much sense for the canal to bypass it.

If Bewdley was not suitable, a junction with the Severn had to be made somewhere. By the middle of 1768 construction had reached Kidderminster, and the need to decide on a location was pressing. In middle of June, Brindley instructed Green to 'go down to Severn and make such remarks on the flood as [he] shou'd think necessary.'[39] It was no idle observation of water levels by the river; the site of the junction, wherever it was to be, had to be spacious enough to accommodate extensive wharves and basins and high enough to avoid the frequent floods. The following day, Green called on a Mr Price who lived in the hamlet of Mitton 'above the Stour's mouth'. From Price, Green ascertained 'where the highest flood he had ever known in Severn' had reached, and began to take the levels from that point. Over the following weeks, he continued to level around Mitton and by 27 October, when his nominal manager, Clerk of Works John Baker, directed him to 'observe where the canal might be brought to the Severn' he had acquainted himself thoroughly with the place.[40] Price's neighbour, the Mitton churchwarden John Acton, owned a field, which was in stubble over the autumn of 1768, 'of large extent' Green observed, 'and quite high enough out of flood's way.' Having surveyed the land 'on lower side of Lower Mitton', he thought it lay 'equally well for cutting for the canal, whether brought below or above Mr Price's house.' On 2 November 1768, a party of committee men came to view the plot, Brindley in their company. Immediately, Green wrote he 'fixed on going through Mr Acton's stubble field above Mr Price's house for making of a Bason & building warehouses etc., on it, and I was then ordered to measure it.'[41] In the absence of anything to suggest otherwise, Mr Acton appears to have sold off his stubble field with good grace, and Mitton (Stourport-on-Severn as it would later be known) grew into a thriving town. If Bewdley lost some of its pre-eminence as a Severn port, it was still prosperous enough to commission a fine stone bridge from Thomas Telford in 1798.

Construction of the Staffordshire and Worcestershire Canal went ahead fast and, in the main, efficiently. Brindley visited the site often enough to give his attention to matters, like the Dunstall Water Bridge, which required it, while at the same time allowing Green scope to exercise his own discretion. It was a species of management which appears to have suited him well, leaving him free to pursue his other work without a nagging agent demanding his constant presence on site, but visiting often enough to keep in regular contact with Green – whom he evidently liked – and encourage and advise him when required. With Green on hand, Brindley could be confident of the canal's satisfactory progress. He would have the considerable satisfaction of seeing it open to traffic throughout its length within his lifetime.

CHAPTER EIGHT

1767–68: Brindley's Zenith

London Bridge

Fame reached Brindley relatively late in his life and brought with it many demands. In the years 1767 and 1768 he took on rather more work than he could satisfactorily manage, but which he was loath to decline. One prestigious appeal for his services came early in 1767, before the Staffordshire and Worcestershire Canal works had advanced far, and arose not from a canal promoter, but the City of London's Court of Common Council who sought his opinion on the condition of London Bridge.

The 1756 London Bridge Act authorised the Common Council of the Corporation of London to purchase and demolish all the shops and dwelling houses on the medieval structure in order to widen it, and as part of the improvements two of the arches were knocked together to produce a single 'Great Arch' in the centre of the bridge. At once problems emerged. With most of the water in the tidal Thames now flowing through the Great Arch, the London Waterworks Company's waterwheels under the bridge's four northernmost arches experienced a drastic loss of power.[1] They sought to increase the pressure on their wheels by damming up two arches called Long Entry and Chapel Locks, but the strategy was not entirely successful and in 1765, 'being yet unable to furnish the citizens and others with a sufficient supply of water at all times', they petitioned the London Corporation for permission to lease, and therefore block, a fifth arch.[2]

By 1767 it had become clear to the corporation that blocking so many arches had severe consequences for shipping. Increasingly, Londoners sought to avoid travelling under the Great Arch that they regarded, with good reason, as a source of peril. Excavation made when the two original arches were knocked into one had weakened the adjoining piers, while the iron water pipes which the Waterworks Company had laid across the bridge leaked and damaged the masonry. While the corporation recognised the need to take remedial action, balancing the demands of the Waterworks Company with the concerns of shipowners called for some tact. Besides supplying the city with water on a daily basis, the Waterworks Company had a fire engine (with a steam-pumping engine) available to meet any sudden demand for water needed to extinguish rogue fires, and fire risk loomed large in Londoners' minds. As recently as April 1758, the timber structure designed to replace the stone bridge while the widening works were in progress had gone up in flames, supposedly torched by opponents of the large-scale changes. (See Illustration 19).

Drawing the Waterworks Company's attention to the Thames watermen's concerns about their vessels being smashed against the bridge fabric under the great arch and insisting that they repair the damage caused by their leaky pipes was prudent, but did nothing to reconcile the competing demands for a steady flow of water and safety in navigation. While the Waterworks Company required a strong current to keep their wheels turning, it was crucial that shipping should be able to pass under the bridge without danger. To resolve the dilemma, in March 1767 the corporation solicited advice from a number of 'eminent surveyors', namely John Smeaton and Thomas Yeoman, who at this time were both working on the Lea Navigation; Robert Mylne, who was engaged on the design and construction of Blackfriars Bridge, and James Brindley who, out of the four, had least experience of conditions on the Thames.[3]

Nothing daunted, he was quick to make his report. For the river, he recommended removing the dams from the two arches on either side of the great arch and installing wheels in the fifth arch at the bridge's northern end and 'the *second arch* on the *Surry* side' – a strategy intended to reduce the force of the eddy which imperilled the shipping. In response to the corporation's wish to have ready access to water supplies for extinguishing fire, rather than employ a fire engine, Brindley advised building a reservoir 'in some convenient part of the city'; 'Fire engines,' he pronounced, 'are machines liable to many accidents, and therefore not to be trusted.'

In their reports Mylne and Smeaton pounced upon his ignorance both of London's geography and its recent population explosion. Since London had 'no void space within or near it' available for a reservoir, Mylne wondered in print at the corporation's even presuming to entertain 'such an idea'. Smeaton agreed that a large reservoir, if it were a practicable option, would indeed be 'the only means of having water at all exigencies of fire', in its absence, a fire engine gave 'the best provision' possible.[4] The corporation decided that on balance, Brindley's possibly rather hasty contributions to the debate were less helpful than they might have been. They presented 30 guineas each to Smeaton, Yeoman and Mylne, for their 'trouble' in surveying the bridge, and 10 guineas to Brindley.[5]

Illness

Wedgwood, whose letters brim with news of the ailments which beset his friends and family, found Brindley's lack of care for his own wellbeing infuriating. On 2 March 1767, he observed in genuine concern that Brindley was 'so incessantly harassed on every side, he hath no rest, either for his mind, or Body', before lamenting that he 'will not be prevailed upon to take proper care of his health.' To judge from the list of remedies he had written down in his notebook of the previous decade, he suffered at intervals from back pain, 'the ague' (probably a form of recurrent malaria) and gravel or stone.[6] Erasmus Darwin, who visited him on his deathbed in September 1772, diagnosed his trouble as 'a Diabetes' – a condition which the eighteenth century did not associate with the body's failure to produce insulin so much as an inability to absorb liquids which resulted in 'constant fever & thirst'.[7] Wedgwood, remembering the engineer's portfolio of salaried posts, soon turns officious. Brindley, he concedes, 'may get a few thousands but what does he give in exchange? His *Health,* & I fear his *Life* too, unless he grows wiser and takes the advice of his friends before it is too late.'[8] Illness had already frustrated Brindley's plans to visit both Ireland and Scotland on canal business. The Irish project, work for Lord Hertford on the section of the Lagan Canal, he delegated reluctantly to Robert Whitworth.[9] The Scottish venture, which concerned the Forth and Clyde Canal as it approached the Carron ironworks, he postponed, judging that his friend Samuel Garbett, Carron's part owner, would be happy allow him time to recover. He eventually visited Scotland in the late summer of 1768.

Health problems notwithstanding, over the summer of 1767 Brindley immersed himself in supervising construction of the Harecastle tunnel. To a certain anonymous and excitable journalist, the project was a total thrill. Several Midlands newspapers printed his 'Letter from Burslem in Staffordshire', which describes the 'Eighth Wonder of the World', namely 'the subterranean Navigation which is cutting by the great Mr Brindley who handles rocks as easily was you would Plumb-Pyes and makes the four elements subservient to his will.'[10] Brindley, the writer adds, 'is as plain a looking man as one of his own Carters, but when he speaks all Ears listen, and every Mind is filled with wonder at the things he pronouhces to be practicable.' He concludes his report with the triumphant, if rash, claim that the men cutting from each end of the tunnel 'intend to meet in the middle by Christmas, when they are to have an ox roasted whole and an hog's head of ale.'

Before long, a riposte arrived from Altrincham, a town which had not forgotten the snub dealt to the nearby Weaver Navigation at the end of 1765. 'Your Burslem correspondent makes Mr Brindley the Sir Isaac Newton of this age,' says the Cheshire writer, 'but seems not to know that the Duke of Bridgewater has another ingenious Man, viz. Thomas Morris, who has improved upon Mr Brindley ...' He proceeds, with a glee that would acquire a certain irony in the coming months, to describe how Morris, a Bridgewater Estates carpenter who held the post of engineer to the Chester Canal Company for a short time in the 1770s, was busy near Dunham, 'raising a valley to the level, by seven double water locks, which enable him to carry earth and stone as if down steps.'[11]

No-one appears to have paid much attention to the press's attempts to manufacture a saga of rivalry between the Duke of Bridgewater's canal men, although according to the Altrincham journalist the duke arranged to be 'towed some miles' along the canal 'to see the progress of his works.' While Morris continued to supervise the men working on the embankment by which the canal approached the River Bollin crossing, Brindley heeded Wedgwood's pleas and took Ann to Derbyshire for a change of scene and a holiday. His decision to visit Matlock suggests he may already have suspected that his health troubles owed something to diabetes, since the town's 'calcareous waters' were regarded as an effective remedy.[12]

They returned to Staffordshire after only two weeks. Wedgwood despaired: 'Mr and Mrs Brindley are returned,' he wrote, exasperated, to Bentley. 'Such a Man is known everywhere & cannot retire,' he added, observing that Brindley 'had little more rest' in the Peaks than he did at home. Even in relaxation, Brindley's thoughts had turned upon practical matters and he had observed the miners around Matlock throwing 'sparr' into a stream, so as to expose the valuable ore.[13] Although Wedgwood allowed that his health was 'a good deal better', than it had been, he could not resist adding that a full recovery would require 'more than a fortnight's rest.'

Coventry's Canal proposals

In the same letter where he fretted over Brindley's wellbeing, Wedgwood also mentions the existence of 'several Navigation schemes in embryo'. Prominent among them in was a plan to build a canal 'from the GRAND TRUNK to Coventry, Banbury and,' Wedgwood adds cheerfully, 'I don't know where.' Despite his vagueness, the statement reveals just how fast and far canal fervour spread. To find Banbury, well to the south of Coventry, named at this time suggests that the notion of connecting the Trent and Mersey Canal to the Thames had widespread support. At the same time, Wedgwood thought the prospective canal's promoters had got somewhat ahead of themselves. 'The money was subscrib'd for surveying,' he recalled, 'and Mr Brindley applied to,' but Brindley gave the Warwickshire coal owners short shrift and told them 'they were too precipitate (for they would have been in Parliam. this Session) although he agreed 'to look over the Country in a year or two if he could'.[14]

They paid little attention. Home from his Derbyshire foray, while Brindley brought his renewed energies to bear upon the tunnel, some gentlemen – probably the same group who had approached Brindley already – met at the White Bear in Coventry 'to consider further of the Navigable Canal intended to be made from that city to near Lichfield.' As a result of their discussion, they agreed unanimously 'that the said design should be carried into execution' without delay and amassed £15,300 for the purpose on the spot.[15] Brindley could hardly ignore the wishes of subscribers who were so visibly eager to part with money in the canal's cause. Exactly what happened is uncertain, but on 26 November 1767, Coventry petitioned Parliament for leave to bring in a bill to make or maintain a navigable canal from Gosford Green in their city to Fradley Heath on the basis of a 'survey lately taken', which suggests the thrusting Coventry coal owners persuaded him into finding time for it after all.[16] Reports of the Coventry Canal Bill's progress through Parliament mention 'a plan published by Mr Brindley' and it is possible that he made what use he could of the work of a forerunner, namely his distant relative Henry Bradford – Quaker timber merchant of Birmingham and half-brother of his great uncle Samuel Bradford – who had surveyed a line from Coventry to Tamworth in 1766.[17]

Whatever its background, the Coventry Canal Bill moved through Parliament fast. Observing from Staffordshire, the Trent and Mersey proprietors were generally inclined to view the enterprise in a favourable light. On 17 December 1767, when the Coventry Bill was due to come up for its second reading, Wedgwood informed Bentley that the Trent & Mersey Canal committee had put their seal 'to a Petition to Parliament in favour of the Coventry Canal, & sent it to London by Express'; several of the committee members, he added, had thought at first 'that the Coventry Navigation would injure ours but they were soon set to rights & agreed to the motion Nem: Con'.[18] On Christmas Eve 1767, Wedgwood confided his pleasure at foreseeing what 'good and great effect' the new waterway would have upon the 'GRAND TRUNK,' now that a 'foundation' was in place 'for extending it to the *Tideway of the R. Thames*'.[19]

If the bill's progress through both Houses was swift, it was not always smooth. The ruthless hurry of the Coventry promoters betrayed a certain lack of sophistication on their part in matters of parliamentary etiquette. In Wedgwood's view, they had 'a lucky escape of losing their Bill [...] by precipitating it too quick through a select Committee', and what was worse, omitting to canvass or send out solicitous *billets-doux* to sympathetic members. Apparently Thomas Gilbert, MP, who would have remembered the 200 letters which the Duke of Bridgewater despatched to garner support for his 1762 Act, was 'greatly disgusted' by Coventry's cavalier attitude to such niceties.[20] Yet thrusting manners reflected thrusting determination. The Coventry Canal would get its Act on 29 January 1768. From the city's first petitioning Parliament, it was only two months before their bill received the Royal Assent.

Floods in Lancashire

Over the early autumn of 1767, Brindley divided his time between the tunnel, the Staffordshire and Worcestershire Canal, which had now reached the area round Devil's Den near Prestwood, and the Coventry men with their demands for a survey. Amid this busy period, October floods destroyed the Stretford and Bollin aqueducts and ravaged Morris's embankment. Brindley was summoned to the site, the messenger who fetched him receiving a 12s tip.[21]

The damage which resulted from what a Manchester correspondent in the *Caledonian Mercury* described as 'the greatest flood here, ever known in the memory of man' was immense. The Rivers Mersey and Irwell both 'exceeded their bounds to the compass of several fields'; at Stretford, 'the bridge ... was, by the weight and impetuosity of the water below, forced from its foundations, and the bricks and stones carried several yards from their place' and at Bollin the aqueduct 'had about one third part carried away.' The total cost of the damage at both places was thought to be in the region of £2,000.[22] John Gilbert had hastened to set works in hand. Having inspected the devastated aqueduct at Stretford, he wrote to his brother saying that he thought it 'proper to have the Foundation Nine foot deeper that it was before', and observing that the bridge might have 'Stood a many years if the ffall of Water above ... had been stilld by a large deep hole at some distance from the entrance under the arch.'[23] The flood, he explained,

> Came with great violence from high ground and the position the water came in with such force when it was checkd at the entrance of the arch it broke up the foundation near 8 foot below where it was set from; the other end of the arch that gave way first was not so deep as the up[p]er end by near 4 foot but the water having liberty to spread at the lower end as it left the arch, it undercut the stream more at that end than the other, which I apprehend was the cause of it giving way first.

If the syntax of Gilbert's letter, composed in the heat of crisis, betrays signs of stress, the gist is plain. Sheer weight of water in the river battered the aqueduct to pieces, the scour of the flood undermining its foundation. Having analysed the cause of the bridge's collapse, Gilbert reflects that it was just as well the disaster occurred before the canal's completion; had it happened afterwards, the inconvenience of having the canal out of commission would be significantly greater. Returning to the subject of the Stretford Aqueduct, he foresees that it may be best 'to take down the pier that stands firm, since 'it will be very troublesome to underbuild it [sic]' while making the new foundation, 'but this,' he says, 'we must talk over with Mr Brindley when he comes.'

After the floods, the weather turned cold and frosty. To work with mortar in these conditions was all but impossible; not only did its moisture content expand unpredictably in the cold, but it could not bond effectively with the wet and icy surface of the bridge masonry.[24] Joseph Banks, who visited the canal in December 1767, watched labourers engaged on the Bollin Aqueduct's repair actually boiling the stones under John Gilberts' supervision in an attempt to combat the effects of the cold. Before long they realised that, cauldrons and pumps notwithstanding, the attempt was vain. It is possible that by this time Brindley, whose practical work as a millwright no doubt gave him some experience of attempting to build in cold and wet conditions, had reached the site. The men, Banks relates, 'were ordered ... immediately to leave off & the water was let in till it covered the top of their work two feet as a security from frost.' It would be pumped out and repairs resumed 'upon the first thaw'.[25]

Trent and Mersey progress

Josiah Wedgwood, meanwhile, at his new and rather grand Burslem home, Etruria Hall, spent much of December 1767 'seting out the Canal' with Hugh Henshall. When he suggested replicating something akin to a Capability Brown vista of water meandering through pastureland in elegant loops, Henshall dismissed the notion out of hand. 'I could not prevail upon the inflexible vandal to give me one line of Grace,' Wedgwood lamented afterwards. 'He must go the nearest, & best way, or Mr Brindley would go mad'.[26] He wrote without rancour, knowing Brindley well enough by this time to make him the butt of a mild Enlightenment joke. Teasing Bentley about his 'raptures' over Jean-Jacques Rousseau's portrayal of the virtue and contentment of primitive or 'natural' man Wedgwood, as it were, in the same breath, continues,

I can make my boasts of reading a *man of Nature* sometimes, though not as often as I could wish, & have my raptures too. Mr Brindley and his Lady call'd here in their way home, lay with us & are just left us this morning. We are to spend tomorrow with them at Newchapel & as I allways edify full as much in that man's company as at Church I promise myself to be much wiser the day following'.[27]

As late as January 1769, he continued to hope that the Trent and Mersey Canal might eventually reach Liverpool and anticipated the erection of a vast aqueduct across the tideway of the Mersey, complete with statue of 'Brindley L'Grand [to] grace the most conspicuous part of this tremendous Fabric'.[28]

Beginning to build the Coventry Canal

With the dawning of 1768 the construction of the Coventry Canal began. It is not easy to form a clear picture of the company of proprietors or the canal committee at this time, since the minutes of their meetings are skeletal, often recording no more than where they met, the sum that Clerk of Works Joseph Parker sought from the company treasurer, and the date of the next meeting. About the progress on the ground, there is hardly a word, although the brief notes give a sense that optimism abounded in the early phases. On 19 February 1768, a day of snow and rain, the sixty or so subscribers present at the first general meeting of the proprietors elected the canal company's officers, despatched 'the necessary business [...] with the most perfect unanimity' and heard Brindley assure them that 'the whole communication with the Staffordshire Canal would be accomplished in four or five years at most'.[29] (See Illustration 20).

Having begun work in good heart, Coventry spirits soon faltered. The company was not rich and financial stringency led the committee into pernickety carefulness. Towards the end of 1768, the minutes clerk noted Parker's representation about the 'insufficiency' of his £150 per annum salary and in December, the committee issued a directive to the effect that,

> That all bills upon the Company shall be from time to time brought before to be examined and allowed by them, before payment be made of any such bills under any pretence whatsoever and the Clerks of the Works are enjoined to attend to this resolution.[30]

For the committee to keep itself informed about where the company spent its funds was hardly unreasonable, but the fussy allusion to 'any pretence whatsoever' and the nagging directive to the company clerks were unlikely to foster much affability between employees and proprietors. Parker made his discontent evident by resigning from his post in 1770, after less than two years' employment, and his former assistant, Samuel Bull, found himself despatched 'for his improvement to the Staffordshire [Trent and Mersey] Canal and other navigations now forming' to give him the chance to increase his experience and hone his skills.[31] In the event, work on the new canal.

Under the terms of his appointment, as the Coventry Canal Company's engineer and surveyor Brindley was required to attend the canal works for at least two months in every year. While this stipulation no doubt reassured the committee of proprietors that he would be on site often enough to oversee more major developments, in practice 'two months' attendance' proved to be an arbitrary and flexible measure. Brindley's visits to the Staffordshire and Worcestershire Canal were typically of about two days' duration and took place at roughly fortnightly intervals, giving a total of approximately forty-eight days in each calendar year – closer to six weeks than two months. Nevertheless, he had no qualms about delegating day-to-day decision making to Clerk of Works John Fennyhouse Green – a most conscientious manager with whom he had an excellent working relationship – and, for the most part, construction went ahead smoothly and well. At Coventry, by contrast, although Brindley may have intended to monitor the works through the early building phase as the canal's construction advanced piecemeal in the hands of many small contractors, his increasing number and scale of commitments, together with the amount of time taken in travel, made frequent attendance difficult if not impossible. Perhaps neither Parker nor Bull were as resourceful as Green. Whatever the cause, it was not long before a note of managerial desperation began to colour some of his instructions.

In May 1769, following an inspection of the works, he gave the Coventry committee of proprietors no fewer than twenty-three separate 'Directions', all of which their clerk carefully noted in the minutes book. Many of them are straightforward. He orders, for instance, 'That the culverts for waste water be fixed in the natural ground where most convenient'; 'That the basin of Bishops Gate be puddled with a loaded broad wheeled cart drawn by Horses abreast', and 'That the ground in Stoke Heath be bricked where it is slipped.' As the list grows, its tone becomes increasingly peremptory. In rapid succession, Brindley demands 'That the workmen in the second depth of the Hill in the tunnelling part be immediately discharged'; 'That there be no more round bricks used in the bridges'; 'That a drain be immediately made through or under Bulkington Lane for the water on the further side of Bedworth Hill, and that the works be laid dry by working up all the dice holes from the said Drain' and 'That the water be turned into the canal immediately in Mr Baxter's land.'[32] Brindley might impress committees, but the list demonstrates his want of the arts of pleasing them. These instructions, issued, no doubt, for good reason, belonged on site rather than in the committee room. A wise contractor assistant or clerk of works would understand the necessity for making a drain without delay, or dismissing unsatisfactory labourers; to gentlemen proprietors, repetition of the word 'immediately' in a volley of orders from their engineer only sounded dogmatic. While it may not have been a strict matter of cause and effect, on 26 September 1769 the general assembly of proprietors resolved that Brindley be discharged from his post.

It is unlikely that the reasons for his dismissal had anything to do with a rather over-assertively worded series of instructions. What is more probable is that the high standard of building on which Brindley insisted promised to prove too expensive for a company that was concerned about cash flow. Accustomed to the duke's readiness to spend freely on extras like stop-gates and ice-breaking vessels in his wish to see the Bridgewater Canal operating as efficiently as possible, Brindley was slow to adjust to the economies practised by a fiscally cautious committee of proprietors. No doubt tempers frayed on both sides before the final breach in relations between engineer and company of proprietors occurred, and a clash with local miners employed in the tunnelling who sabotaged the works when they recognised that the canal would increase competition from other coalfields may have heightened the tension.[33] Without comment, if perhaps somewhat taken aback, Brindley turned his back on Coventry and gave his attention to other ventures.

Beginning to build the Oxford Canal

Since the Oxford Canal was conceived together with the Coventry Canal in order to complete a connection between the Trent, Mersey, Severn and Thames rivers, there is a certain logic in discussing its early development in the light of Brindley's Coventry experience. If his dealings with Coventry were stormy, his association with the Oxford Canal committee was hardly any more tranquil. (See Illustration 21).

The Oxford Canal's leading promoter was Sir Roger Newdigate of Arbury. Founder of a famous prize for poetry, Member of Parliament for the University of Oxford and sometime counsel to the Duke of Bridgewater, he had been largely responsible for piloting the third Bridgewater Canal Act through Parliament in 1762. Like the duke, Sir Roger was a coal owner and canal enthusiast; indeed, both men are reputed to have travelled from their respective homes, Worsley and Arbury, to Westminster entirely by water. In the early part of 1769, he energetically canvassed support from likely allies among the aristocracy who predictably included the Duke of Bridgewater and Earl Gower, the Duke of Marlborough and also his brother, Lord Charles Spencer. He made, he records, 'near 40 visits' in connection with the canal.[34] His conscientiousness paid off; having come before Parliament at the end of November 1768, the Oxford Canal Bill received the Royal Assent on 21 April 1769.[35]

On the Oxford Canal's management committee, influence of the university loomed large, it members including vice-chancellor and master of University College, Nathan Wetherell; former vice-chancellor and principal of Hertford College, David Durell, and George Horne, president of Magdalen.[36] What these donnish proprietors made of Brindley – his unassuming demeanour, his boundless zeal and his canals beginning to cross the country with Biblical verve – history does not relate. What is certain is that Oxford University's interest in the Oxford Canal would be active and long-lived. Although there may be some truth in the allegation that the university's opposition to the GWR in the 1830s arose from a conviction that the railway would be detrimental to the moral wellbeing of the undergraduates, the fact that several colleges owned canal shares no doubt heightened their hostility.[37] In the event, Oxford did not get its rail connection until 1843, six years after the idea had first been mooted.

Having left Coventry, the Oxford Canal was to pass through Ansty, Shilton, Brinklow, Newbold, Hillmorton, Braunston, Napton, Wormleighton, Cropredy, Banbury, King's Sutton, Aynho, Soulldern, Heyford, Shipton, Thrupp, and Wolvercote before it joined the Thames. More or less from the outset, its winding route was to spark some less than appreciative comments which Samuel Simcock, in effect Brindley's resident engineer on the Oxford Canal, would rebut with the argument that a circuitous line clinging to a single level was less expensive to build than a short direct route which tunnelled through hills and required much lockage for ascending and descending.[38] What proved rather more contentious than its loops was the location of its junction with the Coventry Canal.

Initially, the site was to have been Gosford Green, not far from Coventry's city centre. Whether Gosford Green was Brindley's choice of location is not entirely clear. When the Coventry Canal Bill had come up before Parliament, evidence of its practicability was not provided by Brindley but by Coventry city clerk William Dadley, who rather evasively referred to a 'survey lately taken by an able engineer' – the work, perhaps, of Henry Bradford.[39] In February 1769, when the Oxford Canal Bill was making its way through the Commons, petitions from Tamworth, Lichfield, Birmingham and Newcastle-under-Lyme reached Parliament, with a common gist. All argued that building to the line which joined the Coventry Canal at Gosford Green would necessitate some twenty locks, whereas the line terminating at Longford would 'lay the ... Navigation upon a level for above 30 miles together', something they regarded as being 'of great service to Trade and commerce'.[40] It is pure speculation, but the petitioners' conviction about what was best for trade and commerce may have owed a certain amount to Brindley himself, holding forth across the Midlands about Coventry's haste to get its Act through Parliament without waiting for him to consider where its canal should join with the companion waterway intended to run south to the Thames at Oxford.

As a result of the Midland towns' agitation, it was agreed to locate the junction at Longford. It necessitated amendment of the Oxford Bill to include a pair of compensation clauses by which the Coventry Company was to receive the tolls on all coal traffic on the Oxford Canal for the first 2 miles from the Longford junction, while the Oxford Company took the tolls on all articles except coal which came from their canal and travelled up to 3½ miles on the Coventry Canal towards Coventry.[41] So that neither company should lose out, the two canals paralleled one another for a mile or so, making for 'a wasted two miles', as Cyril Boucher graphically observed.[42] As a compromise, it was hardly elegant but it ensured that the Coventry Canal Company received much the same revenue as it would have done had the junction been at Gosford Green. It also paved the way for years of strife between the Oxford and Coventry Canal Companies.

Throughout 1769, Brindley made frequent visits to the Oxford Canal and the mood of his dealings with its scholarly committee of proprietors varied. Frustrated by a succession of small local difficulties with uncooperative landowners, in September 1769 he signed and despatched a note to his rather anxious Clerk of Works, James King, stating that since 'so many obstructions' stood in the canal's way, he advised that 'there be no more progress in the Works till after the next general assembly of Proprietors.' By way of postscript, he added a terse sentence stating that he would not submit any estimate for the works because he knew 'the great difficulty as well as very great expence of making them with any degree of certainty.'[43]

When King showed them this missive, with its writer's tangled admission that providing a reasonably precise estimate of costs was difficult and that the resulting sum would be high, the committee men were unimpressed. They responded by recording their view that 'that Mr Brindley hath in no degree complied with the orders of the committee.'[44] To all appearances, what followed was a brief but ill-humoured spat between a rather remote set of dons, city fathers of Oxford and a few country clergy on the one hand, and the career engineers and contractors on the other, with the hapless King caught between them. In the event, the tempest passed and work resumed, but the following year witnessed another outburst of petty officiousness when the committee passed and minuted a resolution 'That the Engineer-Surveyor and Clerks of this Company do not associate or drink with any of the Inferior officers or workmen employed by this Company under any Pretence whatsoever.'[45] In equally bossy vein, two weeks later they passed heavy handed judgement when a disagreement arose between their appointee, King, and Brindley's on-site deputy, Samuel Simcock. 'It having been represented to the committee,' runs their pompous writ,

> That Mr Simcox … have exceeded the orders given to him by the committee by interfering with Mr King in his offices as surveyor of the work, we do therefore order that Mr King do continue to execute his office … and that a copy of the order be sent to Simcox that he may be apprised of the Trust that was reposed in him.[46]

For Simcock (his name wrongly spelled) it was a dressing-down despatched from a great height. Brindley did not care to see his assistant and brother-in-law humiliated. Although the exact pattern of events that followed this episode is uncertain, a letter copied into the Oxford minutes book gives an idea of their outline. Addressed to Brindley, its contrite sentences tell their own tale. 'Sir', the letter opens,

> We whose names are hereunto subscribed ... have received with great surprise and concern a letter from you to acquaint us of your intended resignation. We are very sorry that anything has happened that has given you offence and shall always be ready to place the greatest confidence in you, as we consider the assistance of your abilities and experience essential to the carrying this Navigation into execution.
>
> Your letter mentions no reason for this sudden step. We therefore desire that you will not fail to meet this ... committee at the Three Tuns in Banbury on Sunday evening ... and that if anything has been done wrong by any of the company's servants it may be thoroughly understood and explained at the general assembly of Proprietors the next day.[47]

Among the signatories are both university vice-chancellor Nathan Wetherall and Thomas Walker, Oxford town clerk. Together, no doubt, with appropriate apologies to Simcock, it was enough to restore Brindley's goodwill. He resumed his post and remained there till his death when Simcock succeeded him.

Bridgewater visitors

Brindley might not have travelled there often during 1768 and 1769, but the Bridgewater Canal attracted had a number of distinguished visitors. Among the more illustrious was King Christian VII of Denmark, a grandson of George II, who made a 'sudden and unexpected visit' to Manchester in September 1768.[48] Having caught the town unaware, rather than stay with any of the local aristocracy, Christian and his entourage put up at the Bull's Head Inn. On the short-notice recommendation of Lord Morton, president of the Royal Society Edward Byrom, a die-hard Mersey & Irwell Navigation man, found himself obliged to give the Danish king a tour of the rival waterway.[49] With this unlikely escort, the king marvelled at the canal's 'ingenuity and facility' and made a candle-lit journey through Gilbert's soughs before leaving a generous tip for the workforce. After inspecting the warehouses, he spent the remainder of his time with his retinue, declining all invitations, including the offer of a ceremonious ball to be held in his honour. Despite his reserve, the press treated his trip as a great success.

Although they attracted less attention, visits by the agriculturalist Arthur Young and the naturalist Joseph Banks left a more enduring legacy. The accounts which appear in Banks' manuscript *Journal of an Excursion to Wales, etc.* of 1767/8 and Young's *Six Months' Tour through the North of England*, first published in 1770, give a clear record both of the canal in its early days and of the various devices evolved to assist in its construction and promote its smooth functioning. Both keen observers with a wish to analyse what they saw, they were visitors with more technological curiosity than either the Danish king or the thrill-seekers who had taken the dare of walking across the Barton Aqueduct.

By 1768, when Arthur Young came to Manchester, the duke's wish to transport coal by water from mine to market had become a reality.[50] Young's account of a boat trip first from Castlefield to Worsley and then, having back-tracked to Castlefield, to Altrincham, graphically indicates why the duke's enterprise should have caught the public's curiosity. Its workings demonstrated human ingenuity writ large. At Castlefield, Young watched as boats, each filled with twelve 'square boxes, fitted in exactly', enter a tunnel. In the tunnel is what Young calls a 'well', more precisely a shaft, and as each vessel comes underneath it, a crane set at street level which, he explains, 'is much higher than the level of the water, being somewhat of a hill', draws up the boxes, each of which is 'ironed' with fastenings for ropes and designed to hold 8 cwt of coal. At the top, the coal is emptied out ready for sale, while each box is let down the shaft into the boat's hold once more, ready for the next trip. A source of particular interest to Young was the waterwheel that powered the crane.

While he was at Castlefield, Young also observed the weir which Brindley had built where the canal met the River Medlock, and which he devised to ensure that excess water returned to the river instead of raising the level of the canal. He designed a vast circular weir with six leaf-like extensions around its rim, in dimension large enough to accommodate an immense quantity of water pouring over it and descending into a well or funnel at its centre. From the well, the water entered a tunnel which returned it to the river at a lower level. Even in its present day form, which is very much less intricate than Brindley's original conception, it is a spectacular structure; Young, who saw the weir in all its foliated glory, found it hugely impressive. At the same time, he admitted that it had 'more than once been totally overflowed' with the result that 'the canal received a much larger portion of water than ever Mr Brindley designed it should, and the inconveniencies of an unrestrained tide either happened or might have done.'

Having admired the aqueducts along the route, attempted to describe the operation of Brindley's stop-gates and remarked upon a pivoting crane 'of very curious construction', used 'for heaving stones out of the quarry into the barges', Young turns his attention to the boats used to move earth in order to build up embankments, which have trapdoors in their hulls. They are, he says, of two kinds. First there are the 'grey boats', which are in most frequent use and which are,

> Constructed by joining two boats together at the distance of about three feet, which is done by cross-beams of timber [.] Upon these is fix'd a trough whose bottom ... is fix'd immediately over the open left between the two boats [.] The bottoms of these troughs are composed of a number of small doors each of which is supported by a chain fasten'd to it ... in such a manner that it is easily let to slip.

Smiles provides detail to flesh out Banks's stark account, indicating that boats would proceed from the canal 'into watertight caissons ... placed at the point over which the earth ... had to be deposited'.[51] Once the boats had entered the caissons and the trough was in the right position, its doors could be raised so as to empty out the earth inside onto the rising embankment. Banks also noticed what he calls 'diving boats', which worked on the same principle but, he explains, 'are single boats divided into partitions, one half of which have doors in their bottoms, while the other half are solid and render the boat buoyant after having discharged her cargo.'

Both Banks and Young wonder at the 'many powers' of the Worsley mill, its 24-foot-diameter wheel driving three pairs of stones which respectively ground corn, powered a boulting mill for refining the flour by sifting out the meal and grist and drove a mortar-making machine.[52] Young also mentions a sand-sifting machine, and vessels adapted as a floating carpenter's shop and blacksmith's forge.[53] Banks, who came in winter, had the pleasure of watching the ice-breaker at work. Things had moved on since Brindley utilised the 'ould 20 tun boat' for ice breaking in November 1763.[54] In January 1766, Sir Peter Warburton, one of the Weaver Navigation trustees, had told Lord Strange that Brindley had 'contrived a machine to be drawn by mules to break the ice.'[55] A year later, Banks watched 'a broad stemmed boat' drawn by a mule forge her way through ice 'near an inch thick' while some seven or eight people on board 'swayed her with great force … & at the same time struck any large pieces of ice in pieces [sic] with clubbs they held in their hands.'[56] He went on to explain how 'swaying a boat' in such a narrow canal affected what he termed 'the whole water', with the result that a 'large wave runns before her which always cracks and often separates the ice before she touches it.'

Among other visitors to the canal, a party from Ireland included both James Fortescue, sometime MP for Louth, and the Sardinian architect and engineer Davis Dukart – born D'Aviso De'Arcourt. Describing his experiences to the Rt Hon. William Brownlow of Lurgan, Dukart claimed to have 'particularly examined' Brindley's work both for the duke and at '*hare Castle*' [sic]. 'The Plan of the Duke's' he pronounces 'excellent', observing that,

> Nature & perverse wrong headed Proprietors of Land could not throw difficulties in the way that the Spirit of that Nobleman & Ingenuity of his Engineer did not overcome rather than to have locks.[57]

'I wish', he adds pointedly, 'I could say as much of the Staffordshire Canal.' To Dukart, the Bridgewater Canal, with its minimal lockage, decisively trumped the Trent and Mersey with more than seventy locks over its 95-mile length. Like Banks and Young, Dukart not only approved of the duke's public-spirited determination to provide Manchester with cheap coal, but marvelled at Brindley's workmanship.

All three men visited Worsley not solely for the excitement of touring the coal workings or walking across the aqueduct, but more with the intention of appraising the canal's construction and the devices which facilitated its working. In the eyes of visitors of this stamp, Brindley's contribution was as significant as that of the duke. It was as though to the new class of industrial tourists and engineering pilgrims, the canal's creators were of different, but equally significant species: the duke who had conceived and financed it, and Brindley who gave it shape. (See Illustration 22).

CHAPTER NINE

New Branches: The Droitwich Canal and the Birmingham Canal

Droitwich

Although the Coventry and Oxford Canals were both projects of national significance, Brindley was also ready to take on less ambitious schemes. Conceived as an outlet for the town's salt traffic, the 6-mile Droitwich Canal would link Droitwich Spa with the Severn at Hawford. It would be wide enough to accommodate the broad-beamed Severn Trows, and its route would include a total of eight locks, to be built by local contractor John Bushel. How Brindley came by this work is not known, although on 13 March 1762, while in London to support the duke's Third Canal Act through Parliament, he noted, 'Salt Work at Dortwhich [sic]', apparently by way of memorandum but without any accompanying explanation.[1] It is a puzzling statement to find in the London setting, but suggests that someone – presumably a Droitwich man aware of the town's need for a better link than the narrow River Salwarpe between its salt pits and the Severn – took the chance of engaging Brindley in what would prove to be a profitable and constructive discussion.

Assuming that there is any truth in this conjectural version of events, it was a considerable amount of time before Droitwich decisively took matters ahead, but on 26 November 1767 a group of petitioners applied to Parliament for leave to bring in a bill to make a canal from the Severn to their town.[2] Two days later, Droitwich man John Priddey gave the House of Commons evidence to support the application, in the course of which he mentioned that 'by an estimate made and signed by Mr James Brindley' the cost of building the canal would be £13,363, 'or thereabouts'; on 29 January 1768 the Droitwich Canal Act received the Royal Assent.[3] In 1769, Brindley was appointed to the exalted-sounding post of inspector of the works. Yet how large a part the Droitwich commission played in his life it is hard to say. The company minutes mention him only twice, which suggests that he attended few of their meetings and to all appearances entrusted supervision of the labour force to Priddey, his *de facto* resident engineer.[4] By 1770, incidentally, Priddey had made himself thoroughly unpopular. His labourers went on strike, claiming that they had 'Bin yoused Very ill' and demanded a wage of at least 11 shillings a week.[5]

Yet these sparse records perhaps give a less than accurate picture of Brindley's interest in Droitwich and its possibilities. While making their archaeological study of Brindley's model lock at Turnhurst, William Klemperer and Paul Sillitoe came across a theory, current apparently among the Droitwich descendants of the canal's original labour crew, that while Brindley was in the area he had experimented with the design of 'self-closing gates', which he conceived in order to save the boatmen's time. Klemperer and Sillitoe found no evidence to corroborate this tradition and they suspect that, even if Brindley had introduced them, the gates would have wasted so much water that their installation on any large scale would have been more trouble than it was worth.[6] Certainly no eighteenth-century visitor to Droitwich Spa ever chronicled their operation in the vein of Arthur Young's and Joseph Banks's descriptions of Brindley's 'ingenious devices' around Worsley.

Birmingham

Beside the Droitwich work, by 1768 Brindley's portfolio of commitments had expanded massively. He was now dividing his time between the Bridgewater Canal as it advanced towards Runcorn by way of Preston Brook; the Grand Trunk with its immense tunnel, substantial aqueducts and numerous locks; he was in regular consultation with Green about the Staffordshire and Worcestershire Canal, and attending to the new canals running from Fradley Heath to Coventry, and from Coventry to Oxford. By now, he had such stature that canal promoters held his involvement with a venture to be a guarantee of its success, and when the leading commercial spirits of Birmingham sought a link from their town to the nascent waterways network they were quick to approach him.

Somehow, over the spring of 1767, with Robert Whitworth's help, he had found time to make an initial survey and the following June recommended that the best line 'would be from near New Hall, over Birmingham Heath to near Oldbury, Tipton Green, Bilson', and then to the Staffordshire and Worcestershire Canal, with branches running to different collieries. The total expense, he estimated, would not exceed £50,000.[7]

Encouraged by a figure which may well have looked modest to a prospering town, the Birmingham manufacturers hastened to convene a committee. They nominated four members – Samuel Garbett, Matthew Boulton, John Kettle and a forceful coalowner named William Bentley – to receive money and make overtures to landowners along the route. Finding them 'unanimously in favour' of the canal, they opened a subscription, and applied to Parliament.[8] The Birmingham Canal Act received the Royal Assent in February 1768.

Energetic and knowing what was required, the committee advertised for contractors 'who perfectly understand the nature of Navigation business' to undertake the 'Cutting of the Canal', and set about recruiting a 'strong able man, perfectly versed in Measuration of all Kinds' to serve as an under-clerk.[9] At the same time, they 'desired' William Bentley to find a source of clay for making bricks, and requested John Baker of the Staffordshire and Worcestershire Canal for advice about timber, requesting him also to 'send a modal [sic] of their Barrows'. They asked Brindley to despatch 'Henshaw [sic] and Whitworth to resurvey the course of the canal immediately'; to instruct them how to obtain 'the necessary implements […] to be used in the Navigation' and, at once hospitable and anxious, added that 'if he [Brindley] comes into this part of the Country soon', they 'wou'd be glad to see him'.[10] Obligingly, he came the next committee meeting where he helped them to appoint a superintendent and a deputy, and recommended that the new recruits spend some time at 'one of the Navigations now compleating' to get some practical experience.[11] Before long, the company appointed Ambrook Stringer and John Brookes to the new office of superintendent. Where, and indeed whether, the two served any period of probation, the minutes make no mention.

After this propitious start, the contractors hit difficulties at Smethwick, where Brindley, working perhaps more from intuition than reasoned analysis, proposed to cross the ridge of high ground by means of a tunnel. Unfortunately, before the publication in 1813 of William Smith's authoritative *Geological Map of Great Britain*, insofar as geology was a recognised field of expertise, neither mine owners nor canal engineers paid it much attention and initial surveys for the canal had included no analysis of the strata through which it was to cut. Discovery of quicksand, or what the company minutes expressively describe as 'running sand and other bad materials' below the Smethwick summit was a major blow.[12] On 8 June 1768, an extraordinary meeting of the committee took place 'in consequence of Mr Brindley's attendance' – a phrase which implies that they had summoned him specially – at which the committee considered how best to proceed. According to the minutes, only after he had 'maturely weighed', the adverb carries a telling charge, 'and considered the consequences attendant upon proceeding thereupon' did he, with apparent reluctance, agree 'to avoid tunnelling'. He clearly believed that the tunnel represented the best means of crossing the Smethwick ridge, not least because by serving as an additional reservoir it would also make a useful contribution to the perennial problem of ensuring that the canal had adequate water supplies. At the same time, although he might be impetuous, particularly in him following his instincts in pursuit of a promising engineering solution to an intractable topographical problem, he was not entirely reckless. If the Birmingham committee viewed his tunnel as a perilous and expensive project, he was ready – albeit with reluctance – to respect their caution. His revised recommendation for Smethwick was to 'to carry the canal over the hill by locks and Fire Engines'.[13] It may not have made for elegant engineering, but it met the proprietors' requirements. In 1786, when the canal's funds were more buoyant, the committee's decision to address the bottlenecks at either end, where traffic queued to enter the locks, by employing Smeaton to lower the summit significantly went some way to endorse the merit of Brindley's original plan.[14]

Scotland

In September 1768, conscious of Garbett's presence and influence on the canal's committee of proprietors, Brindley made his long-deferred visit to the Carron ironworks near Falkirk in which Garbett had a substantial interest. It is likely that that two men were friends as well as colleagues, since their respective backgrounds were sufficiently alike to have drawn them together. Like Brindley, Garbett appears to have had little in the way of formal education. According to the Scottish divine Alexander Carlyle who knew him well, it went no further that 'writing and accounts' but, in a remark which by chance recalls Wedgwood's description of Brindley as a 'sensible friend', Carlyle added that Garbett was 'a man of great acuteness of genius and extent of understanding'.[15] His business career followed an adventurous, stormy path which suggests that he brought intelligence and considerable courage to bear upon his powerful commercial instincts. Besides managing a sulphuric acid factory and a turpentine works, he went into partnership with John Roebuck to refine and assay precious metals and would later help to establish Birmingham's assay office. In later life, Garbett would chair a Birmingham committee opposed to the slave trade; go bankrupt and successfully re-establish himself; raise funds for Birmingham's infirmary and serve as churchwarden of St Philip's Church – later Birmingham Cathedral. He had once been the Birmingham agent of a London merchant named Hollis, and since Brindley recorded spending 30 March 1762 'At Mr Hollis, St Mary Axs', it may have been in Hollis's company that the two of them first met.[16]

Aware that the Forth and Clyde Canal would run close to his Carron works, Garbett did not consider that Smeaton's line came quite as close as he wished. As early as 1765, he told Wedgwood of his intention of 'applying ... to Mr Brindley to review Mr Smeaton's plans and estimates', but Brindley's commitments and bouts of illness meant that three years would pass before he actually came to Scotland. When at last he came to Carron in the early Autumn of 1768, his visit achieved nothing beyond a ride in the rain by way of survey and the recommendation of various changes, none of which the Forth & Clyde Canal Company was inclined to adopt. At least, by way of consolation, he had the honour of being made a burgess of the city of Glasgow.[17]

Birmingham termini

By mid-October 1768, *Aris's Birmingham Gazette* gleefully reported that the new canal was 'in great forwardness', with 'upwards of Five Miles [...] complete'. On 6 November 1769 the first vessels from the Wednesbury pits arrived in the heart of Birmingham, heralding a substantial reduction of the price of coal.[18] Despite this success, Brindley's dealings with the Birmingham committee of proprietors were beginning to show signs of turning into a succession of grudges, grievances and protests. To some degree Brindley himself – particularly revisions he made to the works as they progressed – contributed, albeit unintentionally, to the discord.

In the first round of internecine warfare he played no part other than that of observer. At about the same time that the canal committee was debating the best approach to the heart of the town (in the canal's early stages when it was only a link between Birmingham and Spon Lane, coal vessels did not come into the centre of Birmingham but unloaded at a wharf on Friday Street), Samuel Garbett charged the committee with attempting to side-step their commitment to supply coal as cheaply as possible and accused them preferring to increase the profits of local coal owners. These allegations went to the heart of the canal proprietors' public utility obligations. What was more, Garbett's concern about the bona fides of his fellow proprietors went deep enough for him to take the rather drastic step of resigning from the committee, selling off most of his Birmingham Canal shares, airing his accusations in the press and planning to petition Parliament.[19] As public indignation grew, the rising storm came to encircle a prime target, namely sometime committee Chairman William Bentley.

How far the attacks upon Bentley were justified is hard to say. He had by this time become the focus for a number of comments, suggestions and allegations which combined to suggest that he was less than scrupulous in his commercial dealings. In a typical anti-Bentley gibe, the *Warwickshire Journal*, for example, described him as 'one of the Committee [...] who is most principally concerned in the Direction, hath [...] a Share in some Coal Works, and may order the Canal for his own private Advantage.'[20] Bentley, it is clear, exercised much influence with the other committee men and a rather enigmatic note in the committee minutes of 17 November 1769 apparently authorised him to reach his own agreement 'without waiting for Mr Brindley's' with the contractor Beswick or Turton:

> For cutting to Townes' and Aston's Colliery, and to keep in contemplation his cutting the other part from Bilston to Autherley, but not to conclude that till Mr Brindley hath been in consultation.[21]

Since Brindley was seldom present and pretty much *incommunicado* when travelling or busy elsewhere, allowing Bentley to negotiate with the contractors in his absence may have represented a practical way for the committee to take matters ahead. At the same time, the resolution put much power into Bentley's grasp, which Garbett thought he exploited. His claim that Bentley deliberately redefined Brindley's route so as to keep the canal at a distance from the collieries of two of his competitors gave rise to 'a very sore quarrel'.[22]

These internal squabbles point to a general lack of strong committee leadership. The nascent canal's administration appears to have been excessively lax, as Brindley's complaint in April 1770 about the company clerks being regularly 'called away from their proper sphere of business' bears out.[23] A few months later, the committee summoned him to account for a major breach, the consequence of sub-standard work by the contractor Bannister, 'it appearing to the committee that the water had been turned into that part of the canal before it was ready to receive it.'[24] Exactly how Brindley answered their allegations and whether he thought them valid, the minutes provide no record, but the episode speaks of poor communication between company staff and on-site foremen.

By this stage, the most pressing problem for the proprietors concerned litigation around their planned Birmingham terminus. The committee first signalled a wish to purchase a piece of land called New Hall Ring from one Charles Colmore, and then prevaricated, setting up temporary wharves at locations it found convenient. Brindley informed the committee that he preferred to site his terminus at Brick Kiln Piece (now Gas Street basin). Colmore, not caring for the way the committee men blew hot and cold, consulted lawyers and eventually petitioned Parliament for leave to bring in a bill to compel completion to New Hall, calling John Smeaton as a witness in his support. Parliament decided in Colmore's favour and in February 1771, his bill became law. It allowed the company thirteen months in which to complete the canal to New Hall Ring, 'in as straight and direct a line as the level will admit.'[25]

At this point, new difficulties arose. Rather late in the day Matthew Boulton, James Watt's urbane and usually courteous business partner, realised that the canal's New Hall extension was likely to have a detrimental impact on his Soho Manufactory's water supply.[26] Caught on the raw, Boulton gave vent to an almighty brouhaha in which he bluntly alleged that the canal engineers had no understanding of manufacturers' requirements. 'Let Mr Smeaton or Brindley or all the Engineers upon Earth give what evidence they will before Parliament', he expostulated in somewhat histrionic terms to Thomas Gilbert MP whom he sought as an ally,

> Think of my summer situation, when I have no water, my work people standing-still murmuring. My orders not executed, my foreign friends complaining & countermanding their orders. Think what a distressing situation, what reward is this for my labours and hazards? [...] As a Member of Parliament – as an old acquaintance - - as a friend of your Country – as a good man, I beg you will save me from destruction.[27]

Boulton lets fly again in a letter to Garbett. His tenor is, in essence, that the engineers have no real grasp of local needs. 'I have seen the questioning of [...] Smeaton and Yeoman', he writes,

> And I value the opinions neither of them nor Brindley nor Simcox [sic], in this case, nor of the whole tribe of jobbing ditchers who are retained as evidence on any side which first applies for them.[28]

In the contemplation of possible disaster, his imagination runs riot and he anticipates how 'A mischievous man, or unlucky boy, or a water rat, or a boat pole carelessly used, may at any time in a few hours ruin any canal upon the side of a sandhill.' Even Brindley's ingenious stop-gates, evolved to guard against loss of water in the event of a breach, have only limited usefulness, as Boulton scornfully – if not wholly without justification – observed, remarking 'How easy is it to pin down a stop-gate, or how probable it is that bungling contrivance should not rise if the canal should break down ...' In truth, both Smeaton and Brindley were far too skilled and experienced as millwrights to take a dismissive or cavalier view towards manufacturers' water supplies. Out of temper, and annoyed with himself for not foreseeing the trouble before it became pressing, Boulton was less than fair but his outburst is typical of the division and internal broil that rent the Birmingham Canal committee at just the time when the canal's construction might have benefited from their showing a united front.

Besides reaching New Hall Ring, the proprietors sought to establish a wharf at Brick Kiln Piece. It is hard to know how unanimous or whole-hearted the committee were in wanting two termini from the outset, particularly in view of their apparent readiness to regard the temporary wharfage off Friday Street as fulfilling their Birmingham objectives. Obviously it would not have sufficed for the long term, but since it served their immediate purposes, they gave little indication of establishing anything more permanent and dithered over purchasing the land known as New Hall Ring, near what is now Great Charles Street, which they had previously thought might serve for a terminus and basin. When they took up Brindley's suggestion that Brick Kiln Piece was the better site, as a means of dodging their obligations to Colmore, the proprietors gave out the view that the New Hall ground leaked. Incensed,

Colmore made what obstacles he could contrive in order to prevent them from cutting to Brick Kiln Piece, and eventually a jury resolved the matter, apportioning what they regarded as fair rental to Colmore for land already cut through and required to complete to Brick Kiln Piece, and fair purchase price for the acre needed to complete to New Hall. It was, all told, one wrangle after another; profitable for lawyers, but the source of endless delay before the canal could begin to realise its potential, and in these circumstances, to imagine that Brindley and the contentious committee men could have remained on civil terms beggars belief.

Samuel Simcock by this time had both on-site responsibility to ensure that construction reached an acceptable standard and a free hand to make day-to-day decisions, and perhaps because he was 'family', Brindley seems to have been unusually quick to take his part when he attracted trouble. Trouble descended on Simcock towards the end of 1770 when, marking the way the canal twisted along the contour, the local press ran a story to the effect that the Birmingham Canal's engineers – engineer-in-chief and *de facto* resident alike – had 'lengthened the course of the Canal by turning [looping] so as to increase the tonnage to the proprietors'. As a result, on 11 January 1771 both Brindley and Simcock were required to appear before an assembly of proprietors and asked whether, on their own account or on the instruction of a committee member or other proprietor, they had lengthened the canal in order to increase the tonnage. Their reply was to the effect that they altered the canal's course for two reasons only. First 'where the nature of the ground required' and second, 'to give accommodation to owners of Coal mines who otherwise could not have access to the Canal'.[29]

The reasoning was fair, although as surveyor-in-chief, Brindley claimed for himself a fair amount of latitude. Christopher Lewis suggests, not implausibly, that with works under way on at least six other canals at this time, and his patience with the canal's wrangling proprietors fast exhausted, Brindley may have decided that leaving Simcock to loop along the contours was the simplest way of making progresss.[30] Summoned to face interrogation from an indignant assembly of Birmingham proprietors intent on meting out summary justice, he sought to exculpate Simcock and himself with the least possible trouble. Having reminded them that the more businesses the canal served, the more money it made, the two engineers signed a declaration to the effect that they had had no intention of designing their route to take advantage of their position in order to benefit the company unjustly, and meekly agreed to its insertion in the newspapers.

It was expedient, but less than advantageous to the future utility of the canal which, as Christopher Lewis argues, 'could and should have been more efficiently engineered and surveyed'.[31] Quite apart from the frustrations of negotiating its meandering route, much of the actual workmanship appears to have been downright shoddy, with no towpath, sharp bends and banks unshored and crumbling.[32] It was perhaps as a consequence of the canal's apparently chronic shortage of water that he suggested attaching a piece of lead calibrated in inches to either end of the boats to show 'not only what Burthen such vessel is laden with, but also what water she draws' with a view to avoiding the risk of heavily laden boats damaging lock cills and stop-gates by grounding on them.[33] At the same time, he recommended that no boat 'pass any of the locks or stop gates unless there shall be at least an inch depth of water between the bottom of the boats and the sills of the Locks and stop Gates', and advised that a measure be fixed at the locks and gates' sides. Not so much an ingenious device as a rather drastic attempt to solve a local problem, the committee minutes give no indication of how helpful his lead markers ever were. (See Illustration 23).

Aldersley

The Smethwick Summit, which Brindley had wanted to cross by tunnelling under it, stood near the Wednesbury pits, between Birmingham and Spon Lane. Since running an unambitious if lucrative trade between Wednesbury and Birmingham was clearly to Birmingham's advantage, the proprietors had relatively little incentive to build on to join the Staffordshire and Worcestershire Canal. Nevertheless, a clause in the Birmingham Canal Act bound the company to complete their waterway within six months of reaching Birmingham and, if they failed to do so, made provision for the Staffordshire & Worcestershire Canal Company to build the junction between the two canals themselves, and charge to Birmingham Company the full cost of construction.

Frustrated by Birmingham's preoccupation with the broils surrounding Colmore and Boulton, in January 1770 the Staffordshire & Worcestershire committee enquired precisely when they proposed to complete their canal, and 'make a communication' with the waterway linking Severn with the Trent and Mersey. By way of answer, Birmingham demurred. While there was work assuredly in progress, the progress was slow.[34] Brindley's and Simcock's claim that a meandering line had the means of serving more businesses than a direct one impressed promoters and observers rather less than either engineer might have wished, and the canal's twisty route around Oldbury precipitated a flippant suggestion that it represented Simcock's wish to immortalise his initials.[35] The need for a long flight of locks, twenty-one in total, at the Wolverhampton end may have given Brindley greater qualms than he cared to acknowledge, for it led to a rare hiccup in the headlong confidence of his thinking. Considering the challenge, he appears to have pronounced at first that since there was too little water for 6-foot locks, the locks should be 3 feet deep with an 'extreme lock' of 6 feet. This idea was totally impractical. Not only did Brindley – doubtless hurried, hard-pressed and, in Wedgwood's expression, 'incessantly harassed on every side' – disregard 'the fact that the loss of water is regulated by the largest lock', but he also overlooked the detail that building to these dimensions would necessitate construction of no fewer than forty locks.[36] Small in itself, his stumble here begs the question of whether, regarding locks as a necessary evil which, Bridgewater Canal-wise, he would prefer as far as possible to do without, Brindley did not take rather a dismissive approach to their siting and construction.

Aldersley Junction, where the Birmingham Canal meets the Staffordshire and Worcestershire, shows signs of his learning on the hoof. Broadbridge reckons that Brindley must have reached the point of recognising that building forty-odd locks, each 3 feet deep, would not be practicable 'before the flight was built'; either he failed to mark the point about the largest lock's determining the loss of water, or he marked and disregarded it, since his last lock of the Aldersley flight 'was still of double depth'.[37]

1770 was a year of discontent. Complacent in the face of Staffordshire & Worcestershire needling, the Birmingham committee built themselves a fine navigation office in Paradise Street, with accommodation for company clerks and a coffee house. By August, the Staffordshire & Worcestershire men had sought legal advice upon how to deal with Birmingham's procrastinations. At the same time Brindley, in the not entirely comfortable position of being engineer to both companies, appears to have summoned the Birmingham committee on the ground that the Staffordshire & Worcestershire committee 'desired he would see what orders had been given to forward the Execution of that part of the Canal from Bilston to Autherley [Aldersley]' following assurances Birmingham had made earlier at West Bromwich.[38] Exactly what answer he received is unclear; in fact, the circumstances are decidedly obscure. In his history of the Birmingham Canal Navigations, S. R. Broadbridge states that Brindley was 'called to the committee to see what orders he had given for completion' and reported progress which, he said, 'appeared to me Satisfactory', but it is hard to see how the actual minute supports this interpretation of events.[39]

Discussion turned next to Aldersley and 'Being requested to fix upon the size of the locks in order that proper timber might be provided', Brindley,

> Gave for answer that he wish'd to postpone any Determination thereupon till the quantity of water likely to come upon that part of the Canal could be ascertained, which he promised to do between this time and Michaelmas [29 September], that being the time when the Springs are likely to be in the lowest state, and that any auxiliary supplies are better deferred till the material supply can be as accurately fixed as possible.[40]

To judge from this convoluted statement, it looks as though Brindley's internal deliberations about the best dimensions for the Aldersley Locks may have added to the delay in their construction. His wish to inspect the local springs at the driest season of the year points to constant anxiety over the canal's water supply, which is consistent with his reluctance to abandon his projected tunnel at Smethwick. Mentioning a new difficulty, namely the presence of an 'old Coal Work' on the canal's proposed path between Bilston and Autherley, Brindley asked the committee's permission 'to attend Mr Simcox [sic] when he sets out that part of the canal'.[41] The tactful reason he gives for this request is the need to guard against 'every Inconvenience to be apprehended from the passage of the canal over the imperfect ground.' How far his wish to oversee the work in person related to the difficulty of cutting through poached ground prone to subsidence and how far from a wish – not for the only time – to protect Simcock from potential error is uncertain.

Relentless, Staffordshire & Worcestershire continued to complain about Birmingham's slow progress. After several allegations and denials in the West Midlands press and petitions and counter-petitions to Parliament, the embattled canal companies sought a remedy through arbitration, with 2nd Earl of Dartmouth William Legge as umpire. Eventually, after months of non-cooperation, they lighted on a settlement. Birmingham would pay the cost of the Staffordshire & Worcestershire's application to Parliament. Calls, by the agreed terms, were 'to be made as high and fast as possible'; seven tenths of the revenue raised both through calls and tonnage were to be directed towards 'completing the Birmingham Canal to Autherley [Aldersley]' and, on a final stringent note, no money was to be 'expended in Building Warehouses Etc., till the Junction of the two Canals was made.'[42]

Although effective in ensuring that the Birmingham Canal joined the Staffordshire and Worcestershire Canal at last, Brindley for one found the terms of this 'Deed of Compromise' less than helpful. Building fast was not the same as building well, and in May 1772 he would complain about the poor quality of the iron work and carpentry 'of the Locks at W Hampton under the deed of Compromise', and insist that 'ill tenanted & Mortized' woodwork and 'bad teeth and pinions' in the sluice gear were both improved.[43] Compared with the actual cutting, this remedial work was pretty small-scale. Having agreed to share the cost of building a bridge at the new junction, this time without recourse to litigation, the two companies witnessed the eventual opening of the Birmingham Canal Navigation on 21 September 1772 – less than a week, could they but know it, before James Brindley's death. Its actual cost, in the region of £112,000, was more than twice his optimistic £50,000 estimate. (See Illustration 24).

Darwin, Brindley and the rotating bed

Despite the expense and troubles attending the building of the Birmingham Canal, not to mention constant faction and squabbling among its promoters, Brindley's relations with the Birmingham men were by no means entirely unfriendly. Not only did Samuel Garbett esteem him highly, but he also, perhaps through Wedgwood's influence, appears occasionally to have attended meetings of Birmingham's Lunar Society. The Lunar men customarily met at Soho House, Matthew Boulton's comfortable home, but since the society kept no record of attendance, let alone minutes, it is impossible to be certain who attended each meeting or what they had to say. Nevertheless, there is some documentary evidence, albeit undated, of an extraordinary conversation that took place between Brindley and leading Lunar man, Lichfield physician Erasmus Darwin.

Darwin's *Zoonomia; or, The of Laws of Organic Life* of 1794 is in essence a medical textbook with elements of memoir. In a chapter which discusses the benefits of sleep and methods of inducing it artificially, Darwin recalls that Brindley told him he had 'more than once seen the experiment of a man extending himself across the large stone of a corn mill, and that by gradually letting the stone whirl, the man fell asleep, before the stone had gained its full velocity, and he supposed would have died without pain, by the continuance or increase of the motion.'[44] If there were good medical reasons to induce sleep by whirling, rather than oblige his well-heeled patients to extend themselves across millstones, the obvious step was to design a spinning bed. Enthusing upon the therapeutic possibilities, Darwin persuaded James Watt to produce a drawing to show how it might be constructed.

It was a truly Lunatick idea, and anecdotal evidence indicates that the patients on whom Darwin prevailed to try out the prototype uniting in loathing it. The story's interest lies in its revelation of James Brindley, sociable for once and even eloquent on a subject other than canals. It is a rare moment in which, away from work, he allows himself the enjoyment of friendship and conversation.

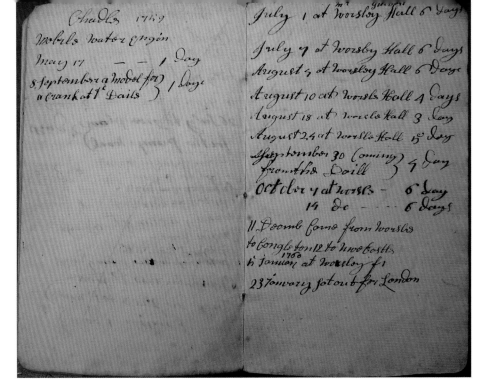

1. Brindley's notebook, 1759–60: his record of early visits to Worsley. (By kind permission of the Institution of Civil Engineers)

2. Francis Egerton, 3rd Duke of Bridgewater (1736–1803) by an unknown artist, 1766. (Copyright of the National Portrait Gallery, London)

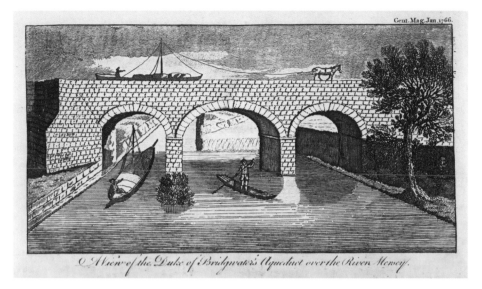

A View of the Duke of Bridgwater's Aqueduct over the River Mersey.

3. Barton Aqueduct, engraved for the *Gentleman's Magazine* 1766. The aqueduct crosses the River Irwell, not the Mersey as the title to the engraving suggests. (Image courtesy of the University of Bristol Library, Special Collections)

4. James Brindley (1716–1772) by Francis Parsons, 1770. (Copyright of the National Portrait Gallery, London)

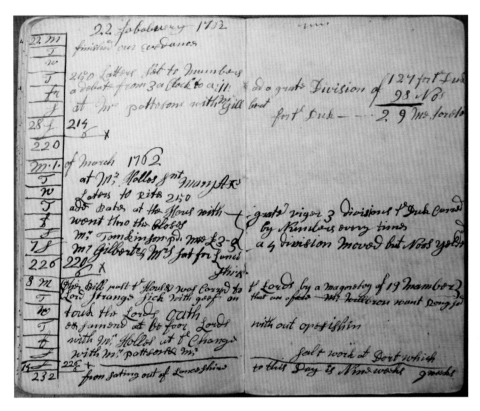

5. James Brindley's account of the parliamentary proceedings surrounding the Duke of Bridgewater's 1762 Canal Bill. (By kind permission of the Institution of Civil Engineers)

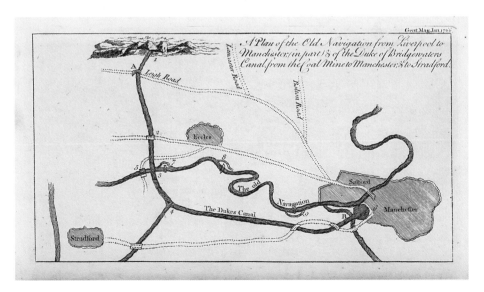

6. An early map showing the Bridgewater Canal in relation to the Mersey and Irwell Navigation, *Gentleman's Magazine*, 1766. (Image courtesy of the University of Bristol Library, Special Collections)

Above left: 7. John Gilbert, (1724–1795), attrib. Michael William Sharp. (Courtesy of Salford Museum and Art Gallery)

Above right: 8. Anonymous map of the Witton Brook, River Weaver Navigation, *c.* 1765. (Image courtesy of John Rylands Library, copyright of the University of Manchester)

Below: 9. Brindley's notebook, October–November 1763, showing his record of time spent with Judge George Perrot, owner of the Lower Avon Navigation. (By kind permission of the Institution of Civil Engineers)

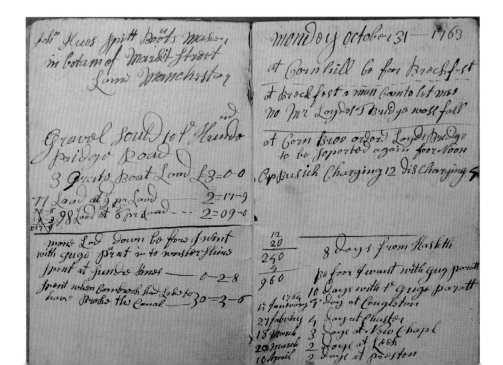

10. Josiah Wedgwood (1730–1795), by William Hackwood. (Copyright of the National Portrait Gallery, London)

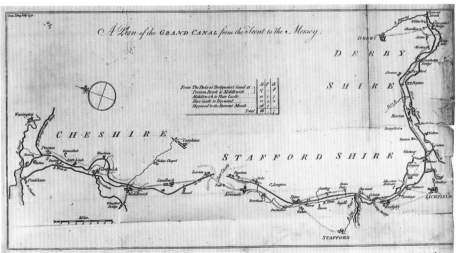

Above: 11. Map of the Trent and Mersey Canal, *Gentleman's Magazine,* 1771. Note the map's alignment, with north on the left-hand side of the page. (Image courtesy of the University of Bristol Library, Special Collections)

Below: 12. The Duke of Bridgewater's canal intercepting the Trent and Mersey Canal at Preston Bridge, *Gentleman's Magazine* 1771. (Image courtesy of the University of Bristol Library, Special Collections)

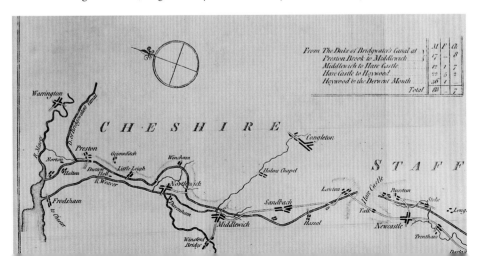

13. A matched race between Mr Fortescue's Ireland and the Duke of Bridgewater's England on Newmarket Heath 1759, by Francis Sartorius. (Image courtesy of Bonhams)

14. James Brindley's home, Turnhurst Hall. Front elevation, from a photograph taken shortly before its demolition in 1929. (Courtesy of Stoke-on-Trent City Archives, ref. SP 865)

15. Turnhurst Hall, side elevation and water feature. From a photograph taken shortly before its demolition in 1929. (Courtesy of Stoke-on-Trent City Archives, ref. SP 865)

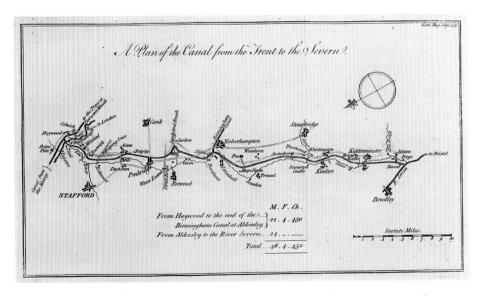

16. Map of the Staffordshire and Worcestershire Canal, *Gentleman's Magazine* 1771. The map is aligned on a south-east/north-west axis, with north in the bottom left-hand corner. (Courtesy of the University of Bristol Library, Special Collections)

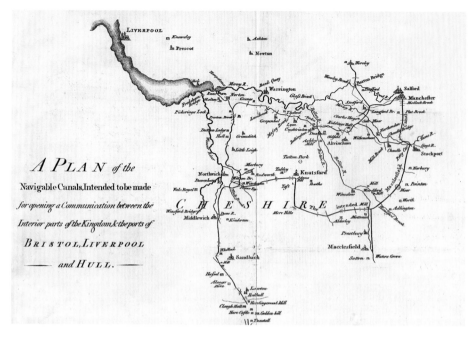

17. Canals of the north West Midlands *c.* 1766, either built, planned or under construction. Note the line of 'The Intended Macclesfield Canal'. (Image by courtesy of Canalmaps Archive www.canalmaps.net)

18. The Dunstall Water Bridge, March 2015. (Author's Collection)

19. 'A View of London Bridge with the Ruins of the Temporary Bridge, 1758', Anthony Walker (1726–65). (Yale Center for British Art, Paul Mellon Collection)

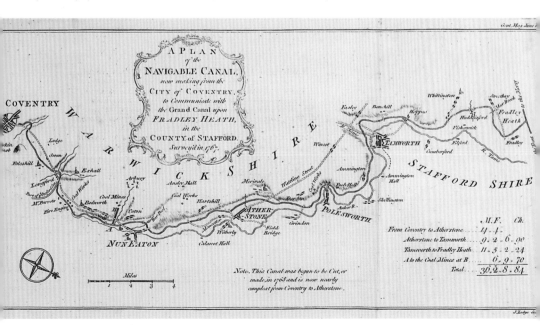

20. Map of the Coventry Canal, *Gentleman's Magazine* 1771. The map is aligned west-east. The 'Grand Canal' is the Trent and Mersey. (Author's Collection)

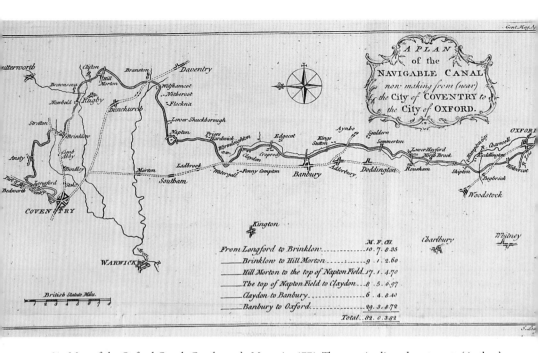

21. Map of the Oxford Canal, *Gentleman's Magazine* 1771. The map is aligned east-west. (Author's Collection)

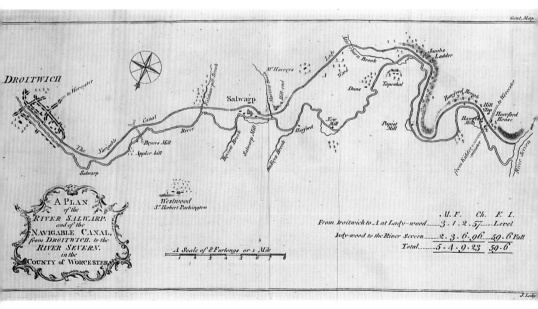

22. Map of the Droitwich Canal, *Gentleman's Magazine* 1771. Note the south/north alignment. (Author's Collection)

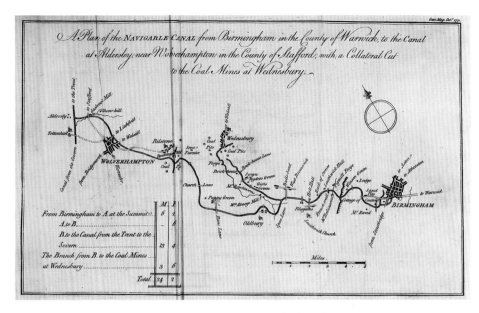

23. Birmingham Canal, *Gentleman's Magazine* 1771. (Author's Collection)

24. The Birmingham Canal becoming increasingly rural as it leaves Wolverhampton. March 2015. (Author's Collection)

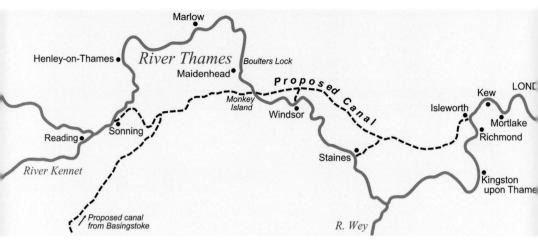

25. Map of the Thames, from Sonning to Mortlake. Drawn and reproduced by kind permission of Richard Dean. (Canalmaps Archive www.canalmaps.net)

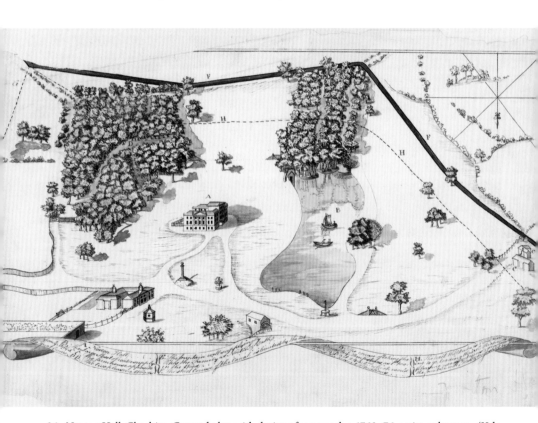

26. Norton Hall, Cheshire. Ground plan with designs for a canal, *c.* 1760–76, artist unknown. (Yale Center for British Art, Paul Mellon Collection)

27. 'The Thames with Montagu House & Westminster Bridge', (undated) Samuel Scott, *c.* 1702–72. Note the size of the sketched barges. (Yale Center for British Art, Paul Mellon Collection)

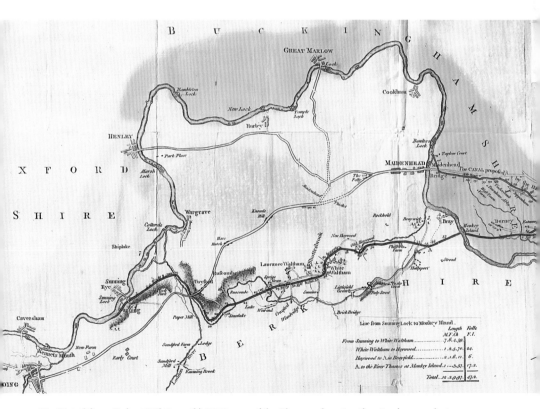

28. Detail from Robert Whitworth's 1770 map of the Thames showing the river's meandering course between Sonning Eye and Monkey Island. (Courtesy of Canalmaps Archive www.canalmaps.net)

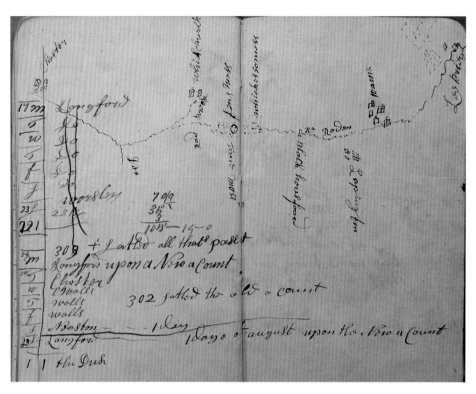

29. Brindley's sketch map of the Shropshire Roden, July 1762. (By kind permission of the Institution of Civil Engineers)

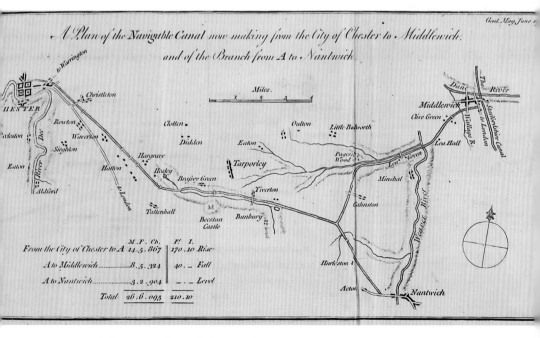

30. Map of the proposed canal from Chester to Middlewich, *Gentleman's Magazine* 1772. (Courtesy of University of Bristol Library, Special Collections)

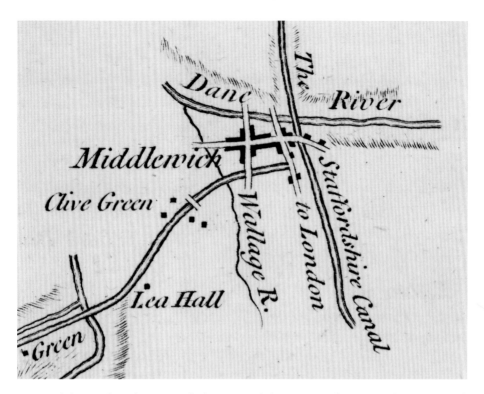

31. Detail showing how the proposed Chester Canal does not join the Trent and Mersey Canal. (Courtesy of University of Bristol Special Collection)

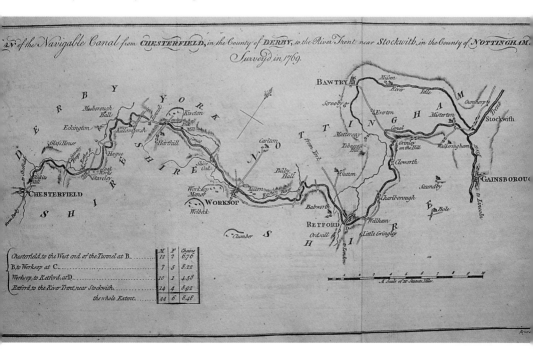

32. Map of the Chesterfield Canal, as surveyed in 1769, *Gentleman's Magazine*, 1772. (Courtesy of University of Bristol Library, Special Collections)

Left: 33. Monument to
Francis Egerton, 3rd Duke
of Bridgewater, Ashridge,
Hertfordshire, May 2015.
(Author's Collection)

Below: 34. Grave of James
Brindley, of Turnhurst,
Engineer, Newchapel,
Staffordshire, April 2015.
(Author's Collection)

CHAPTER TEN

1770: Brindley and the Thames[1]

The threat to Reading from Basingstoke

Towards the end of 1769, acting on behalf of certain unnamed 'Gentlemen of Hampshire', an otherwise forgotten engineer named Benjamin Davis had surveyed the line for a canal to run from Basingstoke to join the Thames at Monkey Island, downstream from Maidenhead. Its prime purpose was for the provision of flour and grain to London, although its supporters also mooted the possibility of its being used 'to furnish timber', presumably from the New Forest, 'for the service of the Navy'.[2] Whatever the intentions of its promoters, the people of Reading (at this time a market town with a dwindling cloth trade) were quick to see how they should be disadvantaged if trading rival Basingstoke were to organise a shortcut for the cheap transport of goods to London. Reading's location on a meandering stretch of the Thames already necessitated a journey past Henley and Marlow for waterborne commodities. Its response to Basingstoke's coup was to call a meeting to discuss the possibility of building a separate canal from the Thames at Sonning, a few miles east of their town, to Monkey Island, near Maidenhead, neatly bypassing the river's northerly loop. (See Illustration 25).

The public meeting took place on 5 January 1770 with local grandee Lord Craven in the chair. A certain amount of information about the discussion emerges in a letter to the *Reading Mercury* from a correspondent with a keen interest in the proceedings, who tellingly signs himself 'A Friend to Trade'.[3] From his account, it emerges that the supporters of the proposed canal were sufficiently knowing to understand what the procedure for promoting a canal entailed. As a postscript to his letter, he appends a list of formal proposals presented at the meeting which deal with practical matters such as getting a survey made, opening a subscription and setting a rate of tonnage. Every indication is that plans for the new canal have already been thought through by intelligent promoters, streetwise enough to understand the need to have solid plans in place for their venture and its finance before petitioning Parliament for enabling legislation. Recognising the worth of influential allies, the Reading promoters authorised one of their number to act as their emissary in London and solicit the support of the lord mayor and aldermen in seeking legislation to enable construction of a canal not merely to Monkey Island, but all the way to Isleworth.

Someone whom the 'Friend to Trade' identifies only as the 'head of one of the most respectable societies in the kingdom' took the persuasive step of inviting James Brindley to the meeting. He appears unassumingly to have taken his place among the couple of hundred or so

Berkshire gentlemen and traders in the Town Hall, and waited to see what decision the meeting reached. Although the letter writer makes no mention of him actually addressing the company, if it was he who first mooted the notion of extending the canal all the way to Isleworth, it would not have been out of character. After all, the potential benefits were striking. Not only would canal-carriage make for shorter journey times, it would also reduce the expense of freight-carriage to London from £1 2s 8d to a modest 4s.

These economic arguments must have carried the day, for the 'Friend to Trade' reports that the gathering resolved to commission Brindley to make a survey 'from Sunning by Monkey Island to Dorney and Isleworth', with the understanding that he would have his estimate ready by 26 February when they planned to meet next. At the same time, amid the optimism there were currents of dissent. Some gentlemen objected that, if built, the new canal would affect them 'in their private property', and there was even an exchange of 'personal reflections and insults'. The 'Friend to Trade' dismissed the episode as an unimportant display of bad manners that he preferred to forget.

Enthusiasm had prevailed and Brindley summoned Robert Whitworth, who had been surveying for a possible canal connection between Andover and Southampton, to join him in inspecting the terrain between Sonning and Isleworth. On 26 February 1770, at Reading's next canal meeting, they produced a plan showing possible routes, and the Reading men at once convened a committee to frame a petition to Parliament.[4] By this time, as a result of Reading's agitation the scheme had come to the notice of the Court of Aldermen and Common Council of London, who appointed a navigation sub-committee to consider its merits.[5]

The Duke of Bridgewater and Sir Richard Brooke: private property

March 1770 found Brindley in London on business other than Reading's. Both the Trent & Mersey committee and the Staffordshire & Worcestershire men sought authority to raise more capital in order to complete their respective canals. The promoters of a new canal proposed to run from Leeds to Liverpool required him to support their petition for an enabling Act. He would have the unsettling experience of having his portrait painted. Furthermore, the Duke of Bridgewater required engineering evidence to support his application to 'remove the statutory protection', which the 1766 Trent and Mersey Canal Act accorded to Sir Richard Brooke of Norton Priory near Runcorn.

In 1750, Sir Richard had built himself a new house on the site of the medieval Augustinian foundation that gave Norton Priory its name.[6] His redesigned home stood amid its fine grounds, which he had also improved, directly in the path of the Duke of Bridgewater's part of the Trent and Mersey Canal – the section which ran from Preston Brook to the Mersey. Seeing no need whatsoever to accommodate the duke's ambitions, Sir Richard had consulted his lawyers and taken every care to ensure that the enabling Act provided both that the canal should not pass within 360 yards of Norton Hall, and that no 'Gravel, Sand, Clay or Earth' was to accumulate anywhere within 500 yards of the house for longer than a year.[7] (See Illustration 26).

On 9 March 1770, the duke petitioned Parliament to vary the terms of the 1766 Act on the ground that the sheer difficulty posed by the 'Nature and Situation of the Ground, and

Springs of Water' made it 'absolutely impracticable' to keep within the course which it prescribed.[8] By chance, a brief account of the MPs' discussion of his application survives in the writings of the Anglo-Irish politician and sometime member for Lostwithiel, Sir Henry Cavendish.[9] Cavendish's record does not so much show a debate in progress, as give a series of opinions. If the circumstances which led the Duke of Bridgewater to ask Parliament to alter clauses in the 1766 legislation look far removed from the proposals emanating from Reading in 1770, the debate offers an insight into landowners' attitude to the challenge of canal promotion – an attitude which would have far-reaching consequences for the Monkey Island scheme.

From the outset, the members were adamant that the House would not allow itself to be inveigled into capriciousness. One Mr Curzon (probably Assheton Curzon, MP for Clitheroe) emphasised that Sir Richard Brooke trusted 'to the faith of Parliament'. 'If Parliament can one day give, and another day take away,' he enquired rhetorically, 'what security is there for property?' Thomas Grosvenor esq., MP for Chester, saw nothing 'peevish' in Sir Richard's refusal to accommodate the duke; Sir Richard, after all, had never wanted to have the canal 'go through his grounds'. Richard Pennant, MP for Liverpool, warned that breaking 'the faith of parliament' for one man's convenience would have the effect of breaching all 'confidence between [...] the public and the legislature'. Lord Strange (James Smith Stanley, MP for Lancashire) took a subtler view, deploring all notion 'that private property should give way to public convenience' and contemptuously described the duke as 'a carrier with privilege on his back', on the one hand, but recommending referral of his petition to a committee on the other. His remark that 'no canal should be undertaken without a plan so drawn that everyone may know how far he will be injured [by it]' was neither unreasonable in itself nor suggestive of total opposition to all artificial inland navigations on principle. Careful to report his own speech to the House, Cavendish himself was at pains to uphold 'the faith of Parliament' while at the same time contriving to support the aims of the duke whom he clearly admired. His suggestion that the canal 'might be carried on in troughs' in order to make it conform to the statutory terms sounds well-intentioned, if far-fetched. Unfortunately, he does not relate what the duke made of his idea.

The debate upon the duke's petition was by no means one-sided and Cavendish's report shows that parliamentary opinion was not wholly critical of his stance. Richard Rigby, MP for Tavistock, contended that Sir Richard Brooke should give way and the 'plan laid down in the Act [be] accomplished', regardless of the expense. Taking the opposite view to Mr Curzon, Robert Henley Ongley, MP for Bedfordshire, insisted outright that 'Private property should give way to public convenience', albeit with compensation. Herbert Mackworth, MP for Cardiff Boroughs, sympathised with Brooke's reluctance to see the canal cut through his woods, but at the same time, by asking 'Can this man [Brooke] control Parliament by his *ipse dixit*?' he raised the question of how far long-established rights of landownership could or should bind future decision-making – an issue which may have given several MPs matter for reflection. Mackworth, not surprisingly, wished to see the duke's petition referred to a committee.

If Brindley was called to testify, Cavendish does not report his evidence. Nevertheless, the MPs knew him by reputation and their discussion produced some colourful reflections upon his character. 'We are to have Mr Brindley,' a 'Mr Burrell' (probably Peter Burrell, MP for Totnes and surveyor-general of the land revenues of the crown) anticipated, 'and what an expense that will occasion!'[10] Yorkshireman William Aislabie, MP for Ripon, asserted bluntly that in petitioning the House, the Duke of Bridgewater was advancing 'the projects of a romantic engineer', a practitioner, in other words, with a taste for building on an extravagant scale. It was the same charge that had come to light in the early days of the Barton Aqueduct's construction, when the scoffers called it a castle in the air. Not only did it resurface in the form of a grinding pun upon the name of the Harecastle Tunnel, but John Smeaton recycled it in his 1768 Report on the Forth and Clyde Navigation, when he suggested that Brindley's aqueduct plans owed more to a taste for spectacle – 'riding his hobby-horse' – than they did to necessity.[11] Nevertheless, at the time of the debate Brindley's influence with the duke and his lavish expenses were side issues. The greater concerns of the House were private property and the faith of Parliament. Put to the vote, 142 members were in favour of referring the duke's petition to committee, with 175 against; the duke's application failed.

Concerns of the London committee

While the House prickled over the rights and wrongs of the neighbourly dispute between the Duke of Bridgewater and Sir Richard Brooke, the Reading plans gathered momentum.[12] At the same time, the aldermen and councillors who made up the London Navigation Sub-committee met in the Guildhall on 7 March 1770 and found they had various questions which they wished to pursue concerning the canal plans, and therefore requested Brindley to meet them and give his answers.

He came, prepared, on 4 June 1770.[13] To their first question, which was whether Isleworth was indeed the best location for a junction between the canal from Monkey Island and the Thames, he answered with in unequivocal affirmative. Since the Thames was tidal as far upstream as Isleworth, high tides would bring vessels right to 'the mouth of the canal'; were the junction to be located further upstream, in neap tides they would find themselves stranded. What was more, and it was a point which future developments would throw into doubt, he was confident that at a point on the Thames known as Rail's Head, the canal could join the river 'without interfering with any house, Gentleman's Garden or pleasure Grounds', and he could not say the same of anywhere else 'below Brentford to above Twickenham'.[14] The line of the canal between Monkey Island and Isleworth would be no more than a fairly modest 17 miles and 7 furlongs in distance, and 'moderately straight' to boot.

The next question, rather more precise and searching, concerned the best width for the canal, considering both its general utility and its 'passage near the metropolis'. Although the committee do not make the point explicit, their question comes with the knowledge that the Thames barges that would use the new waterway were both squarish vessels that were broad in the beam and often used under sail, and very much larger than the Midlands narrow boats. Probably on account of the sheer expense of building combined with the hard labour involved in excavating tunnels, Midlands canals were narrow, with lock dimensions of 7 feet x 70 feet

(2.1 metres x 21.5 metres).[15] The Oxford Canal, under construction at this time, had a bottom width of 16 feet, which as Hugh Compton observes, was 'just sufficient to enable two 7 foot wide narrow boats to pass'.[16] Brindley clearly recognised the need to build the Monkey Island canal to more lavish dimensions. Planning to make it a full 33 feet wide at the bottom, with a depth of 4 feet and 6 inches, he pledged that it would accommodate 'vessels of an hundred tons burthen' and allow them 'to pass each other in every place.' (See Illustration 27).

His awareness of the size and scope of the local boats shaped his answer to the committee's next question, which concerned the amount of water to be taken from the Thames at Monkey Island and at the junction between the Thames and the Colne. The total quantity of water to be taken from the Thames and the Colne would, he indicated, depend 'altogether upon the number of vessels that pass thro' the canal' – in other words, an uncertain figure. In the event of ten vessels passing through per day, each of 100 tons burden, 'according to the present construction of Thames boats' he estimated that each vessel would 'require 495 tons of water to carry it through the locks'.[17] 'And supposing,' he continued,

> The leakage and exhalation to be as much. With 495 tons more (which if the works be well executed can hardly be supposed will amount to half so much) then the quantity of water expended will be 9900 Tons.

While this answer manifested his usual determination to build to high standards, it may have bemused the less technically minded committee members, who may not have found it easy to visualise 9,900 tons of water, let alone the effects of its removal from the river and its tributary.

The committee's next question was whether extracting water from the Thames might be detrimental to navigation of the river, and here Brindley opened with a solid-sounding assurance that 'water taken out of the river for supplying the canal will not be any (sensible) detriment to the navigation of it in the present mode'. In a statement the significance of which may have been clearer to him than it was to the committee, he added that water extraction would not,

> ... reduce the depth [of the Thames] where the river is narrow more than the twentieth part of an inch, and in broader places not half so much, as may be proved by the aforementioned Quantity necessary and the surface of water that glides away in any given time.

The reference to 'the aforementioned Quantity necessary' appears to refer directly to the answer he gave to the previous question (about the amount of water which the canal would require). He implies both that the canal could continue to function with loss and leaks, and that the river could supply it while remaining serviceable to shipping. Yet his remark about the 'surface of water which glides away in any given time' obscures his sense more than clarifying it. Perhaps his thinking outran his writing. The absence in committee minutes of any record of questions or requests for elucidation suggests that the members received this assurance without hesitation or quibble. Whether they followed Brindley's reasoning or whether they hesitated to admit to anything resembling bafflement is open to question.

Their fifth and final question, which concerned the superiority of the canal and its potential advantages to the public in comparison with the river, lent itself to answering in plain terms of a saving in cash and time. From investigations already made, Brindley had gleaned that the cost of taking a vessel of 100–120 tons burden from Isleworth to Sonning was usually in the region of £80. By canal, he argued, it would be closer to £16 – a vast saving by any measure. 'Besides', he adds to drive his point home,

> This is not all the advantage that will accrue to the public from the Canal, for in the present navigation of the River they are sometimes three weeks in going up, and near as long in coming down, often to the great loss and disappointment of the Proprietor in the damage of his Goods.

If it was not graceful oratory, it was bold talk with sound arithmetical evidence to support the case it made. Brindley gave estimates of cost for the two possible routes Whitworth and he had surveyed: £46,899 for the 'Upper Line' which he preferred, and £64,650 for the lower and longer route via Staines. He also gives expenses for individual items such as 'Publick Road Bridges' at £140 each; 'Lesser Road Bridges' at £100 each; a 'small Aqueduct bridge', which comes to £200; swivel bridges 'that may be wanted for preserving communication between the divided Lands' totalling £600 for an unspecified number and 'stop gates, weirs and general sluices', again an unspecified number, amounting to a total cost of £600. One of the larger items of expenditure was £1,467 for 'extra cutting above Ditton Park'. Ditton Park near Slough was home to George Brudenell, 3rd Duke of Montagu and 4th Earl of Cardigan. Since Capability Brown had begun to landscape the gardens and grounds in 1762, a degree of concern on the part of the Duke and Duchess of Montagu about the impact of the canal was only to be expected.

In the face of some close and cautious interrogation, Brindley had made a good enough showing to persuade the committee to give the canal their support. They ordered that a thousand of Brindley's – in reality Robert Whitworth's – plans be printed together with his answers to their questions and estimate of costs for distribution among the members of the Court of Common Council, with a view to joining Reading in petitioning Parliament for a bill.[18]

Around this time, suggestions surfaced in Reading to the effect that instead of building a canal all the way from Sonning to Isleworth, there were good grounds for first improving the Thames between Sonning and Boulter's Lock below Monkey Island, and then cutting a canal from Boulter's Lock to Isleworth. A correspondent to the *Reading Mercury* who signed himself only by initials 'B.H.' argued that this scheme had the merit of avoiding the stretch of the Thames with the greatest number of 'obstacles' and occasions the most 'extravagant expenses', while preserving 'the greatest trading part of the old river'.[19] This description probably refers to the bend by Henley and Marlow, where it seems likely that 'B.H.' lived and worked. By way of improvements, he recommended the introduction of 'Horse towing paths' and the replacement of 'locks', by which he may mean flash locks or stanches with pound locks. His letter expressed what may have been a popular view. Two months or so after its publication, the London committee had second thoughts about the canal plan, and on 26 July 1770 they ordered Brindley to 'observe the most material obstructions and inconveniences' of the river, report on 'the most effectual methods' of improving it and estimate the likely expense.[20]

To all appearances, it would not have been what he wanted to hear. His biographer Christine Richardson argues that undertaking to improve the Thames 'would have impinged upon Brindley's professional identity as the man who built canals and would have nothing to do with naturally flowing waters'.[21] At the same time, he could not afford to give the impression of slighting the London money-men by declining the Thames work outright, and despite his contempt for river navigations, he was not short of experience in making river surveys. Therefore, he complied with the committee's directions and made a full survey of the Thames from Boulter's Lock to Mortlake, with Robert Whitworth, in a literal sense, charting the work with a fine map of the Thames between Caversham and Kew.

Brindley's report

On Wednesday 11 December 1770, Brindley returned to the Thames Navigation sub-committee with the report they had requested. As they soon discovered, it was not so much a report as a polemic. Showing scant patience with their unadventurous inclination to improve the river, he pressed home the virtues of the canal venture with every argument he could muster.

Downright, he opened with the contention that the Thames 'does not lend itself' to improvement of the kind that the London Corporation sought. During the winter months, the flooding that made the river 'impassable for Barges' most years was, in his opinion, 'out of the Power of Art to remedy'.[22] Summer droughts had the same effect, although he allowed that construction of 'dams' (weirs) and 'cisterns' (pound locks) might alleviate the difficulty to some extent. At the same time, he foresaw that the sheer 'expense of improving so large a River in this way' was likely to preclude its being 'put to practice'. As far as the estimate for the necessary works was concerned, he found it 'impossible' to provide an exact sum, although he was confident that it would be 'five or six times the Expense of making a Canal'.

He allowed, if reluctantly, that it might be possible to make some improvement to the river 'by contracting the channel in the broad and shallow places' so as to increase its depth. 'By this means', he continued,

> A sufficient depth of water, I suppose, may be obtained in all places, or at least, may be made much better than it is, but the fall will remain the same, and the current increased by the increased depth of water – consequently will require more strength of man or horses to draw the Barges against the stream, yet by this means it may be rendered much more certain than it is, and an easy Navigation downwards (except in time of flood) but the great labour and expense of taking a vessel upwards cannot be taken away by any method that I know off [sic] but by making a Canal, which if made most places upon the Banks of the River may be supplied by Collateral Cuts, for it is practicable to make Branches from the main Canal to fall into the river wheresoever it may be most useful to the country.

If the passage looks laboured on the page, it may have proved powerful in speech. Obliged to explain his ideas, Brindley does so in a way that is informal, even chatty, and appears very much at ease with the committee with his 'I supposes' and '…that I know of' asides. Crucially, he is no longer content with Reading's argument that the canal would usefully short-circuit the meanders of the Thames. Instead, by emphasising the role of the 'Collateral Cuts' and 'Branches', he seeks to persuade London that the natural and the artificial waterway will combine to provide a more efficient and comprehensive system of transport than anything the area has experienced in the past.

His remedy for the problem of time lost to vessels during neap tides on the shallow stretch of river 'between Mortlake and Richmond Gardens' was to dam the river between Mortlake and Kew Bridge so as to establish a basin for shipping and 'a convenient landing place for all passengers'. Not only did he consider that raising the river would make for 'extremely easy … Navigation' both to the canal's junction with the Thames and downstream to Kingston, but also in a rare fulsome flight, that his developments would 'render that part of the country in general perhaps the most delightful spot in Europe'. The 'perhaps' was tactful; not having travelled in Europe, his opinions on its delights owed more to imagination than experience. At the same time, he was shrewd enough to recognise that his committee audience might find the aesthetic qualities of the scheme as persuasive as its utility.

It was a vision well in tune with the aspirations of the age. In 1768, Isleworth resident George Merchant had visited Liverpool, where he advocated building a pier or barrage from 'above the new Dock to the opposite shore' of the Mersey, of 'sufficient strength to keep out the tide', and installing 'Gates' in it, 'sufficient for admitting ships at low water'.[23] Having sketched his scheme in a letter to the Mayor of Chester – evidently someone whom he expected to welcome his proposals – Merchant added,

Please send Master Bridley a coppy of this and desire his opinion and objections. For my own part, from his character I have no doubt of his acquissence. [sic]

Misremembered surname notwithstanding, the request is not entirely a surprise. Writing to Bentley in 1767, Josiah Wedgwood remarked that he had recently encountered a 'Gimcrackarian … come all the way from Twickenham Common to view our Harecastles, our Tunnels, Grand Trunks and Navigations […]. Do I need tell you', he asks rhetorically, 'his name is Geo Merchant?'[24] If Brindley had indeed heard of Merchant's 1768 proposal for Liverpool, it is not impossible that it had some bearing on his own 1770 scheme for Mortlake. Merchant may even have thought the appropriation rather flattering.

To leave the committee with his estimate of the expense of making the Thames around Twickenham the 'most delightful spot in Europe' – Brindley suggested £17,500 – might be a good note on which to conclude on his report. In the event, having reaffirmed his view that even if vessels proceeding upstream along the Thames needed two tides to reach Isleworth, it was still to his mind 'the most proper place' for a canal junction, he returned to the committee's wish to have an idea of the cost of improving the river. It was impossible, he said, 'to make an Estimate with any degree of accuracy', but he promised that whatever sum they chose to invest – he named £10,000 as a useful amount with which to make a start – it would never be money well spent. While 'the River might be made much better than it is, or perhaps ever was', improving it could never be cost-effective. 'If twenty times that sum be laid out,' he finished, 'it would not make it a good and permanent Navigation.'[25]

For an engineer to turn down a lucrative commission on the frank ground that the proposed scheme is unfit for purpose assuredly made for a fine flourish of committee-room advocacy. Some six or so weeks after they had heard Brindley in full heartfelt flow, the aldermen and Common Council of the city petitioned Parliament on 23 January 1771 for leave to 'bring in a bill for making and maintaining of a navigable canal', on the grounds that navigation of the Thames west of London was 'tedious, inconvenient and expensive'. Their intended canal would run 'from or near Monkey Island to Isleworth, complete with branches to join the Thames above Windsor Bridge and from West Bedfont in the parish of Stanwell to join the Thames at or near Staines'. Perhaps, even when they made their application, lingering doubts about the wisdom of bringing this ambitious network into being remained. At the same time, they also took the precaution of petitioning for leave to repair the 'Channel of the River' between Boulter's Lock near Maidenhead and Mortlake.[26]

To Parliament

It was entirely predictable that such large plans would arouse as much opposition as support. On the last day of January 1771, only about a week after the City of London petition reached Parliament, objections arrived from Henley-on-Thames and Marlow. The two major towns situated on the precise loop of the river which London and Reading wanted to bypass asserted that the canal would 'prejudice them', both 'by rendering the carriage of all kinds of merchandize upon the river Thames much more expensive' and by 'throwing' their trade 'into another channel'. Rather than see the canal built, they pressed for an 'Amendment' of the existing 'Navigation of the Rivers Thames and Isis', which they pronounced to be 'a great public Benefit'.[27] The city's wish to promote trade around the Thames also awakened much indignation among the landowners whose property the new canal looked likely to cross, and they approached Parliament with complaints. On 31 January 1771, Sir John Gibbons of Stanwell lodged his petition against the canal – particularly its West Bedfont branch – on the grounds that if built, it would 'greatly injure' himself and his neighbours 'in their property'; less than a fortnight later, Sir Charles Palmer petitioned the House in much the same tenor both on his own account and on behalf of the residents of Taplow, Eton and Dorney.[28] Richard Willis petitioned on behalf of Daniel d'Anvers Rich of Sonning, who was concerned that the canal would cut through his Holme Park estate.

In view of how contentious the canal plans had become, it is rather surprising to discover that James Brindley did not give evidence in its support himself but entrusted the task to Robert Whitworth. At the time, the decision may not have looked unreasonable. Brindley's health was not good and his visits to London were especially prone to coincide with bouts of illness. Whitworth and he had collaborated often enough in the past to have developed keen understanding of each other's respective styles of work. By 1771, Whitworth had proved an adept surveyor and mathematician, not to mention a mapmaker of supreme skills, and he had addressed the House on several occasions.[29] Further, he had accompanied Brindley on his preliminary surveys of the Thames, assisted in taking levels, drawn up the table of length and fall and had a first-hand knowledge of the river. Although in terms of experience there was no reason to imagine that he should be anything other than an ideal witness, at the same time he was not, perhaps, a ready speaker in public. The writer of the obituary which appeared in the *Newcastle Advertiser* after Whitworth's death remarked that 'what nature had denied him in eloquence and colloquial rhetoric, she more than amply remunerated him in the lucid powers of his pen.'[30] While in essence this reflection is a compliment, it carries the suggestion that as a canal advocate, he had his limitations.

When he came before the House on 21 February 1771, it appears that the canal's opponents trounced him. 'Being cross-examined', Whitworth admitted that,

> He surveyed the land through which the canal is to pass […] That he is not concerned in the execution of it, but only as a surveyor. That the canal may be a permanent navigation except stopt by Frosts, to which both the river and that are equally liable; but the rapidity of the stream has some effect in preventing freezing: that there is a stream in every part of the River between *Reading* and *Monkey Island*, but it has been froze lately, and that the River in its present state, may not be so liable to be stopt by Frosts as the Canal, but if locks are to be built upon it, it will; and that he never knew the obstruction by Frosts at locks removed, except in slight Frosts, but never in a Frost strong enough to freeze the canal: That he is sure the canal may be so executed as by carrying its level above the Floods that they cannot affect it; and knows one so constructed at Birmingham, and several others.[31]

These admissions, many of which are less than robust, suggest that Whitworth was more cautious than confident. The detail about the canal's standing high above the floods was a strong and worthwhile point, his remark about being 'concerned' with the canal 'only as a surveyor' carries the idea that his knowledge has grave limitations. No doubt the caveat represented Whitworth's honest view, but it invited the MPs – many of whom would have had little appreciation of the distinction in the respective expertise of a surveyor and a contractor – to doubt his reliability. Besides, at this stage in the venture's progress the survey team knew the proposed canal better than anyone else. Furthermore, Whitworth's admission that the swift Thames currents stopped it from freezing was a powerful, if inadvertent, piece of river advocacy. As the debate continued, slippery interrogation led Whitworth into increasingly dangerous ground. Asked about the cost of making the canal, always a sensitive subject, Whitworth said it would be 'about £51,000', but added that calculations of this kind often 'turned out fallacious'. Asked specifically if he had ever heard of a canal being executed for the cost given in the estimate, he not only gave the reply that he had not, but went on to say,

> That Mr *Brindley* is concerned in the *Trent* Canal, the estimate for which was £131,000, and that last year there was about £86,000 expended; and that it hath been 4 years and a half in Hand; and he thinks it will greatly exceed the Estimate.

He could hardly have uttered words more prejudicial to the cause of the Monkey Island Canal. His interrogator, whoever he was, was skilled enough to trap Whitworth in his own words. The admission that all canals went over budget – Brindley's Trent and Mersey scheme exemplifying the ease with which their costs could soar out of control – was never going to win the Monkey Island venture much support.

This exchange was not the totality of Whitworth's evidence; having assisted Brindley in compiling estimates, he was able to give the House details of the costs of culverts, floodgates and regulation locks – but it was not a good opening. Whether Brindley, with all his experience, would have parried subtle questioning about costs, frosts and flooding any more effectively, it is impossible to know. Significantly, witnesses with perhaps more local knowledge of the Thames than either Whitworth or Brindley could claim made much in their evidence of the floods which regularly swept through low-lying Bray and the surrounding fields. To introduce a canal which, even in dry seasons, was likely to make the land 'swampy and rushy' hardly promised to improve matters. In the event, the House directed that the report relating to making a canal from Basingstoke to Monkey Island be remitted to the committee for further consideration. As for 'the Question being put that leave be given to bring in a Bill for making a navigable canal from Reading [...] to communicate with the Thames', it passed – unsurprisingly – 'in the Negative.' It was a victory for the landowners who shared Sir Richard Brooke's reluctance to see canals cross their fields and parks.

Afterword

A fortnight or so later, under the headline 'An Authentic ACCOUNT of the DEBATE upon the NAVIGABLE CANAL, proposed to be made between Reading and Monkey Island', the *Reading Mercury* summarised speeches of four Members of Parliament which touched upon the scheme.[32] Barlow Trecothick, alderman, MP for London, Lord Mayor from June–November 1770 and owner of the Addington Estate near Croydon; Hon. Henry Seymour Conway, MP for Thetford, who owned a fine house with its own private theatre near the Thames in Richmond; Lord Strange and Herbert Mackworth MP had both contributed to Parliament's discussion of whether the Duke of Bridgewater should be permitted to cut through the grounds of Norton Priory.[33]

Of this quartet, the south of England's landed gentry, Trecothick and Conway opposed the Monkey Island Canal for predictable reasons. Trecothick thought its construction would 'prove injurious to those interested in the navigation of the river, and be not only useless but prejudicial to the public'. Conway protested that although he was 'a friend to canals in general', he thought there were too many of them; that they were 'intended for places which wanted a navigable stream', and that they were now being made in places 'where nature never intended' that they should be built. This particular canal was likely to 'pass through the garden of a gentleman in Chelsea whose consent had never been asked', and who, at a guess, was a friend of his. 'The encroachment,' Conway continued, 'would [...] be very disagreeable, as it would destroy the pride of situation and mar the pleasures of his life.'

Lord Strange opposed the canal on the grounds that its construction would jeopardise what he took to be the absolute right of landowners to enjoy their private property – a right he was determined to defend. In a rather confused paraphrase of his arguments, the *Reading Mercury* shows him justifying his opposition on the grounds that,

> Because no levels had yet been taken by Mr Brindley, of whom he had not the highest opinion, because it did not appear that the proprietors of the lands through which the canal must pass, had been yet consulted whether they would accept of pecuniary satisfaction.

Since Brindley had provided the Corporation of London sub-committee with copies of Whitworth's profile of the river and accompanying table of lengths and falls, the statement that he had not taken the levels looks mistaken. Furthermore, consultation with the owners of property through which the canal was to pass about whether they would accept compensation tended to occur only once the Canal Act, which would name the commissioners appointed to adjudicate in contested cases, was in place. It looks as though either Lord Strange's animus left him incoherent, or the reporter lost sight of his argument's thread.

Of the MPs whose contributions to the Monkey Island Canal debate the *Reading Mercury* mentioned, it is hardly accidental that Herbert Mackworth, a coal and copper magnate from Glamorgan and thorough-going man of commerce, was the only one to offer the scheme support. Recognising trade's need for reliable transport, he maintained that 'the two schemes', one improving the river and the other building the canal, 'might justly be considered as aids to each other', and saw no reason why these two ventures should not 'be carried on at the same time'. Furthermore, and this view was surely what Reading wanted to hear, he saw the idea of 'supplying the capital more easily and cheaply with provisions and necessaries' as 'a very material object'. But his lone voice carried little weight.

Questions and conclusion

Despite its failure, the history of the Monkey Island Canal raises some intriguing speculation. What social and economic impact might it have had if it had been built? Might the promoters have been more successful if their petition had reached Parliament after rather than before Sir Richard Brooke had given way to public opinion and allowed the Duke of Bridgewater's Canal to take its course through the Norton Priory grounds? And might the parliamentary proceedings have had a different outcome if Brindley rather than Whitworth had come under cross-examination? All these questions are unanswerable.

So too is the question of how much the canal supporters' defeat owed to genuine worry about exacerbating a known flood risk, and how much to ruthless opposition from the Thames Valley landowners. Canal historian Christopher Lewis wonders whether the canal might have contributed to more efficient management of water flow in the Thames Valley. For what it is worth, in 2002 the manmade Jubilee River between Boulter's Lock and Eton opened at a cost of £110 million with the hope that it would reduce flooding around

Maidenhead, Windsor, Eton and Cookham – all of which are close to Monkey Island. Opinions of its success vary.

Debate surrounding the canal at least accelerated improvement of the Thames. In April 1771, the commissioners responsible for the busy stretch between Lechlade and Staines obtained an Act of Parliament which empowered them to build pound locks downstream as far as Maidenhead to dredge the navigation channel and to build a towpath. But the immense loops between Sonning and Maidenhead remained and the Thames boatmen had no choice other than to accept them. (See Illustration 28).

Robert Whitworth's acceptance of the post of surveyor to the Thames Navigation in 1774 suggests that he came to view the failure of the Monkey Island Canal proposal in a philosophical light. With many of Brindley's friends, it would rankle for years. Taking blatant advantage of their guise as contributors to a scholarly work of reference, Hugh Henshall, Josiah Wedgwood and Thomas Bentley smuggled into the *Biographia Britannica* account of Brindley's life and work a stinging comment upon the Monkey Island Canal's opponents. 'These gentlemen', they observed, 'would not suffer their fine villas to be disturbed by noisy boatmen, or their extensive lawns to be cut through for the accommodation of trade and commerce, though it was from trade and commerce that most of their fine villas and extensive lawns derived their origin.'[34]

CHAPTER ELEVEN

Chester and Chesterfield: Mortality

Into Brindley's summer house-cum-office at Turnhurst, many commissions found their way. Quite how they arrived is not entirely clear-cut. By letter? Mounted messenger? Caller dropping by on the off-chance of finding the engineer at home? Sometimes, perhaps, Ann intercepted the summons, musing over what it might mean for her husband. Not all of them came to anything; indeed, abandoned canal schemes strew the autumn of Brindley's life like falling leaves, but there is little surviving evidence of his ever turning work down.[1] Admittedly, in 1765 he declined a commission relating to the Chelmer and Blackwater Navigation, and the fact that Smeaton himself, the Lincolnshire engineer John Grundy and Joseph Nickalls (later a founder member of the Smeatonian Society) all declined it too suggests that some aspect of the work, or perhaps the terms offered, must have been less than attractive.[2] Nevertheless, in a letter dating from November 1772 (after Brindley's death) Wedgwood mentions that Hugh Henshall was prepared to 'send Mr Whitworth or some other proper person' to make a survey for 'the Gentn at Chelmsford, if they desired.'[3] Vague as it is, the statement suggests that in the weeks before he died, Brindley may have agreed to consider the Chelmer and Blackwater Navigation work after all.

By the late 1760s, Brindley's Droitwich, Birmingham, and Staffordshire and Worcestershire Canals were all close to opening. Work continued, inexorably, on the Trent and Mersey Canal and the Bridgewater Canal. Although the Coventry Canal Company had sacked him in September 1769, he remained surveyor-in-chief to the Oxford Canal, its sister waterway. Between 1768 and 1770, together with Robert Whitworth he took an active part in planning the Leeds–Liverpool Canal. When Sir Richard Whitworth MP, who had tried to persuade the December 1765 Wolseley Bridge meeting of the advantages of linking the Trent by means of a canal with both the Weaver and the Severn, brought out a pamphlet proposing a canal to connect the city of Chester with the fast-growing network, Brindley was quick to take up the cause.

The Chester Canal

Concerned that its once-great port on the Dee was silting up, Chester had every reason to fear the future. Goods which once would have travelled down the Dee would soon take the canal to Liverpool by way of the Mersey. The very title of Sir Richard's tract, *A Serious Hint to the Citizens and Merchants of Chester*, reminded them of their commercial vulnerability, and they were quick to heed his warnings. Their city's best hope of future prosperity lay, they decided, in its having its own link with the Trent and Mersey Canal. At much the same time that the Birmingham Canal committee was demanding Brindley's attention, the city fathers of Chester approached him for a survey.

He had some knowledge of the area already. Snaking across the entries in his notebook for a fortnight in late July 1762 is a sketch map of the Shropshire River Roden as it flows between Lee Bridges and Radbrook. Having passed Whixall Moss and Loppington, Brindley's drawing gives the erroneous impression that instead of flowing into the Tern near Walcot, it joins the Dee, and he shows the position of Chester on the western, or right-hand, side of the page. Significantly, his day-by-day entries show that he visited Chester on 24 July 1762 and spent three days there engaged on 'walls' before returning to Longford by way of Neston to meet 'the Duk' on 1 August.[4] True to form, Brindley supplies no information about his July 1762 Chester business, although earlier in the month he mentioned meeting a 'Mr Haskiss' who may have been Henry Hesketh, mayor of Chester for 1762/3. If Hesketh indeed met Brindley at this time, the encounter left him – and, by extension, his fellow-aldermen – well-placed to seek the engineer's advice six years later about their canal plans. (See Illustration 29).

Brindley brought all his energy to Chester's 1768 venture, visiting the city once more where he befriended wealthy silversmith Richard Richardson – one of the scheme's leading proponents – and, in the closing months of year, surveyed a line from Chester to Middlewich, site of the intended junction with the Trent and Mersey Canal. For the leg-work he brought in three assistants: his nephew Thomas Allen, son of his sister Ann and her husband William Allen, the landlord of the Golden Lion Inn in Leek; John Varley, who would soon come to greater prominence on the Chesterfield Canal, and one Thomas Swinnerton.[5] He wrote to Richardson in April 1769, indicating that Chester's initial application to Parliament encountered a hitch. 'I yesterday received the favour of your letter,' he remarks, and goes on to explain that although he has sent a bill for the work of his men, he has charged nothing for himself because, the Chester Bill 'did not go forward'.[6] The letter concludes with Brindley's hope that he will have the chance to meet Richardson at Preston 'o'th'hill', and an expression of good wishes to Mrs Richardson from Ann and himself. It gives the strong impression that although the bill did not proceed as quickly as the Chester men might have wished, relations between Brindley and Richardson remained affable nevertheless.

Whatever misadventures had befallen their 1769 petition, Chester's application to Parliament in 1771 met with some success. Petitions arrived from the Staffordshire pottery towns of Burslem and Newcastle-under-Lyme; salt towns of Cheshire including Nantwich and Middlewich, and from the Company of Proprietors of the undertaking for recovering and preserving the navigation of the River Dee, all in support of the proposed canal. On 24 April 1771, Chester's Bill had its third reading and passed to the Lords. (See Illustration 30).

At this point an objection arose from the Trent & Mersey proprietors, who petitioned against it on the rather presumptuous grounds that the new canal would be an infringement of private property and that it would damage them, or, more precisely, prove 'a Discouragement to a Work in which the Petitioners have risqued their Private Fortunes and from which the

Publick will receive the greatest benefit.'[7] A hearing followed in which counsel for the Trent & Mersey proprietors asked the witness John Chamberlain, a Chester merchant, what objection his city had to the canal which the Duke of Bridgewater apparently proposed to build 'from Ince to Chester'.[8] Chamberlain's answer is not recorded but the barbed question gives the strong indication that the duke was seeking to forestall Chester's intentions. The Bridgewater Canal's Leigh branch, which got its Act in 1795, would indeed take in Ince in Makerfield, but far from going to Chester, it linked the Bridgewater Canal with the Wigan branch of the Leeds–Liverpool Canal. Perhaps, in the early 1770s, the duke genuinely nurtured other plans for it, or wished at least to convey this impression.

Whether Brindley ever anticipated that assisting Chester would bring him into opposing the duke is impossible to say. By the 1790s canal boom, when as many as eighteen new schemes might come before Parliament on the same day, engineers might brush off company rivalries like so many horse-flies. In the 1770s, such detachment was not readily mustered. Once the Trent and Mersey's counsel had summoned Hugh Henshall as a witness in support of their petition against Chester, Brindley appears to have had enough. His decision to break off his Chester connections (his sometime staff holder, Samuel Weston took up the post of engineer to the Chester Canal in his stead) looks like a recognition of the conflicting loyalties. If the duke orchestrated the petition against Chester, as engineer to the Bridgewater Canal Brindley could not comfortably oppose his wishes, least of all if it meant hearing his brother-in-law testify against the Chester scheme.

If Chester bore Brindley any ill-will after his departure, it proved short-lived. The city's canal party persevered in their wish to create a link to the Trent and Mersey and in August 1771, only three months after the House of Lords had thrown out their previous bill, they commissioned a survey from Weston, this time for a canal intended to go from Chester to join the Trent and Mersey at Middlewich, with a branch to Nantwich. Over the following months, articles in the *Chester Courant* talked up its canal cause, promising that it would decrease transport costs, promote manufacture and generally increase the prosperity of the surrounding area.[9] By 31 December, Thomas Yeoman – a vastly experienced engineer – had reviewed Weston's line and, perhaps on his advice, the Chester promoters took the precaution of getting their third petition to bring in a bill 'signed by several gentlemen residing within a moderate distance of the canal's course' by way of indicating their consent to its construction.[10]

Early in 1772, before the city of Chester's latest petition for leave to bring in a canal bill came before the Commons. John Chamberlain of Chester and his friend Mr Turner thought they had succeeded in reaching an agreement with the Duke of Bridgewater to the effect that the Chester Canal would terminate 'at a field on the east side of Booth Lane near Middlewich' through which the Trent and Mersey Canal would run, and there would be 'no ... separation' between the two canals except for the bank of the Grand Trunk.[11] It was not precisely a junction, but the arrangement promised to be workable. It had the merit of allowing for relatively easy transshipment, and since the duke professed that he was 'was pleased to promise that he would not oppose' any bill that Chester might frame in accordance with its terms, the Chester Canal promoters were content with it. Encouraged by the duke's expressions of goodwill towards their city's future 'Trade & Prosperity', they even 'begged' him to use his influence (in the manner most agreeable to himself) 'to induce the proprietors of the Grand Trunk' to allow them to make the Middlewich junction.[12]

On 27 January 1772, they applied rather cautiously to the House of Commons for leave to bring in a new bill, their petition making no mention of any connection with the Trent and Mersey Canal, but referring only to their wish to build a canal from the city of Chester 'to or near Middlewich' and provide a branch to Nantwich.[13] What happened next, the minutes of their 17 February 1772 meeting make all too clear. The agreement they thought they had reached with the duke had evaporated. Despite their deference and courtesy, not mention their unblushing readiness to offer the Trent & Mersey proprietors 'a pecuniary consideration', in other words, bribe, for the 'privilege of joining' their canal, the Chester committee's hopes came to nothing. Far from allowing them to end their canal in a field near Middlewich with only a bank to separate it from the Grand Trunk, the Trent & Mersey proprietors and the duke together had put forward a clause 'to restrain' the Chester party 'from cutting their canal beyond Booth Lane or nearer the Staffordshire Canal than 100 yards.' A hundred yards was a formidable distance for the carriage of a heavy cargo. Smarting, the Chester committee 'reluctantly' consented to give no opposition to this new restriction and convey the news of their decision to John Gilbert.[14] (See Illustration 31).

The Chesterfield Canal[15]

By 1 April 1772, when the Chester Canal Act received the Royal Assent, Brindley had a new scheme on hand on the eastern side of the Pennines at Chesterfield. In comparison with the ambitious Monkey Island plans of the 1770, including the notional transshipment terminal near Kew, passenger dock at Richmond and the promise to make Isleworth the most delightful spot in Europe, the proposed Chesterfield Canal was relatively modest. Its origins lay in the Derbyshire town's mounting frustration with unsatisfactory roads. The idea found particular favour with local lead-mining interests; Alexander Barker, influential mines adviser to William Cavendish, 5th Duke of Devonshire and prominent local mine owner, gave the canal venture his full support. The duke's steward and auditor was one Godfrey Heathcote, an ageing Chesterfield solicitor and clerk of the peace for Derbyshire to whom, by virtue of his Cavendish connections and legal expertise, the administrative business of promoting the proposed canal fell by default. Heathcote delegated the more arduous aspects of the work to his younger colleague Anthony Lax. Lax, eldest of ten children and much devoted to his mother, took to it with seamless, if rather condescending, efficiency.[16]

Approached probably around the close of 1768, Brindley accepted the invitation to make initial route surveys with good will, took stock of the local topography and then handed most of the fieldwork to his on-site assistant, the gifted if inexperienced John Varley. Over the spring of 1769, Varley explored the land between Chesterfield and Bawtry, its nearest inland port which stood some 24 miles north-east on the river Idle, and planned a course for the canal which initially shadowed the line of the River Rother. To the east of Chesterfield were hills which, short of taking a circuitous and costly 10-mile detour, he could wholly not avoid. Fortunately, there was a relatively obvious crossing point at Norwood, between the hamlet of Wales and the village of Killamarsh, where it looked feasible to tunnel through the hilltop before carrying the canal down a deep valley on the ridge's eastern flank and out over flattish land towards Bawtry. Once Varley had mapped his line, he and Brindley – the novice surveyor anxious to make a good showing in front of the master at the height of his skills – discussed their findings, the geography, the availability of materials and labour, and anything else that had a bearing on the canal's likely cost. At some point in the summer of 1769 they met Anthony Lax and the townsmen of Chesterfield; Brindley gave them the waterway's length (28 miles), width (over 28 feet), indicated where and how it would cross the hills and estimated that £100,000 would cover the cost of building.

By now, Chesterfield's canal aspirations had aroused the interest of the neighbouring towns. Both Worksop and, more stridently, Retford requested that the new canal's planned route be amended to come near them. Retford's townsmen included a dogged and highly articulate enthusiast in the person of scholarly squarson Rev. Seth Ellis Stevenson, sometime Rector of Treswell in Nottinghamshire, devoted gardener and headmaster of Retford Grammar School. Like Don Navigation man William Martin of Tinsley, Stevenson had visited Manchester. With his friend Mr Shilleto, he made an extensive tour of the West Midlands in 1767, observing the new canals that were both in use and under construction and learning all that he could about them. Christine Richardson conjectures that as early as Boxing Day 1768 – even before John Varley had surveyed the Chesterfield-Bawtry route – Stevenson began to sound out his fellow townsmen on the advantages of having the canal go through Retford on its way to the Trent.[17] Certainly by the early summer of 1769, possibly even at the same time that John Varley was delineating his fine map of a canal-route between Chesterfield and Bawtry, the leading spirits of Chesterfield and Retford were discussing how the enterprise might be adapted to serve both towns. Bawtry would lose out but Retford needed water transport and Stevenson, for all his clergy scruples, was ruthless in championing his town. The unofficial and off-the-record conversations bore fruit in the shape of an agreement that once the canal company was formally constituted, it would come under the joint control of both Chesterfield and Retford. John Varley made a new route survey, this time for a prospective canal which would still go to the Trent, but now running by way of Retford and Worksop. Worksop, after all, lay right in its obvious path and, being approximately equidistant between the two other towns, promised to be a convenient place for future committee meetings and general assemblies of proprietors. (See Illustration 32).

Over the summer of 1769, Brindley had made site visits to the Staffordshire and Worcestershire Canal to advise on construction of the Dunstall Water bridge (3 May; 11 and 22 June); attended the inaugural committee meeting of the Oxford Canal committee (12 May); inspected and reported on the state of the Coventry Canal's construction (16 May; 6 June) and, together with Whitworth, addressed a Darlington-based committee on the feasibility of making a canal from Stockton-on-Tees by Darlington to Piercebridge and Winston. For good measure, at some point in July he received a request from Richard Dunthorne and John Wing, respectively the superintendent of the Bedford Level and the Duke of Bedford's steward, to advise them on improving the outfall of River Nene, some 4½ miles downstream from Wisbech.[18] The list is indicative of the sheer number of prospective ventures and ventures-in-progress that occupied him at this time, besides which the business of travel from meeting to meeting and site to site was arduous and consuming. He arrived in Worksop in the second half of the summer to attend a meeting held on 24 August 1769 at the Red Lion Inn to promote the cause of a canal 'beginning at or near Chesterfield [...] and to be continued [...] till it falls into the River Trent below Gainsbro', at or near Stockwith'.[19] To judge from the newspaper coverage, when he addressed the local gentry, townsmen, and interested merchants and tradesmen, he was dispassionate and circumspect. 'Mr BRINDLEY', runs the *Derby Mercury*'s account, 'produced a plan [of the canal], with an estimate of the expense of making the same, and a calculation of the tonnage that would yearly arise thereby, and declared it to be practicable'.[20] At this stage, he planned to take the canal to 'join the River Trent at Gainsborough', but that would soon change.

Gainsborough stood just across the county boundary in Lincolnshire, and in choosing it as his junction, Brindley may have followed what he took to be the local interest. Certainly it seems likely that by the time of the crucial August public meeting, a Lincolnshire faction had formed itself around Sir Cecil Wray, MP for Retford, but scion of a Lincolnshire family with the intention of playing an influential role in the new canal's development and administration.[21] If the Lincolnshire party reminded the engineer that the town was an established inland port, well-provided with facilities for cargo-handling and well-known to traders, he had every reason to heed their words.

Nevertheless, late 1760s Retford in Nottinghamshire was not entirely disposed to view the Lincolnshire interest in a favourable light. Sensing Retford's prevailing mood, Seth Ellis Stevenson once again intervened. If Retford wanted to avoid the risk of seeing an overbearing Lincolnshire presence swaying control of its canal commerce (beside the expense of the extra tunnelling which the Gainsborough route entailed) he was ready to weigh in on the town's behalf. If not so well-established an inland port as Gainsborough, the town of West Stockwith was not badly provided with wharfage, storage and facilities for boat building and maintenance. Community spirit, or perhaps the wish to prevent Lincolnshire prospering at Nottinghamshire's expense, led Stevenson to spare 'no effort in achieving his objective ... riding his horse Jockey – in the depths of winter – to the homes of various influential people to put his point of view.'[22] If his conduct looks sharp for a clergyman, and rather close to bringing excessive personal and civic preference to bear on a decision which held sweeping consequences for sizeable tract of the East Midlands, it was not out of tune with Josiah Wedgwood's rides around Staffordshire to promote the nascent canal from the Trent to the Mersey. Just as Thomas Bentley and Erasmus Darwin had produced a promotional pamphlet, *A Short View of the General Advantage of Inland Navigations; with a Plan of a Navigable Canal, intended for a Communication between the Ports of Liverpool & Hull, and a Brief Enumeration of the Peculiar Benefits which will arise from it to the Public*, so in the closing months of 1769 Stevenson brought out a publication of his own, named *Seasonable Hints relating to the Intended Canal from Chesterfield in Derbyshire to the River Trent below Gainsborough*. It was an effective eighteenth-century way of doing things.

A generous host and affable guest, once Stevenson had drawn the greater number of the canal-minded populace of Retford and district round to his opinion concerning the Trent junction, the advantages of Stockwith loomed too large in local thinking for Brindley to dismiss them. Something, be it weight of numbers, the likely cost and difficulty of tunnelling at Castle Hill or the compelling argument from Stevenson, led him to revisit his Gainsborough plan and amend it. Those subscribers, landowners and interested people present at a public meeting held at the Crown in Retford on 25 January 1770 resolved to adopt his new line, joining the Trent at West Stockwith, on the grounds that it was 'capable to be carried into Execution at a less Expense, and in a shorter Time, and', a crucial factor, 'admitting of a more easy Communication with the Trent, than if the same should be taken on to Gainsborough.'[23]

While Stevenson had fought the Stockwith cause, Brindley had resurveyed and approved John Longbotham's proposed line for the trans-Pennine Leeds–Liverpool Canal – a venture whose boldness should have chimed well with his ambition. Yet although he accepted the invitation to become its engineer-in-chief on a salary of £400 per annum, he had second thoughts and asked to be released from this commitment, paving the way for Longbotham to accept the post in his place.[24] Brindley's resignation from the Leeds–Liverpool concern may have stemmed from one of his rare admissions that there were limits to how much work he could do at the same time. The decision may have owed something to his memories of working with rival Yorkshire and Lancashire factions in the Calder Navigation. It had not been his most successful enterprise and in all likelihood, the experience of finding himself obliged to arbitrate between competing Yorkshire and Lancashire interests, leaving one party cocksure and the other resentful, was not something he cared to repeat.

John Varley meanwhile, unpaid to date for his Chesterfield Canal surveying and mapmaking, had begged large loans from Stevenson. By way of earning enough to repay them, in the early summer of 1769 he undertook some independent surveying work on a short canal for the Marquis of Rockingham, intended to connect the Rotherham road with the Don Navigation.[25] Having shown himself to be resourceful and competent, towards the end of 1769 Brindley had drafted him in to help with the Leeds–Liverpool surveying. He took little notice of the winter chill and in January 1770 would inform a meeting of the proprietors of the Trent and Mersey Canal that the tunnellers had advanced about ½ mile through Harecastle Hill and that the work should 'proceed with vigour, notwithstanding the cold weather'.[26]

Obtaining an Act of Parliament

Like the Coventry men whose haste to get an Act of Parliament Brindley considered 'too precipitate', having met on 25 January 1770 the Chesterfield canal promoters rushed to obtain enabling legislation and petitioned Parliament the following month for permission to bring in a bill to make their 'cut or Canal for the navigation of Boats and other Vessels' between Chesterfield and Stockwith.[27] No sooner had they made their red-hot application than they realised something was wrong; within a fortnight it was withdrawn and 'laid aside' for a year to allow the committee to take stock and decide precisely what steps they needed to take. Their mistake appears to have been a failure to define the exact route; the paperwork, such as it was, which accompanied their petition had set out the line in only the mistiest terms. Landowning Members of Parliament, ever-alert to the rights accompanying property ownership, not surprisingly wished to see something rather more closely defined, and in May 1770, John Varley clarified the route by having it staked out. The Chesterfield Canal's promoters had now constituted themselves into a committee consisting of one baronet, nineteen esquires – 'upper gentry', forty-five gentlemen – 'lower gentry', four clergy and a doctor of physic. Over 1770, they met at intervals and did all they could to boost the scheme's public popularity while committee clerk Anthony Lax drafted and re-drafted clauses for inclusion in the Act. On the year's closing day, a meeting at the George in Worksop gave its approval to his new wording of a petition and arranged to apply once more to Parliament.

On its way through the Commons, the revised and improved Chesterfield Canal Bill was to hit three hostile petitions. First came a petition from the Don Navigation commissioners, concerned with good reason about the potential threat the new canal posed to their water. In response to their anxieties, the parliamentary committee charged with examining the bill added a clause to protect their interest.[28] Under its terms no water from the River Rother (which fed the Don), or indeed the Rother's tributaries, was to be taken from the eastern (Chesterfield) side of the hill at Norwood, and all the water that flowed down the western side of the hill into the Rother was to be retained there. That was not to say that the canal might not use it on its way, only that it was to be discharged into the Rother and thence to the Don. The requirement was more finicky than problematic. It necessitated some changes to the siting of the reservoirs intended to serve the canal, but in the overall context of planning the canal's consistent water-supply, these alterations were relatively small-scale.

Secondly, there arose a petition from John Lister, lackadaisical owner of the River Idle Navigation who, it appeared, was entitled to claim damages if he could prove that his business had suffered as a result of the new canal's taking water from the Idle. Although the canal assuredly ruined his trade, the cause of its destruction had nothing to do with the level of water in the River Idle, so Lister's petition never counted for much.

The third petition, by contrast, would bedevil the canal for evermore. One Elizabeth Cavendish owned a thriving ironworks along the route and got her power from the River Rother. Although no record of the discussion of Mrs Cavendish's concern about the risk that the canal posed to her forge at Staveley survives, the committee charged with examining the bill amended it by including a 'clause ... for securing water to Mrs Cavendish's forge'.[29] The fact that Mrs Cavendish's grievance made itself felt relatively late in the bill's passage through Parliament raises the possibility that committee chairman Lord George Cavendish, keen to follow due process of law while protecting a relative's commercial interests, deliberately delayed proposing the new clause so as to discourage unwelcome opposition. Conceivably, rather than air the proposed amendment in committee, Cavendish took it straight to the House, their acceptance being the first the canal party knew of the matter.[30] Whatever the circumstances, the House not only agreed to the clause in the Act protecting Mrs Cavendish's water supply, but stipulated in precise terms that it was, at the Canal Company's expense, 'to be maintained to the standard it had always enjoyed' by the provision of a weir on the canal's edge, which was to be 4 inches lower than any other weir on the section. The provision meant that the canal's water – its life blood – would pour out over the low weir into the Rother and on to Staveley Forge. What was more, if the ironworks should be left without water power, the Canal Company would be liable for damages.

Around the questions of whether John Varley foresaw the implications of introducing the low weir to the canal side and, indeed, whether he had any inkling of the Staveley amendment and its potential consequences before he heard it proposed, there is a vast enigmatic silence. Perhaps, knowing how much the Chesterfield committee wanted their Act, being uncomfortable with the elaborate parliamentary procedures and ill at ease when it came to giving evidence, Varley made an unfortunate error. Whether or not Brindley would have avoided it and approached the matter on a different footing, it is impossible to say. All that is clear is that the Chesterfield promoters now faced the immense difficulty of complying with the terms of the Act, complete with clause safeguarding the Staveley water supply on the one hand, while avoiding their canal's becoming starved of water on its descent from the high Norwood Hill into the Doe Lea valley on the other.

Swarkestone and Runcorn

The Act ratified, cutting began. Around this time, Brindley attempted to promote an extension of the canal south from Chesterfield to join the Trent and Mersey at Swarkestone, but it fell foul of the local landowners' wish to safeguard their property. An aggrieved correspondent to the *Derby Mercury* protested that, for all the supposed advantages of canals which their proponents cried up, 'the Experience of all the Gentlemen and Farmers' whose lands the Trent and Mersey Canal crossed, had been one of 'great Inconvenience and Damage'.[31] The public meeting, held in the George Inn in Derby on 27 June 1771 with the intention of garnering support for the Swarkestone project, ended in the canal party's defeat: 'over-rul'd by a great majority'. The spirit of Sir Richard Brooke of Norton Priory had taken hold upon the gentry of Derbyshire, and for all his conviction and persuasive canal talk, James Brindley could not prevail against it.

At much the same time, he and the duke had a difference of opinion on the subject of locks, structures which both men preferred to do without if at all possible. Here, the disagreement concerned construction of the flight by which the Bridgewater Canal was to reach the Mersey at Runcorn. 'Mr Brindley was with the late Duke of Bridgewater, at making the Locks at Runcorn', reports Rev. Francis Henry Egerton, and apparently,

> ... recommended a dry wall; But, He was Overruled by the Duke Himself, who made a Wall of Red-Rock, 'Pounded,' at the back of the wall.[32]

Brindley's caution had good reason. His brief involvement with the Weaver Navigation had given him the chance to hear about the bulging walls of Henry Berry's lock at Pickerings, which threatened to give way each time water entered the chamber.[33] Should a lock collapse, it would cause a massive loss of time and revenue. Rev. F. H. Egerton reports that Brindley 'used to say of These Locks, '*If these Locks stand, They are the Only Locks that ever stood without a Dry Wall.*' His view, in Egerton's estimation, was altogether too wary. 'They piss', he allowed,

> But they are in Perfect Order and Repair: in continual Use are They, for the Immense Traffic, Which, is passing upon the Navigable Canal; And, They have now stood for over Half a Century.[34]

This record says little beyond testifying to the locks' survival in defiance of Brindley's predictions. Exactly what happened at the site is not easily established, but in October 1771 Brindley was on sufficiently good terms with the Bridgewater Estate management to request the despatch of two wheelbarrows 'to Chesterfield Navig[n]' as samples for the on-site carpenters to copy.[35] The writer of a 'Letter from Runcorn', composed apparently in August 1772 and which the *Derby Mercury* published the following month, names Brindley as 'our great Engineer', but adds significantly that it is the duke who assumes the role of 'chief Director of the Works, and generally overlooks the Men from Morning to Night'.[36] He was to all appearances an effective manager, for the letter writer describes the ten locks, arranged in pairs as being 'chiefly finished'.

From his command of technical detail, the anonymous author appears to have close associations with the ongoing work. He relates, for instance, that the duke 'employs 500 men'; that the 'The lowermost lock is 22 feet and a half in depth, (which is about the heighth of the highest Tides) and will discharge vessels at neap Tides'; that 'each lock' has a fall of seven feet, 'except the lowermost which falls 22 Feet at low water' and that each lock is '27 Feet wide … 70 in length [and] will receive Vessels of 60 Tons Burthen'. It may well be that he is one of the duke's staff, keen to play down Brindley's conspicuous absence from the Runcorn flight, while making much of what promised to be a spectacular structure when finished.

Mortality

Discouraged by his reception in Derby, Brindley abandoned his plans to connect the Chesterfield Canal to the expanding network. Nevertheless, he visited the canal sites at frequent intervals through 1771 and 1772 to inspect the works in progress, much as he did on the Staffordshire and Worcestershire Canal, which by now was nearing its completion under the guardianship of John Fennyhouse Green. Early in September 1772, he made one such visit to Retford ostensibly to encourage John Varley, by now ensconced with his wife Hannah in the village of Harthill, who had the task of overseeing the Chesterfield Canal's day-to-day building: haggling with suppliers of materials; cajoling contractors; encouraging the labourers and conciliating the committee men. While in the neighbourhood, Brindley dined with the proprietors and agreed to subscribe for some canal shares. By now, much of his work was coming to fruition. The Droitwich Canal had opened early in 1771; the Staffordshire and Worcestershire Canal had been open since January 1772 and the Birmingham Canal would open later in the year, its loops immortalising Samuel Simcock's initials until Thomas Telford revised the route in the 1820s and abandoned them. With Henshall's assistance, the great tunnel advanced through Harecastle Hill. Whitworth had surveyed for a canal proposed to link Kendal and Preston by way of Lancaster, and at some point in the late summer of 1772 Josiah Wedgwood suggested constructing a canal to carry stone from the quarries around Ipstones and Caldon through Froghall to the Grand Trunk.

Out with his surveying team in September 1772 to establish a route for Wedgwood's proposed branch, Brindley, so the story goes, got soaked by a shower of rain. Undaunted, he continued working wet-through which, Smiles alleges, he had 'often done with impunity' in the past. After all, he had sanctioned the continuation of work on the Trent and Mersey through the cold winter weather, and he sought no more from his workforce than he was prepared to undertake himself. Unluckily, on this occasion when he retired to spend the night at the Red Lion Inn in Ipstones, they gave him a cold, damp, unaired bed. Ill, he soon realised that he could not continue with the survey. Having somehow got himself home to Turnhurst, he succumbed to what was to be his last illness – a chill, exacerbated by what Erasmus Darwin diagnosed as diabetes, although it was not a condition which he made any claims to understand. Conscious that he was dying, Brindley allowed Ann to purchase his portrait which she had wanted so much. Wedgwood, wretched after his wife's recent miscarriage, visited every day.

Smiles writes,

> It is related of him that, when dying, some eager canal undertakers insisted on having an interview with him. They had encountered a serious difficulty in the course of constructing their canal and they *must* have the advice of Mr Brindley on the subject. They were introduced to the apartment where he lay, scarcely able to gasp, yet his mind was clear. They explained their difficulty – they could not make their canal hold water. 'Then puddle it,' said the engineer. They explained that they had already done so. 'Then puddle it again – and again.' This was all he could say, and it was enough.[37]

At first sight, it looks like a less than believable piece of Brindley folklore – would Ann and Wedgwood really have allowed the men in? At the same time, the story has just enough bearing upon the business of building the Chesterfield Canal to lend it a little plausibility. Once Mrs Cavendish's special low weir was in place, to ensure that the canal had water as it descended from the eastern flank of Norwood Hill into the Doe Lea Valley may well have seemed impossible. Chesterfield's solution to the problem was to build the evocatively named Staveley Puddle Bank – a vast earthwork which straddled the valley floor, halting the canal's descent and creating 8 miles of level pound between Staveley and Renishaw, with reservoirs feeding the vulnerable stretch. A clumsy encumbrance that was expensive to build and maintain, it was at least a way of combatting an unforeseen obstacle.

It is pure conjecture, but if a mob of 'eager', not to say over-importunate, canal builders thrust the problem of the canal's loss of water over the weir upon Brindley's attention as he lay dying, perhaps the Staveley Puddle Bank was his solution. Smiles, of course, was not there and cannot quote, but it is striking that the gate-crashers of his anecdote insist that a section of their canal, despite puddling, will not hold water; significantly, they do not say that it leaked.

Arguably, the circumstances of his story aptly reflect the plight of the Chesterfield Canal between Staveley and Renishaw before the embankment's completion. Besides, introducing the earthwork to circumvent the difficulty caused by Mrs Cavendish's amendment shows a last flicker of Brindley's ingenuity, while in his alleged instruction to 'puddle it again and again' there lurks a rather fitting description of the means of raising the bank. If the grim tale has any foundation, it brings a note of gallows humour to the Schemer's passing.

CHAPTER TWELVE

Immortality

The Duke of Bridgewater

After Brindley died, the Duke of Bridgewater lost none of his canal enthusiasm. A keen observer of the developing network of branches springing and developing from the Grand Trunk, he acquired enough shares in key enterprises (including the Mersey & Irwell Navigation) to keep himself in touch with the direction of their proprietors' thinking.

While an active promoter of late eighteenth-century canal commerce in general, he had no time for enterprises which he viewed as hostile to his own. The early 1780s witnessed a sharp dispute between himself and a number of Trent and Mersey proprietors, Josiah Wedgwood among them, when the new Manchester-based carrying firm which John Gilbert had established with a waggoner named Worthington began to compete with Hugh Henshall's carrying company for the Trent and Mersey trade between Manchester and Stourport. A rumour, mischievous or malicious, that Henshall & Co. intended to cease to transport goods over this part of the network looked like sharp practice by Henshall's up-and-coming Manchester-based rival. When the duke directed that all unconsigned goods at Preston Brook intended for Stourport be delivered to Worthington and Gilbert for carriage, Wedgwood was less than impressed.[1] The gist of his annoyance was that the duke had begun to treat the Trent and Mersey as a branch of his own canal.[2] Meanwhile, the Trent and Mersey's Manchester agent, a Mr Caister, fuelled the fires of discontent by reporting both that local business practice was skewed to ensure despatch of Worthington's boats before Trent and Mersey vessels, and that Trent & Mersey Company porters were 'frequently called off to do Worthington's and his Grace's business'.[3] The dispute lasted for years. The Trent & Mersey proprietors talked openly of establishing a new carrying company dedicated to the Preston Brook–Liverpool trade to rival Gilbert and Worthington, while the duke in disgust called for Mr Caister's dismissal and threatened to sell off his Trent & Mersey shares. At last, perhaps as the result of mutual exhaustion, each faction's position softened and settled to a compromise; the Trent & Mersey men did not establish a rival company (although Hugh Henshall & Co. remained in business) and the duke, his animus losing its edge, retained his Trent & Mersey shares.

In his later years, his youthful interest in bloodstock broadened into a more general concern with agriculture. As early as 1767, Joseph Banks had been aware of his plans to drain parts of Chat Moss, and by 1773 he had reclaimed a large area on which to grow wheat, barley and potatoes, as well as clover to provide hay for the canal mules.[4] Although he continued to purchase paintings, canals remained his abiding enthusiasm. After the death of John Gilbert in 1795 and with Thomas, in Malet's expression, 'almost gone', the duke, if sadly, took responsibility for the direction of his business affairs himself.[5] His readiness to undertake bold ventures never waned. In 1797 he commissioned the American engineer Robert Fulton to build a steam tug for use on the canal.[6] Unfortunately, misadventure dogged this enterprising engagement with new technology. The boat's funnel was too tall for the canal bridges, so it had to be hinged to dip, as Malet says, 'in solemn salutation' of each bridge it passed. Malet relates that the vessel drew some 'eight 25 ton starvationers [from Worsley] to Manchester', 'puffing and splashing' along at a stately 1 mph. At this point, someone raised a concern, no doubt well-founded, that the paddles might damage the canal's clay puddle lining, and the steam tug experiment ceased. In deference to Fulton's service under Napoleon, the boat acquired the name *Buonaparte*, which served, on her failure, as a satisfying gibe at a huffing monster from the derisive Worsley workforce. Often his speculations had happier outcomes. In 1802, the year before he died, he purchased a small estate in Hertfordshire ostensibly 'as a present for Lady Sutherland' for £14,000, before finding that it had a stream flowing through it which 'was found to be so strong and fruitful, its equal was not known.' Shortly after this discovery, the duke entered into negotiation to lease the estate to the New River Company, which at that time supplied the City of London with drinking water and which apparently offered him 'Five thousand pounds a year for the rent of it.'[7]

As he aged, he became increasingly high-handed. On one infamous occasion, he lopped off the heads of the flowers the estate workers had planted at Worsley.[8] Another time, while he watched the men at work near Worsley Bridge, a young woman carrying a bundle of cotton cardings pushed past him in a hurry, and the cotton fibres attached themselves to his hat, tied hair and coat. Seeing her grin in response to his roar of annoyance, he arranged to close the path from the turnpike road to the canalside to 'all females with burdens'.[9] He would not have guests to stay with him because, he explained, 'If they come to me, they may stay as long as they please: if I go to them, I can stay as long as I please'.[10] To this rule there were exceptions, of whom Brindley was one and the duke's young relative Francis Henry Egerton (1756–1829) another. Frank, as the duke called him, was a frequent guest at Worsley, Ashridge and Cleveland House in London, and the duke enjoyed telling him stories of the early phases of the canal.[11] The boy was entranced. The tales he heard were the distant origin of the *Letter to the Parisians*, the tract in which Frank, better known as the Rev. F. H. Egerton, 8th Earl of Bridgewater and eccentric resident of Paris's Rue St Honoré, would compose in response to a French journal's sloppy article which, he thought, over-praised Brindley at the duke's expense. Family honour would prompt him to leave instructions in his will authorising the erection of a monumental column of granite some 40 metres high, topped with a vast copper urn and bearing the inscription 'In Honour of Francis, 3rd Duke of Bridgewater and Father of Inland Navigation.' It stands not at Worsley, but overlooking the Chiltern Hills beyond Ashridge, as though to emphasise that the duke's achievement was not a local matter for Lancashire alone, but touched upon the entire nation. (See Illustration 33).

Guardian genius

That James Brindley should die without having made a will comes as no surprise. Constant, absorbing canal work left little time in which to think over decisions about money, chattels, land and livestock, let alone to sit down with John Sparrow, who, besides his work as clerk to the Trent & Mersey Canal Company, became Ann's family lawyer and drew up a will in correct form. His father, the older James Brindley about whom Smiles wrote in such damning terms, had died in 1770. For all the fecklessness with which Smiles credits him, in November 1763 (just when his eldest son, having given the days' orders to the carpenter and blacksmith took time to record his observation of a strong cross wind blowing on the waters of the a newly completed stretch of the Bridgewater Canal) he had made a will which makes careful provision for what was to happen to his estate and other possession after his death.[12] As executors, he appointed his wife Susannah and, understandably if less than wisely, his eldest son. (see Illustration 34).

In the event, the younger James Brindley, engaging upon his many ventures-in-progress with all the vigour his volatile health permitted, did not regard the legal requirements concerning probate as a pressing priority. His mother, to whom his father bequeathed the family farm for the term of her life, remained resident there; his siblings were grown up and independent. Disbursing £30 legacies apiece to his brothers Joseph, John and Henry and his sisters Esther, Ann and Mary hardly resembled an urgent matter, at least not in comparison with overseeing work on the nascent Chesterfield Canal, or surveying for a branch of the Grand Trunk intended to run to the lime quarries at Cauldon Low. Therefore, whatever he may have intended, he never did anything about it. Commercially speaking, his fortunes continued to rise. The Staffordshire and Worcestershire, the Droitwich and the Birmingham Canals would all open to traffic throughout their entire lengths in the course of 1772. Work on the Bridgewater Canal, the Oxford Canal and Grand Trunk continued steadily, although Brindley's links with the Coventry Canal had severed upon his dismissal in 1769. His direct association with the Duke of Bridgewater might have lost the urgency of the early 1760s but seems to have continued in a quiet way, despite the disagreement on the subject of Runcorn Locks, as his request in October 1771 for Worsley wheelbarrows to be sent to Chesterfield for the canal carpenters to copy bears out.[13] By 1772, the intense work on a variety of sites which had taken so much of his time over the past seven or so years had slowed down. Prudent, he took far-sighted measures to secure the future of the canal network, arguably not so much training a corps of successors as putting opportunities in their way. They were, after all, working in a relatively new field, and if they were to make a success of it they needed to gain experience fast. Charting their adventures in an informative and highly entertaining book, Christopher Lewis had demonstrated how this assemblage of friends and relatives such as Henshall, Whitworth, Simcock and Josiah Clowes; the two nephews, Thomas Allen and the younger James Brindley and colleagues like Varley, Dadford and Weston would complete and develop the work to which Brindley had devoted the last twelve years of his life.[14]

In the months following his death, besides the formal notices, a number of elegies appeared in the press. The *Derby Mercury* offered:

Leek, Cheadle, Chedleton, Delf, Burslem, Woore,
Stoke, Turnhurst, Ipstones, Draycott-in-the-Moor,
All strive for BRINDLEY's birth, but strive in vain
For Brindley rose like Neptune from the Main.[15]

The *Newcastle Courant* proclaimed:

'Tis not in epitaph or formal stone
    Will make they many virtues, Brindley, known.
Be in Elysium then, dear shade, content,
    Thy works shall be an endless monument,

He was the Architect to the Duke of Bridgewater's Canal.[16]

The *Leeds Intelligencer* observed that,

Where many a ploughman till'd the earth before,
Now skilful rowers ply the lab'ring oar.[17]

The fondest tribute owed nothing to poetic language, but took the form of an uproarious celebration to mark the formal opening of a section of the Trent and Mersey Canal in October 1772. 'Our canal was filled with water a few days ago to a temporary wharf not many yards distant from this place', a letter from Burslem informed the *Oxford Journal*,

And yesterday (for the first time) a boat was brought up to it; every part of the boat was adorned with festoons of flowers, which, with an excellent band of music, put us in mind of the famous procession of Cleopatra: The banks on each side were covered, for many miles, with an innumerable crowd of joyful spectators, whose shouts, with the ringing of bells, and the discharge of a few pieces of cannon, seemed to rend the sky. A solemn goblet was drank to the immortal memory of our lamented engineer, the late Mr Brindley, who is now supposed to preside (a guardian genius) over this canal.[18]

Brindley's daughters

Hugh Henshall regarded administering the business affairs of his sister and his nieces Anne and Susannah as part and parcel of his fraternal duty, something which he took seriously. If he did not actively broker Ann Brindley's second marriage, he assuredly did not discourage it. Her next husband was Robert Williamson, a local earthenware manufacturer who may well have been the same 'Mr Williamson' who had the privilege of accompanying the Duke of Bridgewater and Earl Gower of Trentham on a ceremonial voyage into the part-completed Harecastle Tunnel in the autumn of 1773.[19] On 30 December 1775 the couple married, their nuptials witnessed by John Mills, who had witnessed Ann's first wedding. Williamson settled in Longport to become extremely successful, while Ann not only took an active part in his business interests, but also bore him some eight children.

Jane, eldest of Ann and Robert Williamson's children, was born in 1776; her sister Mary in 1778. In what would soon become a sizeable family, the chance that Ann's two daughters from her first marriage would get much attention beyond being asked to mind the steadily increasing number of toddlers and babes in arms was remote, and in June 1778 Hugh Henshall became the young Anne and Susannah Brindley's guardian. The fact that he undertook this duty at the same time as he began to sort out what was to happen to his distinguished late brother-in-law's estate suggests that the guardianship arrangement may have been a device to ensure that his nieces should benefit to some degree from their late father's estate. Despite his numerous commitments, Henshall – engineer-turned-carrier with mining and pottery interests to boot – took a serious and committed view of his duties. He had a wide acquaintance and the opportunity to make useful introductions, so it is not wholly surprising to find Susannah marrying a businessman with a wide range of mercantile interests in her mid-twenties. John Bettington, a Bristolian, described himself as a 'merchant' and owned of a coal mine at Easton.[20] Both he and his father also had a substantial stake in Robert Bayly's white-lead works at Lawrence Hill, where they would install a Boulton and Watt engine in 1789 – the first in Bristol.[21]

Susannah's wedding took place in Burslem parish church on 8 December 1795, thirty years to the day since the marriage of her parents. Once settled in Bristol, she gave to her eldest son, born 1 January 1796, the name James Brindley Bettington, and to her second son, born in 1799, the name John Henshall Bettington. Her proud if pathetic wish to perpetuate the memory of the father of whom, since he died when she was less than year old, she can have had no direct recollection is perhaps the defining action of her short life. In October 1799, the *Derby Mercury* carried a notice of her death.[22] She was not yet thirty and had been married for fewer than four years.

To Anne, the older daughter, under the terms of his will Henshall gave the use of Greenway Bank, a large and rather handsome house near Knypersley, for as long as she remained unmarried. Somehow, her half-brother Hugh Henshall Williamson, coal owner and future high sherriff of Staffordshire, took up residence at Greenway Bank himself and Anne, a lifelong spinster, never lived there. Whatever the circumstances surrounding the house – young Williamson would later attest that Anne had 'renounced her right' to live there – at the age of sixty-four in 1835, she took the momentous decision to visit her nephew, Susannah's son James, in Parramatta, New South Wales, where he had settled to farm sheep, deal in wool and breed race horses.[23]

Before setting sail, on 6 August 1835 she had her friends the Ferneyhough family to dine at her lodgings in Stamford Street, Blackfriars – close, by chance, to the home of the engineer John Rennie. 'Our dinner hour is five o'clock,' she informed Miss Ferneyhough, to whom she addressed the invitation, 'when we hope your father, mother, Brothers and Mrs John Ferneyhough will accompany you.'[24] If providing for a party of this size placed considerable demands upon her landlord or landlady, her impulse was generous nevertheless. Together with her nephew John Bettington, she left London on 30 August 1835 on board the *Lord William Bentinck* bound for Sydney – a voyage which generally took around six months. In fact, they reached their destination on 20 January 1836. Having reached the home of James Bettington and his wife Rebecca, they would remain in Parramatta for the best part of two years.[25] No letters home, nor any family memoir exist to show how they spent the time, but they were on hand for the birth of Anne's great-nephew, also named James Brindley Bettington, on 1 April 1837.[26]

On 14 December 1837, Anne and John embarked on the *William Nicol* bound for Newcastle with only a handful of passengers and a cargo of wool for unloading in London. The *William Nicol* was a ship under a cloud. Commissioned to carry free settler emigrants from the Hebrides, in July 1837 she had departed from Skye to Sydney with 148 adult passengers and 180 children. Of these, one of the adults and ten of the children died on the voyage, and when she docked at the Cape of Good Hope, the British consul Sir Benjamin D'Urban made a scathing report of the conditions he found on board.[27]

There was, therefore, an understandable reason why beside her regular crew and the Australian wool, the *William Nicol* carried only seven passengers, who must have grown to know one another extremely well.[28] It was to prove a leisurely trip, for eight months after the departure from Sydney, the ship with Mr, Mrs and Miss Cory, Dr Holditch, Mr Bettington and 'Mrs Brinley with servent [sic]' aboard, had only reached the straits of Sunda between Sumatra and Java.[29] At some point thereafter, bound for home, Anne died. The cause of her death unknown, her friends in distant Stoke-upon-Trent heard that she had been buried at sea.[30]

The last debt

Brindley's widow Ann Williamson was convinced that despite her late husband's 'plans and undertakings' being so 'beneficial to his Grace's interest', monies owing to him for the years 1765–1772 remained unpaid. In 1774, the year when the Bridgewater Estate settled its outstanding accounts with the 'Representatives of Mr Jas Brindley dec'd' her brother Hugh received £100 from John Gilbert, apparently as an *ex gratia* payment 'on account of Mr Brindley's time.'[31] Unsatisfied by what she regarded as a trifling sum, she indicated in letters first to the Gilbert brothers and then to the duke directly that she thought it inadequate. She received no reply.

Incensed, upon the duke's death, she raised the matter again with his trustee, the newly appointed canal superintendent Robert Haldane Bradshaw. The terms in which he responded, if he ever did, are unknown but in the mid-nineteenth century Ann's letter came to the attention of Samuel Smiles. Dismayed at what he took to be a slight upon a great man and his loyal wife, Smiles quoted Ann's allegation that over the last seven years of his life, her late first husband 'was frequently in very great want'; that he had often had to borrow money to fulfil his obligations to various canal companies; that John Gilbert's £100 was a 'small and inadequate return ... for his services' and, above all, that far his plans and undertakings' had vastly benefitted 'His Grace's interests' in a portentous footnote.[32]

His righteous indignation sparked a storm. W. H. Chaloner sought to demonstrate that Brindley could hardly have been badly off by invoking Davis Dukart's observation that he 'received £500 for the Staffordshire work alone'.[33] Hugh Malet noted the 7s a day, together with occasional board, lodging and grazing for his horse that Brindley had from the duke and said outright that Smiles' remarks about Brindley's being badly paid had 'no foundation in fact'.[34] Peter Lead suggested that Ann 'exaggerated' her late first husband's achievements, albeit unwittingly, to promote her brother Hugh's interests once he had taken over several of Brindley's ventures.[35]

There is another possible explanation, namely that Brindley's own sense of indebtedness to the duke outweighed any payment owing. By 1765, although the duke's canal was far from being finished, Brindley had set its construction well enough in hand to concentrate on new ventures. His formal links with the Bridgewater Estate dissolved probably at some point late in 1765 or early the following year. A man of integrity and good will, mindful of the openings the duke had given him, not to mention for his utter confidence in his engineer despite the scoffing of detractors, Brindley was willing help the duke on whatever canal matters he required without charge. On these terms, he gave evidence in the House of Lords against Charles Roe's Macclesfield Navigation Bill, hastened across country when the Bollin Aqueduct collapsed and made himself available to explain to a decidedly hostile House of Commons why it was necessary to amend the statutory protection accorded to Sir Richard Brooke of Norton Priory.

Eighteenth-century wives were not often party to the intricacies of their husbands' financial arrangements, and it seems unlikely that James Brindley would ever discuss his remuneration with Ann. She had sharp commercial instincts and after Robert Williamson died in 1799, she would take advantage of her financial independence as a widow to purchase part shares in mines and lime works, buy up property in Stoke and nurture a holding in the Williamson pottery business. Perhaps she was always shrewder about business than she was about relationships and James Brindley's dealings with the duke: hatching the idea of building an aqueduct in the early days at Worsley; worried talks of ways and means in remote pubs on Chat Moss, and the solemn and striking gift of the Bible, never entirely conformed to a business-like pattern. The powerful affinity between the two men, an improbable result of their shared canal vision, defied easy explanation, and quite possibly lay beyond Ann's apprehension.

Surveying

Since the business of surveying, both in the sense of looking over a likely canal route to ascertain its practicability and a more detailed taking and marking out the levels of each pound (the stretch of canal between locks), played a crucial and major a part in James Brindley's life at this time, it is worth reflecting briefly on what this work entailed. Indeed, Brindley regarded the surveyor's art as crucial to his work, and it is not accidental that his post on the Trent and Mersey Canal bore the title 'Surveyor General', not 'Engineer'.

With a canal that was emerging from the idea stage into a solid plan, the promoters (as a one-man-band promoter-cum-committee, the Duke of Bridgewater was an exception) would request an initial survey to get an idea of the possible route or, routes. Brindley appears to have made it his practice, before any application had been made to Parliament, to ride over the land through which the planned canal would cut making an 'eye-survey', or what he sometimes termed an 'ocular survey or a reconnitoring'. It played an important part in the preparation. Wedgwood, Bentley and Henshall in their *Biographica Britannica* account of Brindley's life call to mind his early career as a millwright, and observe that his memory,

> Was so remarkable, he often declared that he could remember, and execute, all the parts of the most complex machine, provided he had time in his survey of it, to settle in his mind the several departments, and their relations to each other.

Rides of reconnoitre presumably met a similar need within the context of Brindley's work as a canal engineer in allowing him to memorise and 'settle in his mind' the outline and topography of the country through which he proposed to cut before the chain and level work started. Quite possibly, he acted as an assistant that the promoters could produce when they applied to Parliament in order to show where they proposed to build.

In Francis Parsons's 1770 portrait (this book, illustration 4), Brindley has his surveyor's level to hand; to be more precise, he drapes his left hand over the telescope's brass barrel in a manner which makes much of his fine white shirt cuffs. Mounted parallel to the telescope is a spirit level above a brass circumferentor (a surveyor's compass with folding sights for taking bearings), and the whole ensemble is a subtle reminder of the dignity with which Brindley's skills had invested him.

At the same time, the painting creates its own fiction. Parsons's Brindley stands alone in an unpeopled landscape, monarch of all that he – quite literally – surveys, and while this solitude could be a fair reflection of conditions at the initial reconnoitre stage, taking the levels and establishing the differences in elevation along the canal's proposed line or lines could be a relatively sociable business. Outdoor work, it called for close cooperation between the engineer, his staff-holders, the chain men to measure distances, the on-site clerk and no doubt other assistants to transport the equipment, mark out the line with pegs or chalk and generally make themselves useful. Since it offered ample scope for on-the-spot learning, it was at the levelling stage that several of Brindley's deputies, assistants and pupils honed their skills. In February 1771, when newly appointed engineer of the proposed Chester Canal, Samuel Weston informed the House of Commons that he had 'been employed by Mr Brindley as a staff-holder, and in levelling', which evidently satisfied the House that was he well-qualified for his post.

In uncultivated country, the use and maintenance of surveying instruments required constant care. Over the focal plane of the level's telescopic sight so as to pinpoint the survey-target lay cross-hairs – not engraved lines, but genuine horse-hair positioned so as to be easily accessible for adjustment or replacement. As John Hammond, author of *The Practical Surveyor* (London, 1750), rather unnervingly observes, 'In taking the Theodolite thro' a hedge, it sometimes happens that a thorn or sprig catching the horse-hairs in the sights and breaks them.' The surveyor, he advises, should always 'have spare horse hairs ready, and a piece of dry stick to cut to a sharp point' with which to set them in place. Edmund Gunther (1581–1626), the mathematician who first devised the chain which bears his name, is also credited with introducing the decimal point as a separator in mathematical notation. His chain, fittingly, is a decimal instrument which made for ease of expression; each link, 7.92 inches, being a hundredth part of the length of the whole. Therefore, a measurement given as 4.20 links would be four chains and twenty links. Pegging out chain-stations involved hands-and-knees work over ground which might be either wet and muddy, or cold and unyielding. Robust as it might seem, the Gunther's chain which was used for measuring could not only tangle in storage, but also, as Hammond warns, in country 'where [there] are many furze bushes, thorns, or other short stuff', the links 'will be frequently bent, and the rings opened', or worse, broken. He advises therefore that 'a small hand-vice and a pair of nippers should be ready' for repairs in the field, adding that 'One of the chain-men may easily carry these articles in his pockets.' In theory, a measuring wheel, variously known as a way-wiser, pedometer or perambulator, might fulfil the same purpose as the chain and make for easier usage. In practice, it had the reputation of being less accurate. Besides, it would not have lent itself to use over rough ground, and how far it was used on early canal surveys is open to question. The survey party also needed staves by which to mark each survey station, each being typically about 10 feet long and marked out in sections. Hammond emphasises the wisdom of the surveyor's having 'pieces of tin or other white marks' with him, 'ready to fix on the top of the staves' in conditions of poor visibility. Wet weather could of course cause problems, although Hammond – always more concerned about the survey's outcome than the wellbeing of the survey team while work is in progress – remarks, 'industrious surveyor' would hardly 'leave the field for small mizzling rain'. On a practical note, he suggests that if conditions are so bad as to preclude the surveyor from making entries in his field book,

In ink, yet his observations may be entered with a black-lead pencil, and these wrote over with ink when he returns to his abode.

For transport of smaller and more fragile instruments, Peter Callan, a surveyor active in mid-eighteenth-century Drogheda, advocated purchasing a custom-made pair of saddlebags:

> Twenty inches in depth and twelve inches in width, with straps and loops for a hanging lock, and a long wooden case, with convenient clefts and concavities to slide in, and fix all ... sights, indexes, scales, and sliding compasses; a leather case with a wooden bottom for the box of the circumferentor ... a long leather case for a roll of paper

All which, together with the ball and sockets, screw pins, staves, chain and pins, pencils and colours can safely be kept and carried in the said saddle-bags. 'For the conveniency of travelling', he suggests stowing 'a few changes of linen, shoes and stockings' into the bags along with the instruments. It is counsel which perhaps offers a rather more credible, not to say graphic, commentary upon the conditions of James Brindley's life in the mid-1760s than Parsons's depiction of the engineer-surveyor looking as poised and polished as a country squire at his ease under a benign sky.

For further information about eighteenth-century surveying practice, Finnian O'Cionnaith's PhD thesis, *Land surveying in eighteenth and early nineteenth century Dublin* (Department of History, National University of Ireland Maynooth, April 2011, available online) gives a comprehensive and highly readable account of the subject.

Notes and References

A Note on James Brindley's manuscripts

Of James Brindley's manuscript notebooks that are known to survive in the public domain, the earliest, which covers 1755–58, is in the Brindley Mill in Leek. The notebooks which date respectively from 1759-60, September 1761–December 1762 and October–November 1763 are in the Archives of the Institution of Civil Engineers, London. Birmingham Reference Library holds a photo-stat copy of the 1755–58 manuscript, but its page order differs substantially from the original in Leek.

All four surviving notebooks have been transcribed and are available in printed form, published as Victoria Owens (ed.), *James Brindley's Notebooks* (Gloucester: Choir Press, 2013). For bibliographic convenience, the following notes section supplies page references to this edition.

Abbreviations

JHC: *Journals of the House of Commons*. Re-printed by the Order of House of Commons, 1803, available online digitised by Google.

JBN: *James Brindley's Notebooks*, Victoria Owens (ed.) (Gloucester: Choir Press, 2013).

CJW: *Correspondence of Josiah Wedgwood*, Katherine Eufemia Farrer (ed.), 3 vols. (1st edition published privately, 1903; reissued by Cambridge: Cambridge University Press, 2010)

Chapter One

1. *Journals of the House of Commons*, Reprinted by the Order of House of Commons, 1803, available online digitised by Google (JHC), Vol. 28, December 1757–March 1761, p. 335.
2. J. J. Phelps, 'The Romance of an Old Canal', BBC, 28 August 1925, (Manchester: Phelps Collection, Chetham's Library, unpublished notes for a lecture).
3. Abraham Rees, *Cyclopaedia*, V (1819). Entry for Brindley; the writer is probably John Farey (senior), 1766–1826.
4. For a summary of Brindley's work on mills and steam engines, see Victoria Owens, 'James Brindley's Notebooks, 1755–63: An Eighteenth-Century Engineer Writes About His Work', in *International Journal for the History of Engineering & Technology*, 83, No. 2 (2013), pp. 222–256.

5. Victoria Owens (ed.), *James Brindley's Notebooks* (Gloucester: Choir Press, 2013), (JBN), pp. 10–12.

6. Arnold Bennett, 'The Making of Me' first published in the *Daily Express*, 6 June 1928, repr. *Arnold Bennett: Sketches for Autobiography*, James Hepburn (ed.) (London: George Allen & Unwin, 1979), p. 2.

7. Christine Richardson, 'James Brindley (1716–72): His Simultaneous Commercial Development of Mills, Steam Power and Canals', *Transactions of the Newcomen Society*, 76 (2006), pp. 251–258.

8. Patent No. 730, 1758.

9. Andrew Kippis (ed.), *Biographica Britannica* (1778–93). The entry for Brindley, for which Hugh Henshall provided the information, comes in vol. 2 (1780).

10. Thomas Broade, *A New Scheme for Making Inland Navigations* (London, 1758).

11. Samuel Smiles, *James Brindley and the Early Engineers* (London: John Murray, 1864), p. 142.

12. A. G. Banks and R. B. Schofield, *Brindley at Wet Earth Colliery: An Engineering Study* (Newton Abbot: David & Charles, 1968), p. 143.

13. Recent research suggests that Clifton Colliery in the mid-1750s may not have belonged to the Heathcote family after all. (Author's conversation with staff at Clifton Country Park Visitor Centre, May 2015.)

14. JBN (2013), p. 53.

15. Bridgewater Estate Accounts, June 1759–December 1760, Northamptonshire Records Office, ref. EB 1459/3.

16. Hugh Malet, *Bridgewater: The Canal Duke, 1736-1803* (Manchester: Manchester University Press, 1977), p. 16.

17. Francis Egerton, Earl of Ellesmere, 'Aqueducts and Canals' (untitled and anonymous) in the *Quarterly Review*, LXXIII, No. CXLVI (1844), pp. 281–324. The article also appears with its title in Lord Ellesmere's *Essays on history, biography, geography, engineering, &c.* contributed to the 'Quarterly Review' (London: John Murray, 1858), pp. 201–251.

18. Malet, *Bridgewater*, p. 4.

19. *Biographica Britannica*, II (1780), entry for Brindley; John Aikin, *A Description of the country form thirty to forty miles round Manchester* (1795), p. 139 and Smiles (1864), p. 310.

20. Hugh Malet, *The Canal Duke*, (Newton Abbot: David & Charles, 1961), p. 71. Given source J. H. D. M. Campbell, 'Notes on James Brindley', *Derbyshire Miscellany*, II, February 1959. (NB: Malet (1977) does not specifically mention the Duke's gift, but see note 21 below.)

21. James Brindley's Bible came up for sale at an auction of rare books by Dominic Winter (Auctioneers) of Cirencester on 15 May 2013.

Chapter Two

1. Hugh Malet, 'Brindley and Canals', *History Today*, 23, Issue 4, (4 April 1973); *The Canal Duke* (Dawlish: David & Charles, 1961); *Bridgewater: The Canal Duke, 1736–1803* (Manchester: Manchester University Press, 1977)

2. '... his grace has found so large a Mine of Coal, for which he has so small a consumption, that he is inclinable to make a water road from Worsley Mill to Salford, at his own expence, by which means he will be able to supply Manchester at much cheaper rate.' Malet, *Bridgewater*, p. 32; given source, undated letter of 1758 from Francis Reynold of Strangeways to Edward Chetham.

3. Peter Lead, *Agents of Revolution: John and Thomas Gilbert – Entrepreneurs* (Keele: University of Keele Centre for Local History, 1989), p. 21.

4. Entry for Granville Leveson-Gower, 2nd Earl Gower, Marquis of Stafford (1721–1803), www.revolutionaryplayers.org.uk

5. Malet, *Bridgewater*, p. 115.

6. Michael Chrimes and Susan Hots argue that although 'works of a civil engineering character' (Stonehenge and the Roman road network among them) had been carried out long before the second half of the eighteenth century, Smeaton's 'decision to describe himself as a "civil engineer"' nevertheless played a crucial part in nurturing 'a sense of a new profession'. See Michael Chrime's and Susan Hot's 'Perceptions of Great Engineers II: John Rogers? John Reynolds? John Smeaton? Who Was Britain's First Civil Engineer?', Institution of Civil Engineers, retrieved from www.ice.org.uk, undated, pp. 1, 15.

7. Sir Joseph Banks, *Journal of an Excursion to Wales, Etc., 1767–68* (Cambridge University Library Additional Ms Add. 6294), p. 107.

8. Patent No. 730, 26 December 1758.

9. *Reports of the late John Smeaton, FRS, made on various occasions in the course of his employment as a civil engineer*, I (London: Longman, 1812), pp. 13–16. For Brindley's marriage bond, see Kathleen Evans, *James Brindley, Canal Engineer: A New Perspective* (Leek: Churnet Valley Books, 2007), p. 51.

10. Malet, *Bridgewater*, p. 107.

11. Patent No. 730, 1758.

12. JHC, 28, 1757–1761, pp. 739–40.

13. Ibid.

14. Samuel Hughes, 'Memoir of James Brindley', *Weale's Quarterly Papers on Engineering*, I (1844), p. 47.

15. Ibid.

16. JBN (2013), p. 58.

17. *The Gentleman's Magazine*, XXX, (1760), p. 623. Letter from 'R.W.'

18. Entries for 9 and 16 May 1761 in Bridgewater Estate Accounts, December 1760–February 1762, Chetham's Library, Manchester (unclassified).

19. Entries for 31 May and 20 September 1760, Bridgewater Estate Accounts, June 1759–December 1760, Northamptonshire Records Office, E (B) 1459.

20. See for example 24 December 1762, Bridgewater Estate Payments Book, April 1762–January 1763, Salford University Library Special Collections, DBA/11/549.

21. *London Gazette*, 9 December 1760, p. 7.

22. Smiles, *James Brindley and the Early Engineers*, p. 173.

23. In his will, he would leave £8,000 for the publication of the 'Bridgewater Treatises' – essays written to explore 'the power, wisdom and goodness of God as manifested in Creation.'

24. Strachan Holme, *The Life of the Most Noble Francis Egerton, Third Duke of Bridgewater* (incomplete typescript), Salford University Library Special Collections, DBA/9/524.

25. For Egerton's Brindley stories, see The Hon. Francis Henry Egerton, *A Letter to the Parisians and the French Nation upon Inland Navigation containing a Defence of the Public Character of his Grace Francis Egerton, late Duke of Bridgewater, and including some notices and anecdotes concerning Mr. James Brindley.* (Paris, 1820), Part II passim, but esp. pp. 61–99.

26. Malet, *The Canal Duke*, p. 68. In the 1977 edition, the passage does not appear.

27. Letter from William Brown to John Hussey Delaval, 9 September 1759, Northumberland Record Office, 2DE/6/3/2.

28. Quoted by Malet, *Bridgewater*, p. 13.

29. Egerton, *A Letter to the Parisians*, p. 61.

30. Glen Atkinson, *Barton's Bridges* (Manchester: Neil Richardson, 2002), p. 18.

31. Quoted by H. P. Richards, *William Edwards: Architect, Builder, Minister* (Pontypridd: Pontypridd Museum, 2006), p. 27, given source National Library of Wales, MS 2049B (Panton 84).

32. Smiles, *James Brindley and the Early Engineers*, p. 182.

33. See this book, Chapter Eight.

34. JBN (2013), p. 92 and Bridgewater Estates Payment Book, April 1762–Dec 1763, Salford University Library, Special Collections, DBA/11/549.

35. Sir Joseph Banks, *Journal of an Excursion to Wales, Etc., 1767–68*, Cambridge University Library, MS Add 6294 (2).

36. *Gentleman's Magazine*, 31 (1761), p. 613.

Chapter Three

1. Christine Richardson, *James Brindley: Canal Pioneer* (Burton-on-Trent: Waterways World, 2004), p. 33.

2. Thomas Broade, *A New Scheme for Making Inland Navigations* (London: Printed for R. Griffiths, 1758) esp. pp. 1, 2 and 11.

3. JBN (2013), p. 73.

4. Bridgewater Estates Accounts, December 1760–February 1762, Chetham's Library, Manchester (unclassified). Entry dated 28 November 1761.

5. JHC, 29 (1761–64), p. 43.

6. Ibid.

7. JHC, 29 (1761–64), p. 107, 115.

8. Ibid, p. 169.

9. JHC, 29, (1761–64), 20 Jan 1762, p. 107.

10. Papers of Mary, Countess of Stamford, EGR 3/7/2/1/7, John Rylands Library, Manchester.

11. JBN, pp. 72, 79.

12. Ibid, p. 82.

13. Ibid, p. 80.

14. Entry for Brindley, *Biographica Britannica*, II (1780) and Christine Richardson's email to author, Dec. 2013.

15. Entry for Brindley, *Biographica Britannica*, II (1780).

16. JBN, pp. 102–129, which preserves the spelling and, so far as possible, layout of Brindley's manuscript.

17. Richardson, *James Brindley: Canal Pioneer*, p. 53.

18. Foulkes' map of 1799 shows the aqueduct and gives the span of the arch as 63.9 feet, and the depth from the bottom to the top of the arch as 14 feet 7 inches.

19. See previous chapter; also Smiles, *James Brindley and the Early Engineers*, p. 209 and Egerton, *A Letter to the Parisians*, p. 66.

20. Sir Joseph Banks 'Journal of an Excursion of Wales, etc. 1767–68', Cambridge University Library, ref. Add Ms 6294.

21. By this time, Brindley was apparently lodging in 'a cottage at the top of Pennington Lane' in Stretford. (H. T. Crofton, *History of the Ancient Chapel of Stretford* (Manchester: Chetham Society, 1899), p. 28.

22. Malet, *The Canal Duke*, p. 99 and *Bridgewater*, p. 97.

23. Hugh Potter, 'Brindley Gates', *NarrowBoat* [sic] (Spring 2010), pp. 10–14.

24. Arthur Young, *A Six Month Tour through the North of England* (1770), p. 6.

25. For Banks' description of the ice-breaker, see Chapter Eight, p. 86.

26. Malet, *The Canal Duke*, p. 84; Nick Corble, *James Brindley – the First Canal Builder*, (Stroud: Tempus, 2005), p. 91.

27. Malet, *The Canal Duke*, p. 82.

28. Ibid, pp. 82–6.

29. Malet, *The Canal Duke*, p. 98 and Corble, *James Brindley – the First Canal Builder*, p. 89.

30. Smiles, *James Brindley and the Early Engineers*, pp. 221–222.

31. John Rennie, *The Autobiography of Sir John Rennie* (London & New York: E. & F. N. Spon, 1875) pp. 237–38; Smiles, *James Brindley and the Early Engineers*, p. 220.

Chapter Four

1. John Phillips, *A General History of Inland Navigation* (London, 1792; fifth edition 1805), p. 522.

2. Brindley visited the Don in June and September 1762. (JBN pp. 87, 94–5).

3. Richardson, *James Brindley: Canal Pioneer*, p. 50.

4. Charles Hadfield, *The Canals of Yorkshire and North East England*, I (Newton Abbot: David & Charles, 1972), p. 77 and http://www.rotherhamunofficial.co.uk/

5. Richardson, *James Brindley: Canal Pioneer*, p. 51.

6. Hadfield, *The Canals of Yorkshire and North East England*, p. 77.

7. River Dun [sic] Navigation Company. Minutes of General and Committee Meetings, 1759–1771. National Archives, ref. RAIL 825/5, 24 June, 1762.

8. Hadfield, *The Canals of Yorkshire and North East England*, pp. 76–77 and RAIL 825/5 14 August 1760.
9. RAIL 825/5, 24 June, 1762.
10. Hadfield, *The Canals of Yorkshire and North East England*, p. 78 and RAIL 825/5. Meeting 25 October 1770.
11. Richardson, *James Brindley: Canal Pioneer*, p. 51 and JNB (2013), p. 94.
12. Richardson, *James Brindley: Canal Pioneer*, p. 51.
13. RAIL 825/5, 11 August 1763.
14. Ibid.
15. JBN, pp. 102–3.
16. Entry for George Perrott in the *Dictionary of National Biography* (Oxford: Oxford University Press, 1900 edition).
17. Entry for Andrew Yarranton in the *Biographical Dictionary of Civil Engineers*, I, ed. Sir Alec Skempton et al, (London: Thomas Telford, 2002).
18. Details of the history of the Lower Avon Navigation from http://www.avonnavigationtrust.org/
19. Sir James A. Picton, *City of Liverpool Municipal Archives and Records from 1760–1835* (Liverpool: G. Warmeley, 1886), p. 243.
20. *Biographica Britannica*, II (1780), entry for Brindley.
21. T. S. Willan, *The Navigation of the River Weaver in the Eighteenth Century* (Manchester: Chetham Society, 1951), p. 20.
22. Ibid, p. 83.
23. Ibid, p. 72.
24. Ibid, p. 84.
25. Ibid.
26. Ibid, p. 84, given source, George Heron to Sir Peter Warburton, 18 October 1764, Arley MSS, John Rylands Library, Manchester.
27. Willan, *The Navigation of the River Weaver*, p. 85.
28. Charles Hadfield, *The Canals of Yorkshire and North East England*, 1, (Newton Abbot: David & Charles, 1972), p. 53.
29. West Yorkshire Archives Service's website provides a concise history of the Calder and Hebble Navigation in www.wyjs.org.uk/archives-online-catalogue. Unfortunately no source for Smeaton's statement is given.
30. Hadfield, *The Canals of Yorkshire and North East England*, p. 48.
31. John Watson, *The History and Antiquities of the Parith [sic] of Halifax* (1775), p. 15.
32. Calder and Hebble Navigation Minute Book, National Archives ref. RAIL 815/4, 6 December 1764.
33. Ibid, 31 January 1765.
34. Hadfield, *The Canals of Yorkshire and North East England*, p. 51.
35. JBN, pp. 54, 78.
36. *Reports of the late John Smeaton, FRS., made on various occasions …*, II (London, 1812), p. 115.
37. *Leeds Intelligencer*, 5 March 1765. Charles Hadfield mentions the same, or a very similar, advertisement appearing in the Liverpool-based *Williamson's Advertiser and Mercantile Gazette* (actually *Chronicle*). Hadfield, *The Canals of Yorkshire and North East England*, p. 51, n. 25.

38. Richardson, *James Brindley: Canal Pioneer*, p. 57.
39. *Manchester Mercury*, 23 December 1765.
40. www.myrochdalecanal.org.uk/canal-history
41. www.myrochdalecanal.org.uk/canal-history
42. Hadfield, *The Canals of Yorkshire and North East England*, p. 51.
43. *Leeds Intelligencer*, 1 December 1767.
44. *Leeds Intelligencer*, 15 October, 1776.
45. Letter from James Brindley (not in his own hand) dated 13 September 1766, 'Minutes of the Commissioners of the Loughborough Navigation', National Archives ref. RAIL 849/1.

Chapter Five

1. 'Don't you think we shall set the Trent on fire amongst us?' Josiah Wedgwood to Thomas Bentley, 31 March 1768. Katherine Eufemia Farrer (ed.), *Correspondence of Josiah Wedgwood* (first published privately, 1903, this edition Cambridge: Cambridge University Press, 2010), CJW, I, p. 213.
2. Josiah Wedgwood to John Wedgwood, 1 February 1765. CJW, I, p. 26.
3. Josiah Wedgwood to John Wedgwood, 11 March 1765. CJW, I, p. 37.
4. Eliza Meteyard, *The Life of Josiah Wedgwood from his Private Correspondence*, 1 (London: Hurst & Blackett, 1865), p. 281.
5. JBN, p. 51.
6. Kathleen Evans, *James Brindley – Canal Engineer: A New Perspective* (Leek: Churnet Valley Books, 2007), p. 95.
7. Wedgwood to Bentley, 10 April 1768, CJW, I, pp. 214–5
8. Josiah Wedgwood to John Wedgwood, 3 April 1765, CJW, I, p. 41.
9. Ibid.
10. Samuel Garbett to Josiah Wedgwood, 18 April 1765, V&A/Wedgwood Collection. Presented by the Art Fund with major support from the Heritage Lottery Fund, private donations and a public appeal, Barlaston, Stoke-on-Trent. Barlaston Online Archive, ref. E25-18075.
11. Josiah Wedgwood to Erasmus Darwin, 15 April, 1765, CJW, III, p. 229.
12. Wedgwood to Darwin, 4 May 1765 with enclosure, CJW, III, pp. 236–40.
13. Willan, *The Navigation of the River Weaver*, p. 90.
14. Wedgwood to Darwin, 16 May 1765 with enclosure, CJW, III, pp. 242–3.
15. Wedgwood to Darwin, no date, but probably late May 1765, CJW, III, p. 244.
16. Josiah Wedgwood to John Wedgwood, 6 July 1765, CJW, I, pp. 46–8.
17. Wedgwood to Bentley 1 August 1765, and to John Wedgwood, 7 August 1765. CJW, I, pp. 48–50 and 52–3.
18. Entry for Ann Radcliffe in *The Cambridge Guide to Women's Writing in English* Lorna Sage (ed.) et al, (Cambridge: Cambridge University Press, 1999).
19. Wedgwood to Bentley, 26 and 27 September 1765, CJW, I, pp. 54–8.
20. Samuel Garbett to the Secretary of the Society of Arts, nd, October 1765, CJW, III, p. 263.

21. Wedgwood to Bentley, 2 November 1765, CJW, I, p. 66.

22. Wedgwood to Bentley, 12 December 1765 CJW, I, p. 69.

23. Ibid, p. 70.

24. Ibid. Grose defines 'TO HUM, or HUMBUG' as 'To deceive, or impose on one by some story or device. A humbug; a jocular imposition, or deception. To hum and haw; to hesitate in speech, also to delay, or be with difficulty brought to consent to any matter or business.' Francis Grose, *A Dictionary of the Vulgar Tongue*, (1811).

25. Wedgwood to Bentley, undated continuation of letter begun on 12 December 1765, CJW, I, p. 73.

26. Ibid, pp. 74–5.

27. Wedgwood to Bentley, 28 September 1772, CJW, I, p. 490; Samuel Johnson, *A Dictionary of the English Language*, (1755), definitions of 'sensible' Nos 5, 6 and 7.

28. Wedgwood to Bentley, 2 January 1765. CJW, I, pp. 19–24. The autograph letter is dated '2nd January, 1765' which, in respect of the year, seems unlikely. From Wedgwood's remark: '... everyone join'd in the opinion that if we had not met that evening at Lichfield, nothing could have been done at Wolsley Bridge', it looks as though he wrote the letter after the Wolseley Bridge meeting of 30 December 1765, and made an understandable slip over the ear date at the start of January 1766. Jenny Uglow evidently shares the view that the Lichfield encounter immediately preceded the Wolseley Bridge meeting, remarking how 'That evening' – 30 December 1765 – Wedgwood 'persuaded Gower to back him, and next day his scheme was adopted by a big public meeting.' Jenny Uglow, *The Lunar Men* (London: Faber, 2002), p. 111.

29. In other words, from the landed gentry. After 1732, MPs had to have an estate of £100 pa. Roy Porter, *English Society in the Eighteenth Century* (Harmondsworth: Penguin, 1982), p. 138.

30. Wedgwood to Bentley, 2 January 1765 (probably 1766; see this chapter note 28), CJW, I, p. 21.

31. *Leeds Intelligencer*, 14 January, 1766. Near-identical reports appear in the *Stamford Mercury*, *Oxford Journal* and London-based *Gazetteer and New Daily Advertiser*.

32. John Stafford, solicitor of Macclesfield, to Samuel Wright of Knutsford, 3 January 1766, Weaver Navigation Papers, John Rylands Library, Manchester (unclassified); transcription in Willan, *The Navigation of the River Weaver*, pp. 199–204.

33. *The Liverpool Directory*, 1766 (available online). There is, in Liverpool, both a Tarleton Street and a Colquitt Street.

34. Willan, *The Navigation of the River Weaver*, p. 200.

35. *Reports of the late John Smeaton, FRS., made on various occasions* ..., I (London, 1812), pp. 14–15.

36. *JCH*, 30, (1765–1766), p. 649.

37. *Seasonable Considerations on a Navigable Canal Intended to be cut from the River TRENT, at WILDEN FERRY, in the County of DERBY, to the River MERSEY in the County of CHESTER* (1766), pp. 38–9.

38. Ibid, p. 33.

39. *Supplement to a Pamphlet entitled, Seasonable Considerations on a Navigable Canal Intended to be cut from the River TRENT, at WILDEN FERRY, in the County of DERBY, to the River MERSEY in the County of CHESTER* (1766), p. 55.
40. Ibid.

Chapter Six

1. Malet, *The Canal Duke*, p. 35 and *Bridgewater*, p. 19.
2. Malet, *The Canal Duke*, p. 161–2; *Bridgewater*, pp. 157–8 and www.nationalgallery.org.uk
3. Malet, *The Canal Duke*, p. 37 and *Bridgewater*, p. 21.
4. In answer to an enquiry from a Mr C. M. Prior in January 1934, E. Galen Thompson, Lord Ellesmere's librarian, stated that the 'only known sale by the Duke of Bridgewater of his horses took place on 18 June 1764'. (Duke of Bridgewater Archive, University of Salford, Special Collections ref. DBA 1/12).
5. *Ipswich Journal*, 13 April 1765.
6. *Ipswich Journal*, 26 October 1765.
7. Jane Brown, *The Omnipotent Magician – Lancelot 'Capability' Brown 1716–1783* (London: Chatto & Windus, 2011), pp. 160, 187.
8. www.HistoryofParliamentonline.org.
9. Ibid.
10. Quoted by Malet, *Bridgewater*, p. 106.
11. JBN, p. 94.
12. Christopher Lewis, *The Canal Pioneers – Brindley's School of Engineers* (Stroud: History Press, 2011), p. 39.
13. Meteyard, *The Life of Josiah Wedgwood*, pp. 198, 199.
14. Information about the Henshalls' copy of Browne's *Ars Pictoria* from www.maggs.com the website of Maggs Bros, Ltd, Antiquarian Bookdealers, Stock Code: EA9275.
15. Willan, *The Navigation of the River Weaver*, pp. 90, 197; also this book, Chapter Five.
16. Manuscript note giving measurements, descriptions and values of land. University of Salford Library, Special Collections, ref. DBA 2/130.
17. Wedgwood to Bentley, 13 June 1767, CJW, I, p. 156.
18. For example Richardson *James Brindley: Canal Pioneer*, p. 69 and Corble, *James Brindley – the First Canal Builder*, p. 100.
19. Smiles, *James Brindley and the Early Engineers*, pp. 285–6.
20. Ibid and Lewis, *The Canal Pioneers*, p. 50.
21. Josiah Wedgwood to Ralph Griffiths, 21 December 1767. CJW, I, p. 192.
22. Quoted by Malet, *Bridgewater*, p. 114, given source, Sutherland Estate Papers, Mertoun. Sir Henry Mainwaring, 4th Baronet Mainwaring of Over-Peover (1726–1797), had travelled with Lord Grey of Stamford on his grand tour.
23. Entry for Hester Bateman in Wikipedia.
24. 'Patriotic America: Henshall & Co.' on www.americanhistoricalstaffordshire.com and

Astbury Lime Works Archive in www.mowcop.info/htm/industry/limeworksdocuments.

25. *Oxford Journal,* 19 February 1768.

26. Wedgwood to Bentley, 22 February 1768, CJW, I, p. 203.

27. Gordon Emery`, *The Old Chester Canal – a history and guide* (Chester: Chester Canal Heritage Trust, 2005), p. 16.

28. Joanna Clark, 'Quaker Silhouettes', *The Friend* (28 July 2011).

29. Wedgwood to Bentley, 18 September 1772, CJW, I, pp. 484–5

30. Ibid.

31. National Archives, Kew, ref. PROB 31/657.

32. Amanda Vickery, *Behind Closed Doors: At Home in Georgian England* (New Haven & London: Yale, 2009, p. 214.

33. Despite the name, 'Scotch carpets' appear to have been a staple of the eighteenth-century Kidderminster manufacture. Heather Tetley, '18th Century British Floor Coverings' in www.buildingconservation.com.

34. Dr Johnson's *Dictionary of the English Language* (1755) defines 'cosier' as a 'botcher' that is, a cobbler, although it is easy to see how the word might also signify a saddler. It is possible that the term may also have transferred itself to one of the tools of the trade.

Chapter Seven

1. Bridgewater Estates Payments Book, 5 November 1766, Salford University Library, Special Collections ref. DBA11/548.

2. The sections of this chapter which deal with the Staffordshire and Worcestershire Canal draw extensively on Peter Cross-Rudkin's paper, 'Constructing the Staffordshire and Worcestershire Canal, 1766–72', *Transactions of the Newcomen Society*, 75 (2005), pp. 289–304.

3. *Derby Mercury*, 31 January 1766.

4. Malet, *Bridgewater*, p. 115.

5. General Account Book of the Chief Agent with the Duke of Bridgewater, Northamptonshire Records Office ref E (B)/1460, entry for 28 October 1766.

6. Thomas Congreve, *A scheme or, proposal for making a navigable communication between the rivers of Trent and Severn, in the county of Stafford* (London, 1717).

7. Cross-Rudkin, *Constructing the Staffordshire and Worcestershire Canal*, pp. 289–90, given source ICE Archives, Tract 8vo 25.

8. *JCH*, 30, (1765–66), p. 574

9. Ibid, p. 675.

10. Ibid, p. 675.

11. Ibid, p. 453.

12. Ibid, p. 522.

13. Ibid, p. 668.

14. Ibid, p. 686.

15. www.historyofparliamentonline.org/volume/1754-90/members Entry for Dunning.

16. Manuscript Journal of the House of Lords, Session 1765–66, 17 Dec 1765–10 Sept 1766, Parliamentary Archives, HL/PO/JO/1/137.
17. Smiles, *James Brindley and the Early Engineers*, pp. 226, 7.
18. Charles W. Ingrao, *The Hessian Mercenary State* (Cambridge: Cambridge University Press, 2003), pp. 63, 64.
19. *Leeds Intelligencer*, 14 January 1766.
20. Smiles, *James Brindley and the Early Engineers*, p. 227
21. Ingrao, *The Hessian Mercenary State*, pp. 63, 64.
22. David Patten, www.Taskscape wordpress blog 17 August 2011, and 'Notes re Stourport on Severn, www.davidpatten.co.uk.
23. Cross-Rudkin, *Constructing the Staffordshire and Worcestershire Canal*, p. 293 (c. f. this chapter, note 2).
24. John Fennyhouse Green, 'Orders from Mr Brindley', Staffordshire and Worcestershire Canal, 1767–71, Staffordshire Records Office, ref. 6898/2/4, 5 March 1768.
25. Staffordshire Records Office, ref. 6898/2/7, 9 January 1769.
26. Staffordshire Records Office, ref. 6898/2/9, 20 September 1770.
27. Richardson, *James Brindley: Canal Pioneer*, p. 57.
28. Lewis, *The Canal Pioneers*, p. 103, given source, Minutes of the Staffordshire & Worcestershire Canal Company.
29. William D. Klemperer and Paul Sillitoe, *James Brindley at Turnhurst Hall: An Archaeological and Historical Investigation* (Stoke-on-Trent: City Museum & Art Gallery, 1995), p. 16.
30. L. T. C. Rolt, *Navigable Waterways* (London: Longman, 1969), p. 40.
31. Ibid.
32. 'A brief history of the Droitwich Canals' on www.droitwichcanals.co.uk.
33. Staffordshire Record Office, ref 6898/2/3, 20 July – 1 December 1767,
34. Brown, *The Omnipotent Magician*, p. 189.
35. Staffordshire Records Office, ref 6898/2/7, 3 May 1769.
36. H. W. Gwilliam, 'Redstone Crossing', Worcestershire History Encyclopaedia online.
37. Brian Stephens, 'Orchards in the Manor of Bewdley in 1749', *Wyre Forest Study Group Review 2008*, pp. 32–35 and C. W. F. Garrett, 'Bewdley and the Stinking Ditch' in Laurence Silvester Snell (ed.), *Essays Towards a History of Bewdley* (Bewdley: Bewdley Research Group, 1972), pp. 1–14, esp. pp. 12–13.
38. Garrett, *Bewdley and the Stinking Ditch*, p. 7.
39. Staffordshire Record Office ref. 6898/2/4, 15 June 1768.
40. Staffordshire Record Office ref. 6898/2/6, 27 October 1768.
41. Ibid.

Chapter Eight

1. Patricia Pierce, *Old London Bridge* (London: Hodder Headline, 2001), pp. 258 and 268.
2. *Gentleman's Magazine*, 37 (1767), p. 337.

3. Ibid, p. 338.

4. Ibid.

5. *Leeds Intelligencer*, 26 July 1768.

6. JBN (2013), p. 5 and Mary Dobson, 'The History of Malaria in England', http://malaria.wellcome.ac.uk.

7. Wedgwood to Bentley, 26 September 1772, CJW, I, p. 489; Erasmus Darwin, *Zoonomia; or, the Laws of Organic Life*, Part I (London: 1794), p. 311.

8. Wedgwood to Bentley, 2 March 1767, CJW, I, p. 122.

9. The Institution of Civil Engineers holds a copy of Whitworth's Report, *A Plan and Estimates of the Intended Navigation from Lough-Neagh to Belfast, as Surveyed by Mr. Robert Whitworth: Together with His Report, Concerning the Best Method of Executing the Work. Presented to the Local Committee at Hillsborough, August 24, 1768; and Approved by Mr. James Brindley, Engineer* (Herbert and Robert Joy, 1770), ref. WHI/PE1,T8V/73. ICE.

10. *Aris's Birmingham Gazette*, 5 Sept 1767; *Derby Mercury*, 18 September 1767 and *Jopson's Coventry Mercury*, 28 September 1767.

11. *Derby Mercury*, 25 September 1767.

12. Erasmus Darwin, *Zoonomia* (1794), p. 317.

13. Wedgwood to Bentley, 8 September 1767, CJW, I, pp. 168–9.

14. Wedgwood to Bentley, 2 March 1767, CJW, I, p. 121.

15. *Derby Mercury*, 11 September 1767 and Anthony C. Wood, 'The Diaries of Sir Roger Newdigate', *Essays in Honour of Philip B. Chatwin* (Oxford: Oxford University Press, 1962), pp. 40–54, at p. 45. Given source, manuscript diary of Sir Roger Newdigate, 3 September 1767.

16. JHC, 31 (11 November 1766 to 10 March 1768), p. 427.

17. JHC, 31, p. 488; Charles Hadfield, *The Canals of the East Midlands* (Newton Abbot: David & Charles, 1970), p. 15 and Evans, *James Brindley – Canal Engineer*, pp. 7, 119–20.

18. Wedgwood to Bentley, 17 December 1767, CJW, I, p. 191.

19. Wedgwood to Bentley, 24 December 1767, CJW, I, pp. 195–196. The emphases are Wedgwood's.

20. Ibid.

21. Bridgewater Estate payments book, November 1766–September 1769, Duke of Bridgewater Archive, University of Salford Library Special Collections, Ref. DBA /11/548.

22. *Caledonian Mercury*, 24 October 1767.

23. John Gilbert to Thomas Gilbert, 25 November 1767, Salford University Library, Special Collections ref. DBA/12/556.

24. Christine Richardson's email to author, May 2015, and article 'Cold Weather Masonry', www.masonrymagazine.com.

25. Joseph Banks, 'Journal of an excursion to Wales, etc., 1767–68', Cambridge University Library, GBR/0012/MS Add. 6294.

26. Wedgwood to Bentley, 25 December 1767, CJW, I, p. 197.

27. Wedgwood to Bentley, 22 Feb, 1768. CJW, p. 203.

28. Wedgwood to Bentley, 16 January 1769, CJW, I, p. 242.

29. *Oxford Journal*, 27 February 1768.

30. Minutes of the Coventry Canal Company, National Archives ref RAIL 818/1, 27 December 1768.

31. RAIL 818/1, 6 June 1769.

32. RAIL 818/1, 16 May 1769.

33. W. B. Stephens (ed.), *A History of the County of Warwick*, 8, 'The City of Coventry and Borough of Warwick', Victoria County History Series (Oxford: Oxford University Press, 1969), pp. 34–39.

34. Wood, *The Diaries of Sir Roger Newdigate*, p. 46. Given source, manuscript diary of Sir Roger Newdigate, 4 February 1769.

35. Hugh Compton, *The Oxford Canal* (Newton Abbot: David & Charles, 1976), pp. 11, 14.

36. Minutes of the Oxford Canal Company, 12 May 1769–28 June 1775, National Archives ref. RAIL 855/2. Cyril Boucher, *James Brindley, Engineer 1716-1772* (Norwich: Goose & Son, 1968), pp. 75–76.

37. Jan Morris, *The Oxford Book of Oxford* (Oxford: Oxford University Press, 1978), p. 222.

38. Anthony Burton, *The Canal Builders* (Newton Abbot: David & Charles, 1972), p. 103.

39. JHC, 31, p. 432 and this chapter, note 17.

40. JHC, 32, (10 May 1768–25 September 1769), pp. 221, 238.

41. Charles Hadfield, *The Canals of the East Midlands* (Newton Abbot: David & Charles, 1970), p. 19. JHC, 32, pp. 659, 719.

42. Boucher, *James Brindley, Engineer 1716-1772*, p. 101.

43. RAIL 855/2, 1 September 1769.

44. Ibid.

45. RAIL 855/2, 26 July 1770.

46. RAIL 855/2, 10 August 1770.

47. RAIL 855/2, copy letter dated 12 September 1770.

48. *Caledonian Mercury*, 21 September 1768.

49. Malet, *Bridgewater*, pp. 98, 109 – who erroneously names the Danish monarch as 'Christian VI' and dates his visit to 1778 (p. 89).

50. Arthur Young, *A Six Months Tour through the North of England*, III, Letter XIX (London, 1770). In his autobiography, Young dates the tour to 1768. (Matilda Betham Edwards (ed.), *The Autobiography of Arthur Young* (London: Smith, Elder & Co., 1898), p.49).

51. Smiles, *James Brindley and the Early Engineers*, p. 204.

52. John Aldred, 'Ingenious Devices', in Michael Nevell and Terry Wyke (eds.) *Bridgewater 250: The Archaeology of the World's First Industrial Canal* (Salford: University of Salford 2011), p. 25; Young, *A Six Months Tour through the North of England*, p. 278.

53. Aldred, *Ingenious Devices*, p. 26.

54. This book, Chapter Three.

55. Willan, *The Navigation of the River Weaver*, p. 93.

56. Banks, *Journal* (1767–68).

57. W. H. Chaloner, 'James Brindley (1716-72) and his remuneration as a canal engineer', *Transactions of the Lancashire and Cheshire Antiquarian Society*, 75 and 76 (1965–6), pp. 226-8.

Chapter Nine

1. JBN (2013), p. 81.
2. JCH, 31, p. 428.
3. JCH, 31, pp. 433, 558.
4. Richardson, *James Brindley: Canal Pioneer*, p. 87.
5. Ibid, given source *A Guide to the Droitwich Canals*, (Droitwich: Droitwich Canals Trust, 2000), p. 30.
6. William D. Klemperer and Paul J. Sillitoe, *James Brindley at Turnhurst Hall: An archaeological and historical investigation* (Stoke-on-Trent: City Museum and Art Gallery, 1995); *Staffordshire Archaeological Studies*, No. 6, p. 17. See also Max Sinclair 'Droitwich Canals' www.canalworld.net/forums (History and Heritage), 16 June 2011.
7. *Bath Chronicle and Weekly Gazette*, 18 June 1767.
8. S. R. Broadbridge, *The Birmingham Canal Navigations*, 1, 1768–1846 (Newton Abbot: David & Charles, 1974), p. 14.
9. Ibid, p.17, given source, *Aris's Birmingham Gazette*, 29 February, 14 March and 4 April 1768.
10. Minutes of the Birmingham Canal Navigation Company, 1767–71, National Archives, ref. RAIL 810/1, 12 February 1768.
11. RAIL 810/1, 2 March 1768.
12. RAIL 810/1, 9 June 1768.
13. Ibid.
14. Broadbridge, *The Birmingham Canal Navigations*, p. 83.
15. Alexander Carlyle, *Autobiography* (Edinburgh and London: William Blackwood, 1860), p. 366.
16. JBN (2013), p. 81.
17. Richardson, *James Brindley: Canal Pioneer*, p. 85 and T. J. Dowds, *The Forth and Clyde Canal* (East Linton: Tuckwell Press, 2003), pp. 30, 31.
18. Broadbridge, *The Birmingham Canal Navigations*, pp.17, 19. Given source, *Aris's Birmingham Gazette*, 17 October 1768.
19. Broadbridge, *The Birmingham Canal Navigations*, pp. 20, 21.
20. Broadbridge, *The Birmingham Canal Navigations*, p. 21. Given source, letter from 'Z, – a proprietor', *Warwickshire Journal*, 21 December 1769.
21. RAIL 810/1, 17 November 1769.
22. Broadbridge, *The Birmingham Canal Navigations*, p. 18.
23. RAIL 810/1, 27 April 1770.
24. RAIL 810/1, 16 August 1770.
25. Broadbridge, *The Birmingham Canal Navigations*, p. 23, citing ii Geo III, cap. 67 and JHC, 33, November 1770–November 1772, p. 146.
26. Jenny Uglow, *The Lunar Men* (London: Faber, 2002), p. 119.
27. Richardson, *James Brindley: Canal Pioneer*, p. 93. Given source, Boulton to Thomas Gilbert nd, Matthew Boulton Papers, Letter Book 'D', pp. 34–35, Birmingham Central Library.

28. Richardson, *James Brindley: Canal Pioneer*, p. 93. Given source, Boulton to Samuel Garbett, 12 February 1771, Matthew Boulton Papers, Letter Book 'D', pp. 40–43, Birmingham Central Library.
29. NA ref. RAIL 810/1, 11 January 1771.
30. Lewis, *The Canal Pioneers*, p. 60.
31. Ibid.
32. John Morris Jones, 'Ladywood', available online at www.ladywood-online.org.uk
33. RAIL 810/1, 11 November 1769.
34. 'The Birmingham Canal were taking some steps beyond Oldbury and thinking of more', Broadbridge, *The Birmingham Canal Navigations*, p. 24.
35. Ibid.
36. Ibid, p. 25.
37. Ibid, p. 24.
38. RAIL 810/1, 16 August, 1770. The minute reads 'Mr Brindley having requested that the committee might be summoned he informed them that the W Hampton [Staffordshire and Worcestershire] Gentlemen desired he would see what orders to forward the execution of that part of the Canal from Bilston to Autherley [Aldersley] pursuant to the assurance given by our Committee to the W Hampton Gentlemen at W Bromwich when the orders of the Committee of the 13th inst. were read to Mr Brindley which appeared to me Satisfactory.' This statement does not, with all respect, appear to support the interpretation Broadbridge gives it.
39. Broadbridge, *The Birmingham Canal Navigations*, p. 25.
40. RAIL 810/1, 16 August, 1770.
41. Ibid.
42. Broadbridge, *The Birmingham Canal Navigations*, p. 26. Given source Sir Edward Lyttleton's undated letter to the Earl of Dartmouth.
43. RAIL 810/1, 18 May 1772.
44. Erasmus Darwin, *Zoonomia*, XVIII– 20 (1794), p. 218.

Chapter Ten

1. This chapter is a revised version of my paper 'James Brindley and the (unbuilt) Monkey Island Canal', which first appeared in the *Railway and Canal Historical Society Journal*, No. 223 (July 2015), pp. 278–290.
2. *JCH*, 33 (13 November 1770–17 November 1775), p. 33.
3. *Reading Mercury*, 15 January 1770.
4. *Reading Mercury*, 5 March 1770.
5. Ibid.
6. Lucy Lead, '"They flow for Country and People": landowners and early canal development in England', *Railway and Canal Historical Society Journal*, No. 220 (July 2014), pp. 73–89.
7. Malet, *Bridgewater*, p. 124.

8. JHC, 32, p. 768 and Malet, *Bridgewater*, p. 124.

9. Sir Henry Cavendish, *Debates of the House of Commons during the thirteenth Parliament of Great Britain, commonly called the unreported Parliament* (London: Longman, 1840) pp. 500–504.

10. In 1770 there were two sitting MPs with the surname 'Burrell'. Peter Burrell, MP for Totnes, and William Burrell, MP for Haslemere.

11. 'That my brother Brindley should prefer the Printfield passage, I can readily comprehend: a late author has very solidly demonstrated that every man, however so great his genius, has a certain hobby horse that he like to ride. A large aqueduct bridge over a large river does not happen to be mine, whom am of opinion that a given sum of money is as solidly laid out for posterity in cutting through the neck of a hill as in building a bridge to carry water over water, though admirers of the wonderful may not be so loud in their applauses.' *Reports of the late John Smeaton, FRS, made on various occasions*, II (London, 1803), p. 119.

12. *Reading Mercury*, 5 March 1770.

13. Thames Navigation: Committee of the Common Council, Minutes 1770–1777, London Metropolitan Archives, Microfilm MCFP/303, vol. A/1.

14. The Rails Head took its name from the stakes (rails) driven into the upper end of Isleworth Weir. Susan Reynolds (ed.), 'Shepperton, Staines, Stanwell, Sunbury, Teddington, Heston and Isleworth, Twickenham, Cowley, Cranford, West Drayton, Greenford, Hanwell, Harefield and Harlington', *A History of the County of Middlesex*, vol. 3, (London: Victoria County History, 1962), pp. 85–94.

15. The London Canal Museum website suggests that the adoption of narrow dimensions 'almost certainly came from the need for the Trent and Mersey to tunnel under Harecastle Hill, just north of the Potteries. The expense of digging a 2,880-yard tunnel manually deterred Brindley from building the canal to a gauge to carry the wider flats trading off the Mersey and its linked rivers.' www.canalmuseum.org.uk/history *Hugh Compton traces the decision to adopt these dimensions across the Midlands to a meeting held at the George Inn, Lichfield, on 14 December 1769. Compton, The Oxford Canal, p. 19.*

16. Compton, *The Oxford Canal*, p. 19.

17. That is, 106,920 gallons.

18. Brindley's record of surveying from Tapley (Taplow) Mill near Boulter's Lock to Isleworth dated 15 June 1770 is in the London Metropolitan Archives (LMA) ref. CLRO MCFP/303 Vol A/1, (microfilm). LMA also holds one of the printed pamphlets together with an engraved and printed copy of Whitworth's map, ref. ACC 36/1.

19. *Reading Mercury*, 7 May 1770.

20. LMA ref ACC 36/1.

21. Richardson, *James Brindley: Canal Pioneer*, p. 92.

22. LMA ref. ACC 36/1.

23. George Merchant to the Mayor of Chester, 17 December 1768. University of Salford Library, Special Collections ref DBA/5/409.

24. Wedgwood to Bentley, 27 Sept 1767, CJW I, p. 174.

25. LMA ref CLRO MCFP/303 Vol A/1, (microfilm).

26. JHC, 33, pp. 81, 82.
27. JHC, 33, p. 119.
28. JHC, 33, p. 153.
29. Whitworth appears to have given evidence in 1767/8 in connection with the Coventry Canal; he also testified in support of the Staffordshire & Worcestershire Canal Company's petition for leave to raise new capital in March 1770 when Brindley was too ill to attend. Lewis, *The Canal Pioneers*, p. 70.
30. Lewis, *The Canal Pioneers*, p. 83.
31. JHC, 33, p.190 ff.
32. *Reading Mercury*, 11 March, 1771.
33. The information about the MPs comes from www.historyofparliamentonline.org.
34. *Biographica Britannica*, II (1780), entry for Brindley, p. 602.

Chapter Eleven

1. Among the unrealised canal projects whose promoters consulted Brindley were schemes based around Taunton (from the Bristol Channel to Exeter and from Langport to Exmouth); from Stockton to Darlington in the north-east; between Andover and Redbridge – a canal which eventually came into being, with Robert Whitworth as its engineer-in-chief, and the Salisbury and Southampton Canal which had been intended to connect with it; extensions of the Bridgewater Canal, both a branch to Stockport and from Runcorn to Liverpool. (Boucher, *James Brindley, Engineer 1716-1772*, p. 120.)
2. See History on the Chelmer and Blackwater navigation on www.Jim-Shead.com/waterways.
3. Josiah Wedgwood to Thomas Bentley, 5 November 1772, www.wedgwoodmuseum.org.uk, online archive, ref E25-18417; V&A/Wedgwood Collection, Presented by the Art Fund with major support from the Heritage Lottery Fund, private donations and a public appeal.
4. JBN (2013), p.91.
5. Gordon Emery (ed.), *The Old Chester Canal – a history and guide*, (Chester: Chester Canal Heritage Trust, 2005) p. 29, given source, Cheshire Records Office, (Treasurers' Vouchers, 1553-1836) ref Z/TAV/55. For Thomas Allen, see Evans, *James Brindley – Canal Engineer*, p. 107.
6. Emery (ed.), *The Old Chester Canal*, p. 16, given source, Cheshire Records Office (Treasurers' Vouchers, 1553–1836), ref Z/TAV/55. The letter is not in Brindley's handwriting.
7. *Journal of the House of Lords*, 33, 24 April 1771. (Journal of the House of Lords, British History Online, www.british-history.ac.uk/lords).
8. Ibid, 2 May 1771.
9. Emery (ed.), *The Old Chester Canal*, pp. 22, 50.
10. Minutes of the Chester Canal Company 1771–1813, National Archives, RAIL/816/2, 13 December 1771.
11. Emery (ed.), *The Old Chester Canal*, p. 29.

12. RAIL/816/2, 24 January 1772.

13. JHC Vol 33, p. 419.

14. RAIL/816/2, 17 February 1772.

15. This section and the remainder of this chapter draw extensively on Christine Richardson's book, *The Waterways Revolution – From the Peaks to the Trent 1768-1778* (Hanley Swan, Worcs.: Self-Publishing Association, 1992).

16. Ibid, p. 31.

17. Ibid, p. 47/8.

18. Brindley did not publish his recommendations until August 1770. *The Report of James Brindley … for improving the navigation and drainage at Wisbeach* [sic] (Wisbech, 1770).

19. *Derby Mercury*, 18 August 1769.

20. *Derby Mercury*, 6 October, 1769.

21. Richardson, *The Waterways Revolution*, p. 55.

22.. Ibid.

23. *Derby Mercury*, 2 February 1770.

24. *Leeds Intelligencer*, 4 September 1770.

25. Richardson, *The Waterways Revolution*, p. 43. The Marquis did not actually build his canal until 1775, when he approached John Smeaton to direct the work.

26. *Leeds Intelligencer*, 30 January 1770.

27. Richardson, *The Waterways Revolution*, pp. 66–7.

28. Ibid, p. 80.

29. JHC, 33, p. 265.

30. Richardson, *The Waterways Revolution*, p. 83.

31. *Derby Mercury*, 5 July 1771.

32.. Egerton, *A Letter to the Parisians*, p. 65. In an explanatory note, Egerton says that the wall is 'made of Bricks and … ribbed, only in large compartments, with Stone.' How much his words add in terms of information about the locks' construction is debateable.

33. Willan, *The Navigation of the River Weaver*, p. 82.

34. Egerton, *A Letter to the Parisians*, p. 65.

35. Booklet, 'Worsley Accounts', Salford University Library, Special Collections, ref DBA 7/517/4.

36. *Derby Mercury*, 4 September 1772.

37. Smiles, *James Brindley and the Early Engineers*, p. 293.

Chapter Twelve

1. Jean Lindsay, *The Trent and Mersey Canal* (Newton Abbot: David & Charles, 1979), pp. 88–9.

2. Peter Lead, *Agents of Revolution*, p. 80.

3. Lindsay, *The Trent and Mersey Canal*, p. 89.

4. Denise Kenyon, *The Origins of Lancashire* (Manchester: Manchester University Press, 1991) p. 9; Malet, *Bridgewater*, p. 132.

5. Malet, *Bridgewater*, p. 146.
6. Ibid, p. 151.
7. *The Times*, 17 February 1902: centennial reprinting of a passage first published in *The Times* of 1802. Salford University Library, Special Collections, DBA 8/521.
8. Malet, *Bridgewater*, p. 144.
9. Ibid, p. 148, given source Charles Hulbert, *Memoirs of Seventy Years of an eventful life* (Shrewsbury: 1852), pp. 82, 83.
10. Rev. F. H. Egerton, 8th Earl of Bridgewater, *Family Anecdotes* (Paris, *c.* 1825).
11. Strachan Holme, *The Life of the Most Noble Francis Egerton, Third Duke of Bridgewater*, unpublished draft in fifteen typescripts, Salford University Library, Special Collections DBA 9/526a.
12. Boucher, *James Brindley, Engineer 1716-1772*, pp. 1, 2.
13. 'Memorandum from the Representatives of Mr Jas Brindley dec'd, to His Grace the Duke of Bridgewater', 28 February 1774, Salford University Library Special Collections, DBA 7/517/4.
14. Christopher Lewis, *The Canal Pioneers: Brindley's School of Engineers* (Stroud: The History Press, 2011).
15. *Derby Mercury*, 16 October 1772.
16. *Newcastle Courant*, 31 October 1772.
17. *Leeds Intelligencer*, 10 November 1772.
18. *Oxford Journal*, 17 October 1772.
19. *Leeds Intelligencer*, 16 November 1773.
20. Bristol poll books covering elections 1774–1790, Bristol Central Library Reference Collection (unclassified).
21. Nicholas Kingsley, 'Preliminary list of Boulton and Watt Engines Supplied to Gloucestershire', www.gsia.org.uk.
22. *Derby Mercury*, 24 October 1799.
23. Evans, *James Brindley – Canal Engineer*, p. 85 and letter to author, January 2014.
24. William Salt Library, Stafford, ref S. MS. 478/2/107.
25. 'Shipping Intelligence – Arrivals', *Sydney Monitor*, Wednesday 20 January 1836.
26. Australian Dictionary of Biography Online, entry for James Brindley Bettington, 1796–1857.
27. Copy of the sick book of the emigrant ship William Nicol for 3 July to 28 October 1837, National Archives ref ADM 101/79/7/4 and item 'Search Free Settler or Felon?' on www.jenwilletscom.
28. www.ozships.net; *Sydney Monitor*, 14 December 1837.
29. 'Shipping News', *Morning Post*, 2 August 1838.
30. John Ward, *History of the Borough of Stoke-upon-Trent* (London: W. Lewis & Son, 1843), p. 175.
31. Duke of Bridgewater Archive, Salford University Library Special Collections DBA 7/517/4.
32. Smiles *James Brindley and the Early Engineers* p. 227.
33. W. H. Chaloner, *James Brindley (1716–72)*, pp. 226–8.
34. Malet, *The Canal Duke*, p. 71 and *Bridgewater*, p. 57.
35. Peter Lead, *Agents of Revolution*, p. 55.

Bibliography

Manuscripts

'A true plain perfect and particular inventory of all and singular the goods the chattels and credits of James Brindley late of Turnhurst in the county of Stafford deceased ...' Probate inventory of James Brindley's estate compiled 1778 by Hugh Henshall, National Archives, ref. PROB 31/657.

Banks, Sir Joseph, *Journal of an Excursion of Wales, etc. 1767–68*, Cambridge University Library, ref. Add Ms 6294.

Bridgewater Estates Accounts, June 1759–December 1760, Northamptonshire Records Office, Northampton, ref. EB 1459/3.

Bridgewater Estates Accounts, December 1760–February 1762, held on long term loan by Chetham's Library, Manchester.

Bridgewater Estates Payments Book, 5 November 1766 ff, Duke of Bridgewater Archive, University of Salford Library, Special Collections, ref. DBA 11/548.

Brindley, James, Notebook 1755–58, Brindley Mill and James Brindley Museum, Leek.

Brindley, James, Notebook 1755–58, photocopy made by D. W. Dickinson, Birmingham Central Library.

Brindley, James, Notebook 1759–60, Institution of Civil Engineers, Archives, London.

Brindley, James, Notebook September 1761–December 1762, Institution of Civil Engineers, Archives, London.

Brindley, James, Notebook 31 October–27 November 1763, Institution of Civil Engineers, Archives, London.

Brown, William, letter to John Hussey Delaval, 9 September 1759, Northumberland Record Office, ref. 2DE/6/3/2.

Committee Order Book of the Staffordshire & Worcestershire Canal Company, 1766–1785, National Archives, ref. RAIL 871/1.

Green, John Fennyhouse, 'Orders from Mr Brindley', 1767–71, Staffordshire Records Office, ref. 6898/2/1-18.

Green, John Fennyhouse, Manuscript Notebooks, Staffordshire Records Office, ref. 6898/2.

Holme, Strachan, *The Life of the Most Noble Francis Egerton, Third Duke of Bridgewater*, Unfinished typescript, Salford University Library Special Collections, ref. DBA /9/524.

151

Minutes of the River Dun Navigation Company, General and Committee Meetings, 1729–1825 National Archives, ref. RAIL 825/5.

Minutes of the Birmingham Canal Company, 1767–1771, National Archives, ref. RAIL 810/1.

Minutes of the Proprietors and Committee of the Calder & Hebble Navigation Company, 1758–1797, National Archives, ref. 815/4.

Minutes of the Chester Canal Company 1771–1813, National Archives, ref. RAIL/816/2.

Minutes of the Chesterfield Canal Company, 1769–1780, National Archives, ref. 817/1–2.

Minutes of the Coventry Canal Company, 1768ff National Archives, ref. RAIL 818/1.

Minutes of the Oxford Canal Company, 1769–1775, National Archives, ref. RAIL 855/2.

Minutes of the Thames Navigation Committee of the London Common Council, 1770–1777, London Metropolitan Archives, Microfilm MCFP/303) Vol A/1.

Minutes of the Commissioners of the Loughborough Navigation, National Archives, ref. RAIL 849/1.

Miscellaneous papers, typescripts, drafts etc., in the Duke of Bridgewater Archive, University of Salford Library, Special Collections.

Papers of Mary, Countess of Stamford, John Rylands Library, Manchester ref. EGR 3/7/2/1/7.

O'Cionnaith, Finnian, *Land surveying in eighteenth and early nineteenth century Dublin*, (PhD thesis, Department of History, National University of Ireland Maynooth, April 2011, available online).

Phelps, J. J. *The Romance of an Old Canal*, unpublished notes for a lecture. Chetham's Library, Manchester, Phelps Collection.

Weaver Navigation Papers, John Rylands Library, Manchester (unclassified).

Published Sources

Articles

Bennett, Arnold, 'The Making of Me', *Daily Express*, 6 June 1928.

Campbell, J. H. D. M., 'Notes on James Brindley', *Derbyshire Miscellany*, February 1959.

Chaloner, W. H., 'James Brindley (1716–1772) and his remuneration as a canal engineer', *Transactions of the Lancashire and Cheshire Antiquarian Society*, 75/56, (1965/6), pp. 226–8.

Cross-Rudkin, Peter, 'Constructing the Staffordshire and Worcestershire Canal, 1766–72', *Transactions of the Newcomen Society*, 75 (2005) pp. 289–305.

Egerton, Francis, Earl of Ellesmere, Untitled article including review of Samuel Hughes' 'Memoir of James Brindley', published anonymously in the *Quarterly Review* (1844), pp. 281–324.

Garrett, C.W.F., 'Bewdley and the Stinking Ditch', in Laurence Silvester Snell (ed.), *Essays Towards a History of Bewdley* (Bewdley: Bewdley Research Group, 1972) pp. 1–13.

Hughes, Samuel, 'Memoir of James Brindley', *Weale's Quarterly Papers on Engineering*, I (1844), pp. 1–49.

Lead, Lucy, '"They Flow for Country and People": landowners and early canal developments in England', *Railway and Canal Historical Society Journal*, No. 220 (July 2014), pp. 73–89.

Malet, Hugh, 'Brindley and Canals', *History Today*, 23, Issue 4 (4 April 1973), pp. 266–275.

Owens, Victoria, 'James Brindley's Notebooks, 1755–1763: An Eighteenth-Century Engineer Writes About His Work', *International Journal for the History of Engineering & Technology*, 83, No. 2 (2013), pp. 222–256.

Owens, Victoria, 'The Private Property Debate', *Journal of the Railway & Canal Historical Society*, 38, Part 4, No. 222 (March 2015), pp. 258–59.

Owens, Victoria, 'James Brindley and the (unbuilt) Monkey Island Canal', *Journal of the Railway & Canal Historical Society*, 38, Part 5, No. 223 (July 2015), pp. 278–290.

Potter, Hugh, 'Brindley Gates', *NarrowBoat*, (Spring 2010), pp. 10–14.

Richardson, Christine, 'James Brindley 1716–72: His Simultaneous Commercial Development of Mills, Steam Power and Canals', *Transactions of the Newcomen Society*, 76 (2006).

Wood, Anthony C., 'The Diaries of Sir Roger Newdigate' in *Essays in Honour of Philip B. Chatwin* (Oxford: Oxford University Press, 1962), pp. 40–54.

Books

Aiken, John, *A Description of the Country from Thirty to Forty Miles Round Manchester* (1795).

Anon, *Seasonable Considerations on a Navigable Canal Intended to be cut from the River Trent … to the River Mersey* (1766).

Anon, *Supplement to a Pamphlet, entitled, Seasonable Considerations on a Navigable Canal Intended to be cut from the River Trent … to the River Mersey* (1766).

Atkinson, Glen, *Barton's Bridges* (Manchester: Neil Richardson, 2002).

Banks, A. G. and R. B. Schofield, *Brindley at Wet Earth Colliery: An Engineering Study* (Newton Abbot: David & Charles, 1968).

Boucher, Cyril, *James Brindley: Engineer 1716–1772* (Norwich: Goose & Son, 1968).

Broade, Thomas, *A new scheme for making Inland Navigations* (1758, ECCO print editions).

Broadbridge, S. R., *The Birmingham Canal Navigations, Vol. I, 1768–1846* (Newton Abbot: David & Charles, 1974).

Brown, Jane, *The Omnipotent Magician: Lancelot 'Capability' Brown* (London: Chatto & Windus, 2011).

Cavendish, Sir Hugh, *Debates of the House of Commons during the Thirteenth Parliament of Great Britain, commonly called the unreported Parliament* (London: Longman, 1840).

Compton, Hugh, *The Oxford Canal* (Newton Abbot: David & Charles, 1976).

Corble, Nick, *James Brindley: The First Canal Builder* (Stroud: Tempus, 2005).

Crofton, H. T., *History of the Ancient Chapel of Stretford* (Manchester: Chetham Society, 1899).

Darwin, Erasmus, *Zoonomia* (1794).

Egerton, Rev. Francis Henry, Eighth Earl of Bridgewater, *Letter to the Parisians, and the French Nation, Upon Inland Navigation, Containing a Defence of the Public Character of His Grace Francis Egerton, Late Duke of Bridgewater: And, Including Some Notices, And, Anecdotes, Concerning Mr. James Brindley* (1819).

Emery, Gordon (ed.), *The Old Chester Canal: A History and Guide* (Chester: Chester Canal Heritage Trust, 2005).

Evans, Kathleen, *James Brindley: Canal Engineer: A New Perspective* (2nd edn, Leek: Churnet Valley Books, 2007).

Hadfield, Charles, *The Canals of Yorkshire and North East England* (Newton Abbot: David & Charles, 1972).

Hadfield, Charles, *The Canals of the East Midlands* (Newton Abbot: David & Charles, 1970).

Jenkins, Rhys, *Links in the History of Engineering and Technology from Tudor Times* (London: Ayer Publishing, 1936).

Journals of the House of Commons, Vols 28–35 (Reprinted by the House of Commons, 1803. Digitised by Google).

Journal of the House of Lords, digitised on British History Online.

Kenyon, Denise, *The Origins of Lancashire* (Manchester: Manchester University Press, 1991).

Kippis, Andrew (ed.), *Biographica Britannica* (London, 1778–93).

Klemperer, William D. and Paul Sillitoe, *James Brindley at Turnhurst Hall: An Archaeological and Historical Investigation* (Stoke-on-Trent: City Museum & Art Gallery, 1995).

Lead, Peter, *Agents of Revolution John and Thomas Gilbert: Entrepreneurs* (Keele: Centre for Local History, University of Keele, 1989).

Lewis, Christopher, *The Canal Pioneers: Brindley's School of Engineers* (Stroud: The History Press, 2011).

Lindsay, Jean, *The Trent and Mersey Canal* (Newton Abbot: David & Charles, 1979).

Malet, Hugh, *The Canal Duke* (Dawlish: David & Charles, 1961).

Malet, Hugh, *Bridgewater: The Canal Duke 1736–1803* (revised edition, Manchester: Manchester University Press, 1977).

Meteyard, Eliza, *The Life of Josiah Wedgwood from his Private Correspondence and Family Papers* (London: Hurst & Blackett, 1865).

Nevell, Michael, and Terry Wyke (eds.), *Bridgewater 250: The Archaeology of World's First Industrial Canal* (Manchester: Manchester Metropolitan University, University of Salford; Council for British Archaeology – North West Industrial Archaeology Panel, 2012).

Owens, Victoria (ed.), *James Brindley's Notebooks* (Gloucester: Choir Press, 2013).

Phillips, John, *The General History of Inland Navigation* London, (1803, digitised by Google).

Picton, Sir James A., *City of Liverpool Municipal Archives and Records from 1760–1835* (Liverpool: G. Warmeley, 1886).

Pierce, Patricia, *Old London Bridge* (London: Hodder Headline, 2001).

Porter, Roy, *English Society in the Eighteenth Century* (Harmondsworth: Penguin, 1982).

Raistrick, Arthur, *Dynasty of Ironfounders* (Revised 2nd edn, Ironbridge: Ironbridge Gorge Museum Trust, 1989, 1st published 1953).

Rees, Abraham, *Cyclopaedia*, (1819).

Rennie, Sir John, *The Autobiography of Sir John Rennie* (London & New York: E. & F. N. Spon, 1875).

Reynolds, Terry S., *Stronger than a Hundred Men: A History of the Vertical Water Wheel* (Baltimore and London: Johns Hopkins University Press, 1983).

Richards, H. P., *William Edwards: Architect, Builder, Minister* (Pontypridd: Pontypridd Museum, 2006).

Richardson, Christine, *James Brindley: Canal Pioneer* (Burton on Trent: Waterways World, 2004).

Richardson, Christine, *The Waterways Revolution: From the Peaks to the Trent, 1768–78* (Hanley Swan, Worcs.: Self-Publishing Association, 1992).

Rolt, L. T. C., *Navigable Waterways* (London: Longman, 1969).

Skempton, Sir Alec W. (ed.) et al, *Biographical Dictionary of Civil Engineers in Great Britain and Ireland*, 1, 1500–1830 (London: Thomas Telford, 2002).

Skempton, Sir Alec W., et al, *Biographical Dictionary of Civil Engineers*, 1, 1500–1830, (London: Institution of Civil Engineers, 2002).

Sleigh, John, *History of Leek* (1883, digitised by Google).

Smeaton, John, *Reports of the late John Smeaton, FRS, made on various occasions in the course of his employment as a civil engineer* (London: Longman, 1812).

Smiles, Samuel, *James Brindley and the Early Engineers*, (London: John Murray, 1864).

Smith, Elizabeth, *The Compleat Housewife*, (1st published 1753; facsimile edition Alton: Chawton House Library, 2009).

Snell, Laurence Silvester (ed.), *Essays Towards a History of Bewdley* (Bewdley: Bewdley Research Group, 1972).

Uglow, Jenny, *The Lunar Men* (London: Faber, 2002).

Vickery, Amanda, *Behind Closed Doors: At Home in Georgian England* (New Haven and London: Yale, 2009).

Victoria County Histories, digitised on www.britishhistoryonline.

Ward, John, *A History of the Borough of Stoke-upon-Trent* (1843, digitised by Google).

Watson, John, *The History and Antiquities of the Parith [sic] of Halifax*, (1775, digitised).

Wedgwood, Josiah, *Letters of Josiah Wedgwood*, 3 vols., edited by Euphemia Farrer (1st published privately 1903–6, reprinted Cambridge: Cambridge University Press, 2010).

White, William, *History, Gazetteer and Directory of Staffordshire* (1851).

Willan, T. S., *The Navigation of the River Weaver in the Eighteenth Century* (Manchester: Chetham Society, 1951).

Young, Arthur, *A Six Month Tour through the North of England* (1770).

Index of People and Places